THE
ADMIRAL'S
DAUGHTER

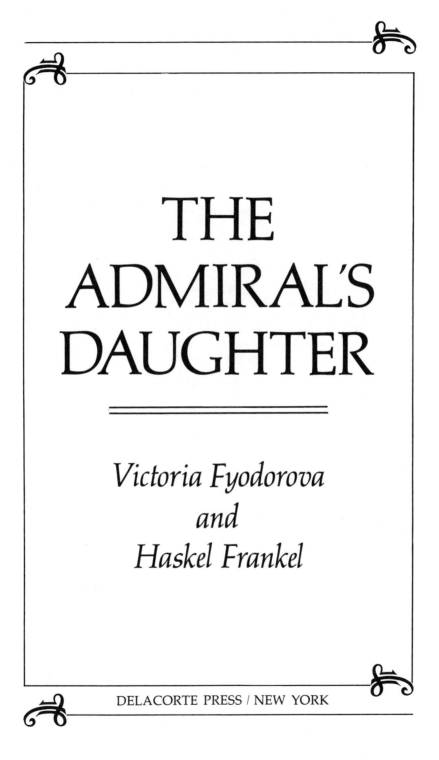

THE ADMIRAL'S DAUGHTER

Victoria Fyodorova
and
Haskel Frankel

DELACORTE PRESS / NEW YORK

Published by
Delacorte Press
1 Dag Hammarskjold Plaza
New York, New York 10017

LIBRARY OF CONGRESS CATALOGING IN PUBLICATION DATA
Fyodorova, Victoria, 1946–
    The admiral's daughter.

    Includes index.
    1. Fyodorova, Victoria, 1946–   2. Russia—
Biography.   3. United States—Biography.   I. Frankel,
Haskel, joint author.   II. Title
CT1218.F88A33   947.084′092′2   [B]   78-26664
ISBN 0-440-00366-0

ACKNOWLEDGMENTS

A few words of appreciation are in order to the busy men and women who took the time to help with memories, facts, clippings, advice, all of which were needed in recreating the story that follows.

I am extremely grateful to Gloria Trimel and the staff of the Westbrook Public Library, Westbrook, Connecticut, who made both in- and out-of-print books available to me throughout my research.

I would also like to thank Dr. Paul J. Coppola, Dr. Alan H. DeCherney, Carol Graves and the Eugene O'Neill Theatre Center, Faina Krais, Deborah Pfaffmann, Judy Lynn Prince, Alfred Simon, and especially Louise B. Smith, whose assorted comments on tape transcriptions often featured bits of personal research or pointed out discrepancies that forced me into further research.

Above all, I wish to thank both Dr. Irina Kirk and Henry Gris, both professional writers who were individually involved in the history that became *The Admiral's Daughter*, for sharing their memories with me.

It should be noted that those parts of the text devoted to Zoya Fyodorova were remembered by her daughter, Victoria, who had recorded them in her diary as her mother had told them to her.

Last, but never least, I must thank my wife, Marilyn, for putting up with a house awash with scraps of paper and assorted newspaper clippings, and for putting up with the assorted moods of a writer at work. I also thank her for reading the manuscript as it progressed and for her questions throughout which greatly improved the text.

HASKEL FRANKEL

To my dearest Mamatchka, whose love has
guided me through good times and bad,
whether near to me or far away, and
who is in my thoughts forever.

V.F.

For my parents,
Sally and Tobias Frankel,
who always believed.
And for
May and Harold Freedman,
who believed, but couldn't wait.

H.F.

PROLOGUE

VICTORIA

Even now, there are still moments when I first awaken that I find myself confused by the view outside the bedroom windows. My life has taken me more than halfway around the world, and I have to think to remember where I am.

But then I remember. This is Connecticut, and I am home and safe. I have to smile at that. Those are such funny words to me. *Home. Safe.* Home is only *home-for-now* to me. I do not know the deep meaning of that word, because life has left me too fearful that what is good will not stay, and what is bad will return.

I guess that explains *safe*, too. There is too much cruelty from my childhood that I remember, too many terrible people whose faces I can still see for me ever to feel safe.

And yet I am now home and safe. People keep telling me this so that I accept it. But I don't really feel it. I wonder if I ever will.

This is such a strange time for me. I am in the United States, but I am not yet American. I have left Russia, but I am still Russian. It is something like sitting in a train watching the world go by your window. You are sitting still, but your world is moving.

I often think that if people could see me when I am alone in the house they would think I am mad. There are times when I am walking and I suddenly stop, and other times when there is nothing funny and I laugh. But I know what these moments are about.

Once I was walking through the dining room and I stopped in the middle of a step. It was because I had passed a bowl of fruit without really noticing it. Apples and oranges, and I had grown so used to them that I didn't even notice them. Incredible when I think back to the time when an orange was something to dream about, something to build fantasies around.

And one day, I found myself in front of the open door of the refrigerator, laughing. I had decided to make myself a sandwich and I was trying to choose between ham and bologna. Imagine such a problem! I, who had never tasted meat until I was over eight years old. And then I began to cry, as I thought of all the people I had left behind me who would never have the opportunity to worry about ham or bologna.

I know I am a very lucky woman. I have been told that, too, many times. And in a way it is so. But only in a way. God has given me many wonderful gifts, but they have come to me in such strange ways.

I can still hear words—and feel the pain of them, too—like *bastard* and *illegitimate* and *orphan*. Those are words that stay sharp and hurting even after life has revealed them to be untrue. I have two parents, but deep inside of me I do not. I did not meet my mother until I was almost nine, and my father until I was almost 30. In my entire life I have never been in a room in which I could turn my head and look from one parent to the other. There has never been a moment when my whole world was together in one place. That remains a dream, and one that will never come true.

But so many dreams that I was told were impossible have come true, that I cannot feel sad over one little dream. I can look back in my life and find miracles, and that is more than enough. And if my childhood was filled with faces that turned from me with hatred, faces that wished me dead, I can also now look back on some faces that have smiled at me, on hands that have reached out to help me. I remember so many letters from people all over the world who wrote to wish me well and to tell me I was in their prayers. People I have never met.

I remember a lady who came up to me in a department store when I first came to this country. She said she knew who I was, and she handed me a small American flag. Tears filled my eyes. Such a little kindness, such a big gesture. I carried the flag with me everywhere, a proof that a dream had come true.

Above all, there is Irina Kirk who gave so much of herself to find my father for me. Others have involved themselves in my life for all sorts of reasons—I was a good newspaper story, I had publicity value—but Irina just seemed to care, and she acted on that alone. Now, when the bad memories with the evil faces come too close to me, I think of Irina, and I know that those people are not the whole world. There are good people, too, and I am here because of them.

And I have my father because of them.

If what you have just read makes you think of me as an unhappy person, in a way that is so. But only in a way. I am happy today, but I cannot free myself completely from yesterday. It has crawled deep into my bones and it clings there, and every so often it moves a little to remind me that it is with me and will not go away.

I think the thing that startles me most is when someone says to me that I have had a unique life. I know that is so, but I always have to stop and think a moment before I agree. If I stand outside of my life and look at it, I can see the uniqueness, but it was never really that way for me. I lived it a day at a time, and it had a progression, even in its worst moments, that made sense. What happened one day led into what happened the day after, and so for me, it was a life. Perhaps it is one that Russians can understand better than other people.

Inside my private self, I think of my life as a jigsaw puzzle I have always been working on. Other people seem to live their entire lives inside complete pictures that may change or grow larger, but are always complete. My life has been one in which I have always been searching for pieces and fitting them in so that I could see the picture of me.

The puzzle has been unfinished for 30 years, but at last, I have a complete picture like everyone else. And finally, I can look back into my life and see it all, and know the whys of what has happened to me, and to my mother, and to my father.

BOOK
I

JACKSON ROGERS TATE

It is legend in the Tate family that Ernest Carnes Tate was with Teddy Roosevelt and his Rough Riders approaching Cuba at the time that Leola Tate was giving birth to their son. But the boy was born on October 15, 1898, and the Spanish-American War had ended in July.

Then where was Ernest Carnes Tate? It doesn't really matter. He wasn't with his wife at Tates Island, Florida, when his child came into the world. But he had rarely been with her since their marriage. Ernest Tate probably should never have married. It was too confining a situation for a man with an itch to travel, a yen for the whole world. Ernest Carnes Tate was what they used to call "an adventurer," and maybe that was what attracted Leola Rogers to him when they met in Clearwater, Florida.

He had dash to him, she said that from the start. And while Leola told her friends she didn't really care about such things—it was just that her parents did—it was nice to know that Ernest came from such a fine American background. A Tate had been governor of Tennessee and Ernest's father had been a colonel in the Civil War. Why, if you traveled west from Memphis, you would come to three plantations one after the other named Jacksonborough, Rogersville, and Tate Springs, and they were all part of the Tate family history. (It seemed only right and proper to Leola that she use the plantation names when she had her son christened Jackson Rogers Tate.)

After their marriage, Ernest was always off somewhere in Central or South America, and Leola would be left behind to wait at Tates Island. The longer he stayed away, the deeper her resentment grew. But then one day he would turn up and her bitterness would melt away in the excitement of seeing him. They would talk late into the night, and he would tell her of things he had seen and done—so many things that his stories became blurs in her mind, and the pictures he created for her were fuzzy. He had been made a general in the Nicaraguan army, and he was an admiral in some other navy. There was no doubt of it, he told her, Central America was going to be a part of the United States of America, and he was in on the ground floor.

And then he was gone again. But what about me, she would ask herself? And she would cry herself to sleep listening to the water scratching its way back and forth on the shore. It only deepened her bitterness. When they had decided to marry, they had talked about a life together on a tropical island, so Nanan, as she liked to be called (Lizzie Carnes Tate, Ernest's mother), had bought them one—Tates Island—for a wedding present. But for a woman alone, an island didn't make for a tropical paradise. For Leola Rogers Tate, the island became a tropical prison.

Leola's becoming a mother didn't seem to turn Ernest into a father. Oh, he took pride in his son when he was home. He would bounce the infant on his knee, and he would often disappear for an hour at a time in the evening to stand by the sleeping child's crib. Sometimes Leola sneaked up the stairs and watched her husband from the hall. The tender, loving look on his face almost gave her hope for their marriage, even though she knew there was none.

The tropical-island dream ended with the hurricane that blew so fiercely across the island that Leola feared it would bring down the house. She took her child outdoors away from the house and with rope tied him to the trunk of a tree and put herself between the boy and the wind. Ernest, who was at home at the time, was trapped on the mainland, away from his family as usual. He couldn't get back in the one-cylinder naphtha launch until the waters calmed.

He met a badly shaken Leola who told him flatly that she was done with islands. They moved to Lizzie's house in Tampa, and sold Tates Island for the sum of $7,400. It seemed like a decent profit at the time considering Nanan had bought the land for $1,500 from the federal government. Today, Tates Island is called Clearwater Beach.

Tampa made no change in the Tate marriage. Shortly after he had helped to settle his wife and child, Ernest Tate was off again.

When Jack was three years old, Leola had had enough of being a married woman with only a sometime husband. Divorce wasn't quite proper in 1901, but Leola saw no other way. Better to be a divorced woman than to dry up in the Tampa sun with nothing to show for it.

Nanan agreed with her. Ernest might be her own flesh, but she disapproved of him and his ways. Truth to tell, he deserved to lose a fine woman like Leola. But Nanan, who was to live to the age of 103, had no intention of losing her grandson.

She made both Ernest and Leola sign an agreement giving up all claim to the young Jackson Rogers Tate, and then she adopted him as her own son.

Ernest Carnes Tate took to the waters of the world. For a time, he was captain of a fishing smack off the Yucatán banks and then first mate on a schooner that plied the South Seas. For five years he served as captain of the steamer *Haitian Prince*, running between New York City and Singapore. During World War I, he was a captain on a torpedo boat. Afterwards, he retired to Laguna Beach, California, with his second wife and their son.

Leola Rogers Tate went first to Salisbury, North Carolina, and from there to Philadelphia where she met and married John Howard Haines, who stayed at her side until his death.

Jack Tate grew up in the confusing position of being his father's brother, his mother's brother-in-law (albeit ex), his grandmother's son, and technically his own uncle. Nanan gave her new son the best of everything, and she never quite forgave Ernest for his wandering feet. When she died, she left her money to "my two sons, Jackson and Ernest," naming Jack ahead of the son she had borne. But the bank in which her money was kept failed early in the Depression, and her sons received nothing.

Jack's first school was Mount Washington Seminary, outside of Baltimore, Maryland, a Catholic school run by nuns. Apparently Nanan chose the school because it was good, certainly not because it was Catholic. At birth Jackson Rogers Tate had been baptized in the Episcopalian faith. But in the two or three years he was at Mount Washington Seminary, he was rebaptized Catholic. The two baptisms had little effect on him. Today, he tells people: "I never was very religious. I believe very sincerely in God, but I don't believe any religion has any special inside track."

The next school was the Money School in Campbell, Virginia, where he stayed until he was 12. Nanan then transferred him to another private school in Boulogne-sur-Mer, France. At 14 he came back to the Phillips-Brooks Academy in Philadelphia. During this time, he lived with his natural mother, now Mrs. John Haines.

Jack brought something back with him from France that was to set the pattern of his entire life. He had seen men leaving the ground in those strange things called aeroplanes, and the boy was fascinated. Perhaps it was the subliminal memory of the water off Tates Island, but at 16 Jack knew that he wanted to go into the navy and he wanted to fly.

This determination grew as he entered his last years of high school—West Philadelphia High School, the only public school he was ever to attend. Looking back, it appears that the transfer to a public school was Leola's decision, but it was Nanan who sent him on to the Columbian Preparatory School in Washington, D.C., which was noted for sending its young men to Annapolis and West Point.

Jack was 19 and had been appointed to Annapolis when the United States entered World War I. Young, feisty, and impatient, he sent a note to the first alternate for his appointment, a man named Jim Nolan, who was later to serve under Jack as a junior officer: "You go to Annapolis. I hereby give up my principal appointment to you. I'm going to France to win the war."

What Nanan thought is not recorded, but Jack enlisted in the navy as a second-class seaman and began his climb up through the ranks. Though he applied for flight training several times, he never got his transfer during the war. But he did make ensign by the time he sailed for France, and the end of the war found him serving as an interpreter to the Peace Commission.

While most young American men were itching to get back home, Jack told his superior officers: "I'd just as lief stay in Europe. I'm having fun."

Whether he realized it or not, the decision was typical of many that Jackson Rogers Tate was to make throughout his life. Quick, clean, and unsentimental. Perhaps it was all the shunting around during his childhood, but he had learned to think for himself, without worrying about what others might want of him. He wasn't selfish; he merely decided things in terms of what was right or wrong as he saw them.

Nanan was an old woman, his mother had a life as Mrs. Haines, and the footloose navy style suited Jack Tate just fine. That's all there was to it.

Neither at this point nor at any other while he was serving all over the world did he ever stop to consider if the life he was leading bore any resemblance to the life of his father. That wasn't Jack's sort of thinking. A man was, and a man did, and that was that.

If Nanan had any great plans for her adopted son, Jack never learned of them. And it was just as well, because Nanan had always dreamed that he would work for and eventually inherit the Tampa Hardware Company in which she had a great deal of money. The company went under in the crash of '29.

In 1919 the young ensign was ordered aboard the destroyer *Borie*, which was being commissioned at Cramp's Shipyard in Philadelphia, for what was to be his first trip to Russia. Jack was at sea for over two years.

On his return in 1921 he was ordered to the *Langley*, the former collier ship *Jupiter*, which was being converted to the

U.S. Navy's first aircraft carrier. He left the *Langley* for flight training at Pensacola, and then returned to the ship and sailed with her to Panama.

At the Panama Naval Air Station, he served as commanding officer of Torpedo Plane Squadron Three. From there, he went to Fighter Squadron One aboard the *Saratoga,* and then to Pensacola as commanding officer of the Advanced Training Squadron.

During these years of wandering he acquired a wife, Hilda Avery, who bore him a daughter, Jacqueline. Hilda lived with him whenever possible and waited with their child when he was at sea. She died of high blood pressure some five years after they were married—while he was away. Jacqueline was raised by her grandmother, Hilda's mother, and drifted out of his life—again, an echo of Jack's own childhood.

Becoming a test pilot, Jack gained a reputation as a man who could and would fly anything. He tested the first plane that Roy Grumann ever built. He was part of the famed Hi-Hats at the Cleveland air races in 1929—nine single-seater Boeing biplanes tied together, performing stunts and formations. On his own, in Panama, Jack flew upside down from the Atlantic to the Pacific Ocean, a distance of 46 miles, in 12 minutes.

In the early 1930s he was loaned to M-G-M and did the stunt-flying on a film called *Hell Divers*, which made Clark Gable a star. The two men became friends. In later years he was to know and like Gable's wife, Carole Lombard, as well as Lucille Ball and Desi Arnaz. It wasn't because they were movie stars. Celebrities per se meant nothing to Jack. They were just people he liked. After all, he could look back on incidents in his life involving names of equal or greater luster. He knew Howard Hughes. He had once co-hosted a duck dinner with navy buddies for Aimee Semple McPherson. And there was the time he had flown the Sunday papers out to the presidential yacht, taken off, and then flown back again to collect the money he had laid out from Calvin Coolidge himself.

In the 1930s he married again. Helen Harris Spann was a widow with four children. But as in his previous marriage, emotional ties had little effect on his life-style. He served two years aboard the *Yorktown* as air-group commander, and then went to Alaska to put the station at Sitka into commission.

When World War II began, Jack took the carrier *Altamaha*—a Creek Indian word meaning "leaky canoe"—to the South Pacific. After a year he returned to the States and then sailed with a deck filled with P-51's from San Diego to Karachi, India. He was now a captain.

He saw action at Guadalcanal and Tarawa. And somewhere along the way, his marriage to Helen came apart. They separated.

After Tarawa, Jack was sent home to be deputy commandant for the training station at Corpus Christi, Texas. He disliked it. It seemed almost dishonest to be sitting out a global war in Texas. Jack wanted to be back in it.

Through his connections in naval intelligence, Jack knew that Roosevelt and Stalin had agreed at Teheran that the U.S.S.R. would join the war against Japan 90 days after the cessation of hostilities in Europe. Looking at the way things were going on the Continent, Jack figured that by the time he could arrange to have himself transferred there, the war might well be over in Europe. But the war against Japan was something else.

Jack flew to Washington to see his friend Paul Foster, who was close to Roosevelt. It was F.D.R. himself who had had Foster recalled to service. Paul Foster arranged Jack's orders to Moscow.

Jack was assigned to be the naval representative of a special military mission to Moscow under General John Dean called Operation Mile Post. They were to set up the bombing of Japan by American flyers who would operate from an American-run field to be built in Siberia.

Jackson Rogers Tate, age 46 and separated from his wife, arrived in Moscow in January of 1945.

ZOYA FYODOROVA

In 1912 Alexei Fyodorov was a man who could look around him with satisfaction and say life had been kind to him. He had a good job as a metal worker in a factory in Saint Petersburg. He had a fine apartment—four rooms—and what man needed more than that? The czar, of course, but his days were numbered. The revolution was near—it was spoken of at every meeting Alexei attended.

And best of all, Alexei had a fine wife and a fertile one in Ekaterina. He loved their two daughters, Alexandra and Maria, but this time Ekaterina would present him with a son. Surely it was so.

So all things considered, Alexei was pleased. There was love in his home, and he had respect at the factory. Any man who worked with him knew that Alexei Fyodorov was a man of intelligence and honesty who spoke his mind, a man worth listening to.

On December 21, 1912, his third child was born. It was a girl again, and they named her Zoya Alexyevna. If there was a moment of disappointment at her birth, it was quickly forgotten in the beauty of this newborn child, more beautiful than either of her sisters had been. Alexei was pleased. And after all, he and Ekaterina were still young. There was time yet for a son. (They were later to have a fourth child, a son, who would die in World War II.)

Two years after her birth, Saint Petersburg became Petrograd. Five years after her birth, the revolution, in which her father took part, occurred. But Zoya remembers none of this. Her first memory is of the man who came to the apartment and helped the family to load their belongings into his carriage, and of her mother, with tears in her eyes, kissing a neighbor woman good-bye. She remembers the horses that pulled the carriage and how she could see them when her father took her on his lap. And there was a neighbor's dog, to whom the child often gave bits of food, who followed them for blocks.

They were moving to Moscow, a reward to her father from Lenin himself. He was to work for the government inside the Kremlin, to be in charge of the documents that allowed people to enter and leave the Kremlin.

Alexei was pleased to be able at last to work with his mind instead of his hands. An avid reader, a self-educated man—how often had friends and relatives made remarks about his reading? What did a factory worker need with it? His eyes would burn out of his head, and all for nothing.

But it wasn't for nothing, he thought as he and his wife and three daughters walked through the six-room apartment in Moscow that had been assigned to him. He had never seen such furnishings in his whole life. Furniture that gleamed like oil in sunlight, and fine paintings in beautiful frames. Truly wonderful, but Alexei Fyodorov could not accept it. As he explained to Ekaterina and later to the officials who were in charge of such things, "I cannot take this furniture and all of these other things, because they do not belong to me. I didn't earn them."

Zoya remembers when all of the beautiful things were carried out. For days afterward the family ate their meals sitting on the floor with their dishes set on newspapers. And the children slept on the floor like gypsies. In time, they had their own things, but nothing so grand as what had been. And two of the rooms were rented out to strangers, because Alexei did not feel it was right to have so much room. He wasn't being difficult. He just knew what was right and wrong, and four rooms for a family of five people was more than enough.

Perhaps it was not always easy being the child of a man of such honesty and such principles, but it was an honor. Even as a child Zoya sensed that. But in later years, under Stalin, Alexei's honesty and his outspokenness would cease to be virtues and would become crimes to be used against him.

Early on in her school years Zoya fell in love with the theater and the magic of make-believe. At school she saw fairy tales and folk tales performed, and she found it all dazzling, a world unlike any she had ever known. To be a part of such a world was almost beyond imagining.

The fascination with theater stayed with her as she progressed in school. There was no feeling to compare with the excitement that raced through her body as she stepped out onto the stage in a school play. And her fascination expanded to include motion pictures, which showed even more than the theater could. She wanted to be an actress more than anything in the whole world.

But was she pretty enough? She wasn't certain. When she asked her parents, her mother would say, "All of my daughters are beautiful," and her father would just laugh and pat her on the head, so they were no real help. But she sometimes caught boys looking out of the corners of their eyes at her, and she thought they looked pleased.

Zoya couldn't quite decide how she felt about herself. A *maybe* was the best she could come up with. Her figure was good, she thought, though she did have a tendency to put on weight. And probably five feet two was as tall as she was going to grow. Was that too tiny? Her nose was sort of snubby, but her green eyes had a nice sparkle. And her blond hair was definitely attractive. Well, good or bad, it would have to do. She was determined to be an actress.

Zoya went straight from high school into the theater school conducted by the great Zavadsky, a disciple of Stanislavsky's and a noted director in his own right. But after two years, his school closed, and Zoya was back at the beginning again. With the school gone, there was no way she could get the papers she needed in order to work as an actress.

Starting again, she entered the Theater of the Revolution, and began what she thought would be four years of study with the famous actor Popov.

But when she was only in her second year, her film career began. One day, she was called out of class. An assistant film director was waiting for her. She had been seen in a small part in a play staged at the school. A film was to be made called *Concertina,* and it had been decided that Zoya was right for the heroine. She thought she would faint. Barely 20, not even out of school, and it was happening.

Well, maybe. *Concertina* was to be a film with singing and dancing. Could Zoya sing? Could she dance? She sang for the man right there in the empty classroom. Happily, the dancing turned out to be nothing more difficult than folk dancing. Yes, she could do that. "But what about my nose?" she heard herself saying to the assistant director, and she wanted to bite her tongue off. "I mean, look. It is short and it goes up."

The director only laughed. "You are a silly girl. It is because of your nose that we want you."

It was an adjustment playing in front of a camera, because Zoya's training had been for live audiences in the theater, but she caught on quickly. Even before *Concertina* was finished she was receiving offers for other films.

Concertina was a successful picture, and it made the public aware of the sweet-faced blond, but nothing more. It was her second film, *Girlfriends,* released in 1934, that established Zoya Alexyevna Fyodorova as a star for all time.

Girlfriends was the story of three women friends during World War I who volunteer to go to the front as nurses. The picture was wildly successful. It seemed to contain a special inspirational message for Russian women.

They lined up to see it over and over again, and the fictional nurses became life models to emulate. A Russian woman could look at one of the "girlfriends" and measure herself against her. Had she given as much to her country? the film seemed to ask. *Girlfriends* so caught the female imagination that it was brought back and was popular all over again when World War II started. The picture inspired women to volunteer for service in all branches so they could be like their screen heroines.

With the release of *Girlfriends* Zoya, at the age of 22, knew what it was like to be a star in her native land. When she walked in the streets now, some woman was always screaming "Zoya Fyodorova!" and rushing to embrace her. Or there were telephone calls from fans to her parents' apartment where she still lived. And men would smile at her wherever she went. She had become "Our Zoya," the "lyrical heroine" of the movies—forever sweet, always good, always in love, and always ending up with the hero in the closing scenes. She was every man's dream-wife.

And in 1934 Zoya almost saw herself that way. After all, she was in love, or she thought she was. Though she couldn't see it at the time, Zoya knew more about love from the film scripts and plays she had studied than from actual experience. His name was Vladimir Rappaport, a cameraman on *Girlfriends*. They were together every day while the film was shooting. He was a good man and he was attentive to her; and they had their work in common. It was easy to fall in love with Vladimir. In a way, it seemed to Zoya as if she had stepped into one of her films with Vladimir as her leading man.

When the day's filming finished, she strolled the streets of Leningrad, where *Girlfriends* was made, with Vladimir. She dined with him in the evening, lunched with him at the studio. Wherever she looked he was there, smiling his love at her from behind his camera.

When he told her he loved her and wanted to marry her, it was so easy for her to agree. They were married before it was time for Zoya to return to Moscow. Vladimir assumed she would stay in Leningrad where his work was. But Zoya had a film waiting for her in Moscow, and her career had only just begun. She couldn't be expected to give it up.

At first Vladimir understood, and they saw each other on weekends or whenever one could get the time to make the trip to the other's city. But despite the cliché, absence did not make the heart grow fonder. At first the reunions were warm and loving, but as the months passed, too often the weekends ended in anger. Vladimir expected his marriage to be like everyone else's, and he found himself a married man without a wife. It was Zoya's place to be with him. They even had an apartment granted to them in Leningrad, a proof from the government itself of where they were meant to live. What did Zoya have in Moscow? Only a bed in her parents' apartment.

Zoya would respond to his tirades with sighs, occasionally with tears, but rarely with words. There was nothing she could say. Secretly she thought Vladimir was right, but she couldn't go to him because she didn't love him. It wasn't a choice between love and a career. For a man she loved, a career would mean nothing. She just did not love Vladimir Rappaport. Whatever she had felt for him at the beginning was now gone. Yes, she liked him, she respected him, but that was all. And it was not enough.

Each time she knew they were to see each other, she promised herself she would tell him the truth. No matter what he would think of her, it was better than this. But she always lost her nerve. The pain in his eyes always undid her.

They were married for almost five years before he gave up, and they divorced.

In 1936 Zoya's mother was discovered to have cancer. The doctors that Alexei consulted said there was no hope for her. He could not accept that. Ekaterina could not die. In a city the size of Moscow, there had to be someone who could cure her. He asked everyone he knew to give him the names of doctors. One day in the street, he stopped a German musician who lived in his apartment building. Maybe a German doctor, if that is who served the musician's family, would know of something that the Russian doctors didn't. The German took a piece of paper and a pencil from his jacket and wrote the name and address of his doctor on it and gave the paper to Alexei. Alexei rushed off down the street to find this new hope for his wife.

But Ekaterina died. For months afterward Alexei, normally a social and talkative man, would sit home night after night speaking with no one, often not noticing the coming of darkness in the room. Zoya or one of her sisters would come home and find her father sitting in the dark.

In time Alexei began to drop in after work at the taverns where the men would spend the hours discussing the world around them. But it was the time of Josef Stalin, and one spoke only with caution. This was not an age in which a wise man was outspoken against the government. Alexei Fyodorov, however, was never a man to hide his thoughts.

One night he was at a table with five other men, and he thought they were all talking nonsense about how pleased Lenin would be with Stalin and all he had done for the people. Hadn't Lenin himself said that Stalin should succeed him? they were saying. Alexei couldn't believe what he was hearing. Didn't these men ever think for themselves? He stood up and slammed his fist on the table. The entire room grew silent and turned to him as he said in a voice that everyone could hear, "I worked for Lenin. Who should know better than I? I know for sure, and I can put my head on the guillotine that Lenin never said that Stalin should take his place after his death. That was Stalin's own idea. It was not Lenin's wish."

Throughout the tavern men stood up, said quick good-nights, and left. With a madman among them, it was not a safe place to be. Alexei looked at these men, their collars pulled up around their necks, as if they were hunching their faces out of sight. He felt contempt for them. If Russia was a free country under Stalin, why were they running?

Nothing happened to Alexei until 1938, two years after Ekaterina's death. Then a new wave of arrests swept the country, and Alexei was taken away during the night. The charge against him was "58." Every Russian knew that number. It stood for a charge based on nothing, with manufactured evidence to back it up.

Alexei Fyodorov was accused of digging a tunnel under the Kremlin wall in order to kill highly placed men in the government. Alexei's protests were in vain. "Where is this tunnel?" he demanded. "Show it to me! Why should I do such a thing? Have I not worked long and hard for the government?"

But no one listened to him.

Furthermore, he was told that he was a German-Japanese spy. "Incredible!" he shouted. "I have never even met a Japanese in my entire life."

Night after night, when his interrogators were through with him, Alexei would force his exhausted brain to think. And finally, he remembered the German musician who gave him the slip of paper in the street. And he remembered times when, after company had left their apartment, Ekaterina would beg him to watch what he said. "These are bad times. Anyone could be an informer. Even a friend in our home."

And he would pat her cheek. "My beloved one, I cannot live if I do not speak what I think. I am not even a man without that."

He knew his crimes at last. He had dared to think aloud, and he had tried to save his wife's life. Alexei Fyodorov was sentenced to ten years in a hard labor camp. Zoya did not know to which camp her father was sent but she knew it would be north, in or near Siberia, where the winter slashed at a man like knives of ice. Alexei was wearing only thin trousers and a light summer jacket when he was arrested.

To try to get an overcoat to him was impossible, to plead for him, futile. Zoya and her sisters could only pray for him.

The years passed, and Zoya's career reached new heights. In 1941 she was awarded the Laureate of Stalin for the film *The Musical Story*. As usual, she played the lyrical heroine the Russian people had come to expect from "our Zoya," a simple girl who works in a garage and falls in love with a taxi driver who becomes an opera singer. The Laureate was the highest honor an actress could hope for, a silver medallion with a gold profile of Stalin on it, suspended from a red ribbon. Zoya turned over the prize money to charity. (In 1942 she was to win the Laureate again, this time for *Girlfriends at the Front*.)

Zoya now had power in Russia, enough power that she could ask to see and be granted a meeting with Lavrenty Beria, the Commissar for Internal Affairs, head of the dreaded NKVD, and number two to Stalin himself. There were even those who thought that Beria was more to be feared than Stalin. But Zoya went to him to plead for her father. "I do not even know for certain that he is alive," she said.

Beria was standing behind his desk, sun streaming in from the windows in back of him so that she could barely see his face. "I will check on him," Beria said, "and we will see what, if anything, can be done."

Zoya saw his features for only a second as he turned away from her to stare out the window. Sunlight caught on the lenses of his pince-nez and wiped out his eyes, but she thought she saw a smile at his mouth. "But he was not a spy for anyone. My father is a loyal, patriotic man. You must know that."

The head nodded, but he did not turn to look at her. "Perhaps that is so, Zoya Alexyevna, and perhaps you will see your father very soon. And now this meeting is at an end."

In June of 1941 the German army crossed the Russian border. As one of Russia's most popular actresses, Zoya was in great demand wherever there were troops. In between pictures she was forever going to the front lines, to hospitals to sing, to tell stories, to cheer up battle-weary men. Years later, she can still cry at the memory of a room filled with hammocks, each holding a man, and of a young voice calling to her after she finished a song, "Forgive us, Zoya Alexyevna, if we do not applaud you, but none of us here has hands."

Ever since her divorce from Vladimir Rappaport, Zoya had wondered about herself: Was she capable of loving someone? To this minute, she could not explain to herself what had gone wrong. How had she confused affection, attraction—what was it?—with love? Maybe whatever it was that made her want to become an actress also made her incapable of real, sustained emotion. She had known a few actresses who were that way, women who had lived so long in a world of manufactured emotions that they were incapable of the real thing. Was she one of these sad creatures?

But in 1941 she met Ivan Klischov, an army pilot, and all of her fears ended. She loved him, there was no doubt of it. And he loved her. In only a matter of days, they were speaking of marriage. Should they, with Russia at war? Should they wait until after? They decided to wait, and for a foolish reason: Ivan's vanity.

That's really all it was. Zoya was a winner of the Laureate of Stalin. Ivan promised her that he would be awarded the Hero of the Soviet Union twice before they married. "Be *my* hero," Zoya said. "It will be enough."

Ivan kissed her. "Yours and the Soviet's, Zoyatchka."

He only won the Hero of the Soviet Union once before his plane crashed in the Battle of Stalingrad. He was pulled, badly wounded, from the wreckage of his plane, but he lived. He was in the hospital for a month and Zoya visited him every day. He was bitter that he would never be a combat pilot again.

When he came out of the hospital, he was assigned to the investigation of flight accidents. Zoya was relieved. It meant her Ivan would live.

But it was not to be. He had been out on an investigation, and rather than stay overnight, he had decided to fly back to Moscow through a storm because he was anxious to get back to Zoya. His plane crashed near the town of Tambod. The Pioneers, a Soviet youth organization, attend his grave which Zoya visits to this day.

In late summer of 1941 Zoya went to Beria again. "You promised me to find out about my father?"

Beria was again behind his desk, but this time there was no sun. She could see the face with the cold eyes behind the pince-nez. They never seemed to blink. "I promised you, Zoya Alexyevna, what did I promise you?"

She had to dig her fingernails into her palms to keep from striking him. This man was playing games with her, games with her father's life. "You indicated that I might see my father soon. You promised me that."

"Soon." He seemed to consider the word. "And how long is 'soon,' Zoya Alexyevna? How many days, weeks, months?"

She burst into tears. It was hopeless. This man was without feeling.

"And then perhaps 'soon' is now."

She looked up, and there was the faintest of smiles on his lips. "Go to your house. I am not certain who will be the first one there, you or your father."

She ran through the streets. Her father was already there when she arrived. She recognized the thin summer jacket in which he had been arrested before she recognized him. Three years in the camp had turned him into an old man. He was only 56 but he looked 70. There were deep lines in his face and he was painfully thin. As she entered the room, he stood and placed his hands behind his back as if he were a prisoner on line for inspection. "Papatchka!" She ran to him and threw her arms about him and covered his face with kisses. Their tears ran together.

"My little Zoya." He whispered it into her hair.

She felt his hands against her back, but the moment she released him, he quickly hid them again. "Papatchka," she said. "The prison is over. You do not have to stand that way anymore. You are home now."

His smile was sick. "I do not know how to show you."

She didn't understand. "Show me what?"

Slowly, he brought out his hands and held them up. He had only part of both thumbs. All of his fingers were gone.

Zoya screamed. She pressed her hands over her mouth to silence herself. The floor seemed to move under her, and she sat down abruptly, feeling faint and dizzy. There was a sour taste rising in her throat.

Alexei sat opposite her and buried his hands between his knees. When she had pulled herself together, he told her about his hands.

It had happened last winter, a bitter cold day with an angry wind cutting at the men as they worked along the road. How he had lived through the previous winters in his thin prison clothes, Alexei didn't know, but that day he felt ill. His throat ached. His chest felt as if there were straps tied across it, and there were moments when his face seemed on fire even as he felt the wind cut against him. He tried to go on working. To complain could bring severe punishment.

Finally, he gave up. He felt too ill. The guard looked at him with contempt. "There is no medical help here. You know that. We will have to transport you to the next camp where there is a doctor."

He was marched to an open truck on which corpses were being loaded. When the truck was filled, they covered the bodies with a canvas, and he was ordered to climb on board. The truck pulled out, and Alexei shrank down against the back of the cab wall to protect himself as much as possible from the wind.

It was a long ride, several hours, he thought, but he couldn't be certain. The fever that raged within his body, plus the intense cold that made him want to sleep, confused him completely. Somewhere along the way, he felt his hands going numb. He tried moving his fingers but it was painful. In desperation he forced his hands down between his legs and against his crotch for what little warmth was there.

When the truck pulled into the camp where the doctor was, the guards had to lift Alexei down. He was too stiff to stand. In the doctor's office, an assistant had to help Alexei to strip. His feet were red with cold, but the doctor said they would be all right. His temperature was 104. Perhaps pneumonia, the doctor said, and injected him with something. Then he took hold of Alexei's hands. The fingers were black with frostbite.

The doctor reached for a pair of medical shears and, as if he were pruning a rosebush, snipped off his fingers one after the other. Alexei passed out.

Zoya and her sisters took turns staying with their father. There was so little that he could do for himself. Not that he complained. The old Alexei who spoke out, who was afraid of nothing, was gone. The Alexei who came back from prison trembled at each loud noise from the street, leaped to his feet and stood at attention when anyone came to the door.

He was only home a few weeks when it was discovered that he had cancer of the lymph nodes. The hospitals were all overcrowded because of the war, but Zoya, because of her position, was able to get her father a bed. He died on September 22, 1941.

The day after his death, Beria called Zoya. "I was sorry to hear of your father's death."

Sorry? Zoya wanted to spit into the telephone. Who killed him? Who put him in the camp that killed him? But she could not say any of that. Instead she said, "You know my father was an innocent man."

There was a brief pause, then Beria said, "But he was quite a chatterbox."

The stories about Beria that circulated through Moscow were frightening. He was a drunkard, a debaucher of women and young girls. A girl would disappear from the streets and one would hear that it was because Beria wanted her. One also heard that Beria had only to tell Stalin that so-and-so was planning to assassinate him, and that man would be arrested immediately. Stalin, it was said, trusted Beria so completely that he believed everything Beria told him.

Every few months there would be a call from Beria. It chilled Zoya. This was a friendship that she didn't want. He was always polite. He had seen a film of hers and wanted to tell her how much he enjoyed it. Or he had gotten an excellent report on her last concert tour. She had done much for Soviet morale, and he wanted personally to thank her. Was there anything she needed that perhaps he might be able to get?

Zoya always thanked him and said she needed nothing.

One day he telephoned. At the request of his wife, he said. There was to be a large party at their house for her birthday, and she specifically asked that Zoya Fyodorova be invited.

Zoya thought it odd to be invited to a birthday celebration by a woman she had never met, but she accepted. One did not refuse an invitation from Lavrenty Beria. He said he would send a car and driver for her that evening.

The driver assisted Zoya into the back seat of the limousine. It was a car such as she had rarely seen, and never since the beginning of the war. It moved swiftly and silently through the nearly empty streets of Moscow. These days, only military vehicles had gasoline.

It seemed to Zoya that she had barely settled herself when the car turned onto Kachalova and through the gates in the stone wall surrounding Beria's house. As the driver helped her out, Zoya looked around the courtyard for signs of other guests. There were none.

The house seemed surprisingly silent. There were only a few lights showing, and why were there no sounds of music or laughter?

Zoya felt fear. She hesitated, then turned, but the driver was standing between her and the car. He tilted his head. Was there something the lady had forgotten? Zoya shook her head and went to the front door.

She was admitted by a colonel who served as Beria's secretary and bodyguard. He helped her with her coat, hat, and boots. When he opened the door to the guest-closet Zoya saw that there were no other coats hanging there. She felt a leap of panic, but she forced it back. Perhaps it was only that she was the first to arrive.

Beria came down the staircase that curved into the entrance

hall. He paused near the landing for a moment to smile at Zoya. She smiled, but not in greeting as he must have thought. As an actress, she recognized the pause on the staircase for what it was, a calculated theatrical effect. But she didn't know what effect he was trying to achieve.

His smile was a cold one, as if it were something he had not had much experience in doing. The pasty white skin, the light making his eyes invisible behind his pince-nez, the dull gleam on his bald head, all made Zoya think of a fat, frightening frog. He came to her and took her hand. "Zoya Alexyevna," he said, looking into her eyes, and he led her into a room off the entrance hall, holding her hand all the way.

The room was small, a waiting room of some sort, she thought. There was a lamp on a round table in the center, its light too weak to cut the gloom that crept out from the dark corners. This was no room for a party. She wanted to run, but she didn't dare. Instead, she turned quickly to sit down so that her hand pulled free from the cold, damp clasp of his. "The party?" she said, making her voice sound casual. "Where is your wife? Your other guests?"

Beria turned away to light a cigarette so that she couldn't see his face. "My wife offers you her apologies. She has a painful headache and went for a brief drive to get the winter air. She will soon return."

Zoya waited. Beria took his time. Then he turned. The smile on his face seemed to say to Zoya, Of course I am lying to you. We both know that, but does it matter between us? "Naturally, I immediately telephoned my other guests to delay their coming until my wife returns. But since the car had already gone for you, there was nothing I could do. I am certain you understand?"

It was a question. Zoya nodded. She understood.

"And now you must excuse me, dear Zoya Alexyevna. There is an emergency meeting I must attend, but I will return in no time. You understand, one is never free of the Kremlin. But my maid, Tanya, is here should you require anything. And there is our cat who may drop in to amuse you. And there is a record player in the corner, with, I think, a good selection of records." He nodded and left the room.

Zoya waited to hear the front door open and close behind him, but there was no such sound. She was certain he was still somewhere in the house.

Zoya walked around the room. The light was too dim to read the titles on the books, but when she touched one, her hand came away dusty. She found the record player, but she wasn't certain how to work it. And what if she broke a record? There were enough stories around Moscow about Beria's violent temper.

The time dragged by in heavy silence. No cat came. No maid. Fifteen minutes, twenty, a half hour. How long did he intend to play out this farce? Zoya was firmly convinced that Beria's wife wasn't even in Moscow.

The silence and the closeness of the room were getting to her. Zoya wiped her palms on her handkerchief. Surely a guest, no matter for what purpose, had some rights. She walked to the door and opened it. The hall was empty. She listened for sounds from upstairs. Nothing. Nothing but the tick of a clock somewhere.

Farther down the hall, away from the front door, there were other doors. Should she, could she, go and look? What if someone saw her? Zoya thought of her father. These days anyone could be accused of being a spy, and to go poking about in the house of Lavrenty Beria. . . . But she was a guest in this house, and she was being treated shabbily. In the poorest apartment in Moscow a guest would be offered something, yet here, in a house of wealth, no one had paid any attention to her.

Zoya felt a flush of anger. She stepped out of the room and started down the hall. If anyone stopped her, she was looking for the maid to bring her a coffee. The first door she came to was locked, but the second door opened, and Zoya saw proof of what she had known since she had entered this house.

It was the dining room, and the table was set for the kind of banquet that had disappeared with the war. The tablecloth was old lace, and there were silver candelabra at either end with candles ready to be lit. A crystal decanter of vodka sat in a crystal bowl of ice. Beside it in another bowl was a black pool of caviar. But there were only two settings at the long table. Two chairs were at right angles to each other at one corner.

Zoya quietly closed the door and went back to the small waiting room. She was shaking so, that she had to sit down. She was flooded with emotions: shame, anger, fear, and outrage. How dare he, this monster-frog, how dare he import her to his house like some prostitute? How dare he decide that she would give herself to him?

Tears of rage came to her eyes, but she forced them back. He would not see red eyes from her. And she must be calm, she told herself. She must think. Anger would not help her. She forced herself back against the chair and breathed deeply.

There, that was better. Now, what was to be done? By all rules of decency, she had every right to leave. It was almost an hour since he left her. There was no wife, no guests, no party. That was obvious. As obvious as what he had brought her for. But he was mad if he thought Zoya Fyodorova would put up with this. If he had power, so did she. She wanted to leave but she knew that she couldn't. In the little room just alongside the vestibule there would be an adjutant whose function was to keep out unwanted visitors, and to keep in those whom Beria wanted to stay.

Further thought ended as the door opened and Beria came in. "A thousand apologies, Zoya Alexyevna, but there is always someone at these meetings who feels the need of speech-making."

Zoya nodded. But she had not heard a car drive up, had not heard the front door open, and his boots showed no trace of snow.

He smiled. "This evening, I fear, is a shambles. I have just spoken with my wife and her headache has worsened. She sends her apologies, but she has decided to go to our dacha in the country where the air will be better for her. I have instructed my aide to cancel our other guests."

Zoya stood up. "I trust your wife will be better by morning. And now I must go."

Beria laughed and put his arm about her shoulder. "But that is foolish, dear lady. We have here a dinner for fifty. Surely, you will stay. I have already instructed the maid to adjust the seating."

He led her to the dining room and seated her on his right at the corner. The candles were now lit. Beria placed a mound of caviar on her plate and though she protested, filled her glass with vodka. He toasted her greatness in films and her beauty, and drank deeply. Zoya, who was not a drinker, took only a sip. She had to be in command of herself. Beyond the candle flame that danced in his lenses, she caught his eyes, cold and watching.

Beria refilled his glass. Zoya placed her hand over hers. He smiled. She smiled back. A Georgian, she thought to herself, big drinkers, every one of them.

Then he launched into a general discussion of the film industry. For a moment, Zoya felt relief. Perhaps she had been wrong about this evening. After all, films were powerful propaganda, especially in wartime. Maybe that was why she was here.

But then his conversation took a turn that offended her. He talked of the Jews in the film industry. Did Zoya know many of them? What did she think of them? How dangerous did Zoya think they were?

For Zoya this was too much. He was an animal without taste or sensitivity. As head of the secret police, Beria had access to the files on every citizen of the Soviet Union. He knew that the man Zoya had been married to was a Jew who worked in films.

The maid had removed the caviar plates, and now a bowl of hot, golden *chikhirtma*—the Georgian chicken soup, rich with egg yolks and lemon juice beneath a film of olive oil—was placed before her, and from the kitchen Zoya could smell lamb. The aromas were dizzying. She hadn't known such smells since the beginning of the war. Oh, if only she could control her anger with this animal of a man until she had eaten this meal.

She looked at Beria. Was he mocking her, baiting her? The face was inscrutable. Zoya chose her words carefully. "Forgive me, Lavrenty Pavlovich, but I am surprised to hear you speak this way."

He looked at her over his glass as he emptied it for the second time. "Tell me why, Zoyatchka." He leaned toward her and dropped his free hand on her knee.

She turned to him and in the deliberate shifting of her body caused his hand to fall away. "Because when you speak like this, you sound like an ignorant street boy. And that is beneath a man of your power in our government. A man like you is for all the people in our country, surely."

She watched his face for a clue. Had there been enough sugar in what she had said? Had she offended him? There was nothing. He refilled his vodka glass and sat back in his chair, ignoring the soup.

She found his silence unnerving. "You know, of course, that my husband was Jewish?" she said.

He smiled. "But you are not married now." He leaned toward her again and placed his hand on her thigh. "Do you miss marriage and the pleasures it offers, Zoya Alexyevna?"

Zoya picked his hand from her as if she were picking off lice. "Stop that, or I will leave."

"I do not want you to leave," he said as if that settled everything.

His absolute assurance infuriated Zoya. She stood up. "What do you think I am? And where do you think we are? This is not the Russia of a hundred years ago where you could pick out a little actress and have her brought to you."

"Bravo!" Beria said and applauded her. Then his face grew stern. "And now sit down. You look foolish, like some little monkey."

Zoya lost all control. It wasn't the attack on her vanity, but the absolute certainty of this ugly man that she was his for taking. "And if I am a monkey, what are you? Get up and go to the mirror and look! You will see an ape!"

Beria's face darkened. "How dare you speak to me this way? Do you think I am even slightly interested in you, a short nothing of a woman? It is ridiculous. You were invited here as an actress whose films I have enjoyed. That is all. Physically, you repel me."

"I am delighted to hear that," Zoya said, "and now I would like to go home."

Beria reached with his foot to a bell beneath the table. The colonel came to the door. "This woman is leaving."

Beria reached for the decanter and refilled his glass. He sat back in his chair and twirled the glass in the candlelight. Zoya was forgotten. He paid no attention as she left the room.

The colonel got her coat and helped her with her boots. The car and driver were waiting in front of the house. As the driver opened the door for her, Zoya saw a bouquet of roses carefully placed on the rear seat. She reached in and picked them up. She almost laughed. The great commissar hadn't had time to tell his driver that there was no reason to thank this woman. The nerve of the man to be so sure of himself!

She turned to the house and saw Beria standing in the doorway. Zoya held up the flowers. "For me?"

She couldn't see his face because the light was behind him, but his voice was icy. "They could be for your grave."

The massive door closed, and Zoya was left in the driveway, shivering. She placed the flowers in the car, as far away from herself as possible. She left them there when the driver helped her out in front of her apartment building on Gorki Street.

In January of 1945 Zoya Alexyevna Fyodorova was only a few weeks past her thirty-second birthday. She was one of the Soviet Union's most beloved film stars, she earned a decent salary by Soviet standards, and she had her own apartment on Gorki Street, only a few blocks from Red Square. Considering the hardships of the war, she had a good life. Except that she was alone.

BOOK
II

MOSCOW, 1945

By some miracle, the apartment was empty. Jack Tate was grateful for the quiet. Where the two other American officers who shared the apartment were, he didn't know, and frankly, he didn't care. Luba, the cook and housekeeper who took care of them, was either home or turning in her weekly report on the *Americantzis* to the NKVD. That wasn't guesswork. Luba had told them openly that she was ordered to spy on her employers. It was the one good thing Jack Tate could say for her. She was unattractive, sour-faced, a rotten cook, but at least she was an honest spy.

Moscow was getting him down. It wasn't the city, or the constant snow, or the wartime hardships. It was the day-after-day haggling over the most minor details of Operation Mile Post that was eating at him. The Russians had agreed that they would come into the war against Japan 90 days after the war ended in Europe. They had agreed to the building of an American airfield in Siberia from which bombing raids against mainland Japan could be launched. With all that settled, the whole project should have gone ahead like gangbusters, yet it was continuously getting caught in petty bureaucracy. Every Russian he dealt with was terrified of making any positive statement, of taking the slightest responsibility on his own. To work with them was like trying to run through quicksand. You kept getting bogged down.

He had arrived in January, and now it was February. One whole month gone, and he wasn't certain he had accomplished one goddamn thing. He might as well have stayed in Texas.

He stared into the bathroom mirror and rubbed at his face. He decided that he could get away with not shaving again, and finished knotting his tie for his dress uniform.

What he really wanted to do was just stay in for the evening, eat whatever was in the kitchen, probably cabbage soup—the only thing Luba seemed capable of cooking, or maybe of being able to buy to cook—and then go to bed. But an engraved invitation from Molotov was not something you turned down lightly. Not that he knew him. Every American in Moscow had received one. But there had also been a note from the American ambassador, W. Averell Harriman, calling attention to it, which was a polite way of saying "show up."

Jack went into the living room to take another look at the invitation. It lay on the grand piano, where there was some open sheet music for "Begin the Beguine." Who had moved the piano into the apartment, who had bought the sheet music, Jack didn't know. None of the current occupants could even play "Chopsticks."

The invitation said 8 P.M. at Spiridonivskaya Dom and called for "formal dress with orders." The occasion was the twenty-seventh anniversary of the Red Army, and that meant a big blowout. Jack checked the fruit salad on his jacket—three rows of ribbons. They represented a lot of years, though tonight they wouldn't look like much, Jack thought, up against the Russians who would show up clanking with every medal and ribbon they owned.

As he turned to leave, he caught sight of Red Square in the moonlight out of the bay window in the living room, and it riveted him as it always did. He had been in Moscow for a month and he still couldn't get used to the spectacle of it all, especially St. Basil's Cathedral rising and curling upward in Byzantine splendor. Maybe working with the Russians could drive a man crazy, but it was worth it just for the sight of the domes of St. Basil's, or the feeling of power that pressed down on a man when he walked in front of the red Kremlin wall.

He glanced at his wristwatch. Time to get moving. He went to get his coat and checked for his car keys. Anyway, the food had to be better than Luba's cabbage soup.

Zoya stood in front of the mirror and turned from side to side to check the wear on her navy-blue velvet dress. There was no denying it, there was definitely a shine beginning at the elbows and where the arms rubbed against the sides. Well, it would have to do. It had been a long war and decent new dresses were close to impossible to get. Perhaps if she draped the wool stole loosely so that it hung low? Yes, that would help.

Then she checked her stockings. Nothing showed below the calf-length hem. And if the little snag near the top of the right leg didn't develop into a major run, she'd be fine.

She looked forward to the reception at Spiridonivskaya Dom. It was correct to call that place *dom;* it truly was a palace. She remembered it well from the previous year's anniversary celebration. And it was an honor for an artist to be invited. And the food and drink! Not that she cared much about the drinking, but the food! Good food, especially nowadays, was always a matter of importance. But best of all were the exciting, intelligent people who would be there. Everyone of any importance in the arts, surely. They interested Zoya the most. She knew and cared little for politics.

Zoya felt a need for new people. The war had hurt her and driven her into herself. It had taken away her brother, and then Ivan, and her father. She knew that her father's death really had nothing to do with the war, but somehow the brutality of what had been done to him linked him with the war for her. For too long now she had lived only with her work, a few photographs of the men who were gone from her life, and three graves to visit.

But now it was time to come alive again. She could feel the stirrings within herself. Happiness was a more natural state to Zoya, and she was fighting her way back to it.

She took a last look at herself in the mirror. The deep blue of the velvet went well with her blond hair. She went to get her coat and boots.

The line of cars was half a block long as Jack arrived. When he finally came abreast of the NKVD men guarding the gates, they just waved him in without asking for credentials or invitation. He had no doubt that they knew every American inside Russia right down to his undershorts.

When Jack had checked his coat and hat, he entered the first of what turned out to be a string of enormous rooms, with marble walls and floors and many large crystal chandeliers. In the first ballroom stood Molotov and his wife, and a receiving line stretched out from them all the way across the room. Jack got on line behind a tall man in a tailcoat and a lady in a red silk gown. From their looks and the sound of the language they were speaking, Jack decided they were from one of the Scandinavian countries. He spotted Ambassador Harriman farther up the line in a double-breasted business suit. He also thought he saw Dimitri Shostakovich, but he couldn't be certain. The man looked somewhat like the picture of Shostakovich he had seen on concert posters. He recognized none of the Russians on the line, though he was certain that all the top brass in Moscow would be here tonight.

The noise was deafening as voices bounced and rebounced off the marble walls. Jack could see a string quartet at work across the room, but he couldn't hear one note of what they were playing.

Finally, he was up to the Molotovs. Madame Molotov barely touched his hand with her pudgy one. She smiled, but did not speak. Molotov, then Commissioner for Foreign Affairs, was a big man, with everything wide about his face. Jack didn't know if he was supposed to shake hands or what. He waited for Molotov to make the first move. It was *his* shindig. Molotov merely nodded his head and said, "Velcome." No smile crossed his face. His eyes slid over Jack's epaulets and moved on to the next person. Jack said, "*Spasibo*," thank you, and left the line.

He moved into the next room, where there were tables along the back with decanters of vodka and small glasses, as well as bottles of Russian champagne, both the white and the pink.

The rest of the room was filled with rows of folding chairs arranged in front of a raised platform where there was a piano. Obviously there was going to be some sort of concert first. Jack grabbed a vodka and headed for the next room. He wasn't in the mood for songs he didn't understand.

Back in the days when the Dom was a working palace, this had undoubtedly been the main ballroom. A band was setting up at one end, and banquet tables ran the full length of both sides of the room. At the moment, they only displayed vodka and champagne and some small things to nibble on that Jack didn't recognize. He tried one and didn't like it. He finished his vodka and got himself another, making a mental note to watch himself. There was nothing the Russians liked better than seeing an American drunk and making a fool of himself.

Five men, all in Red Army uniforms, entered the room in a cluster. They were coming straight toward Jack when they hesitated for just a second and then veered off and away from him.

It's crazy, Jack thought. Here we are allies, and yet there is no real trust between us. It was something he was aware of all the time wherever he went. The top brass was always stiff and formal. Lower down on the chain of command you saw fear in the eyes. The lesser men knew they had to deal with you, but they never wanted to be put in a position of responsibility. If at all possible, they avoided signing even the simplest receipt, which could become evidence against a man at some future date.

Only the people in the street seemed friendly. When he wore his uniform he saw the curious stares and the faint smiles when he caught their eyes. He always had the feeling they wanted to speak with him, but that they didn't dare.

Of course, when he wore the civvies he had been told to bring with him to Russia—the dark blue suit, the cap, and the ankle-high boots—and looked like most men in Moscow, he was treated like any other Russian, which meant rudely. Then he was jostled or bumped into on the street with never an apology, only an annoyed glance.

He sipped at his vodka and looked around the room for someone to speak to. He didn't spot anyone who looked as if he spoke English. The five Russians had just completed one of their many toasts. Jack watched as they downed their drinks, then held the upturned glasses over their heads to prove that they were empty before refilling their glasses. The band, despite peasant blouses, turned out to be a jazz group. When they swung into their opening number, a current Moscow favorite, "Don't Sit Under the Apple Tree with Anyone Else but Me," it sounded twice as loud, crashing against the marble walls, and all conversations automatically escalated in volume.

Jack was about to go on to another room when a tiny blond woman in a dark blue dress entered. The five Russians raised their glasses to her. She acknowledged their toast with pleasure. As she moved toward the serving table, Jack noticed that people turned to stare at her. He decided she was somebody of importance, but he had no idea who she might be. She didn't look political.

He found himself interested. He let his eyes roam over her body. She had a good figure, not big-boned like so many Russian women, and she moved gracefully. She shook her head when a waiter offered her a vodka, and accepted a glass of champagne. A man came up to her and leaned over to whisper something. She smiled, but whatever he said didn't interest her much. The man went away.

At that moment she became aware of someone staring at her, and she looked up. Jack saw that her eyes were green, and he liked that. She smiled at him, then turned away.

Jack was just starting to go over to her when the room fell silent. He noticed that a man in a uniform heavy with medals was standing in front of the band with his glass raised. Another toast. The Russians all tilted back their glasses. Jack took one swallow of his.

Men pushed in around him to refill their glasses. Jack stepped away from the table and looked for the woman, but she was gone.

Jack started in the direction of where she had last been. A hand slammed down on his shoulder. "How you doin', sport?"

It was an American major who lived in the same building as Jack, but he didn't know his name. "Just fine. You?"

The man held up his empty glass. "I'm getting there."

"You'd better watch it, pal."

The major laughed. "Something's going to kick up my ulcer tonight, and I'd rather it be vodka than Russky food. I'd sell my sister for a plain old hamburger right now."

Jack nodded and moved on, searching for the woman. There was something very appealing about her. She stuck in his mind, and it had been a long time since anyone had affected him that way.

He was certain she hadn't left the ballroom, but it was filling up rapidly as the food appeared on the tables. And what food. There was a lavish *zakuska,* a Russian smorgasbord of epic proportions. Huge bowls of caviar, so large that they looked like pools of ink; platters of roast beef, sturgeon, and pressed duck; serving trays heaped with piroshki stuffed with meat and cheese. The best-dressed people pushed into the tables like starving ragamuffins. Jack stepped back to avoid the crush and began working his way around the room.

He was almost three quarters of the way when he found her. It was the light, tinkling laugh that made him turn. At first he didn't see any woman, only three tall burly men in a semicircle. But then the laugh came again, and he moved so that he could see between the men, and there she was. The conversation was in Russian, so he waited.

The American had turned and gone to the serving table. Was he going to go away? She didn't want him to. She smiled radiantly at the men with her. "Now, I must leave you, my three heroes. I do not know why I was invited to this grand reception, but I am certain it was not to devote myself exclusively to you three, no matter how charming I may find you. I think we women are supposed to circulate."

What could they do? They saluted her with their glasses and moved aside. Zoya stepped to the table and held out her glass for more champagne. The American was just a little way down the table. Zoya turned to him. He was looking at her. She smiled, and he came over.

"Hello."

Zoya nodded. "Hal-lo."

"I'm Jackson Rogers Tate. Captain. Navy."

His smile was nice, she thought. It went with his puppy-dog eyes. But what was he saying? If only he would speak more slowly. She gave him the charming laugh. It didn't work. He looked puzzled.

"I said my name is Jackson Rogers Tate. What is your name?"

Now she understood what he was asking. "Zoya Alexyevna Fyodorova." She laughed. Now it was his turn to look confused. "Zoy-YAH. Zoy-YAH."

He tried it out and she nodded enthusiastically. But what was he called? "Say for me now you name, please."

"JACK-son. JACK-son, or Jack if you . . ."

She motioned him to silence. "Jackson, yes?"

He took the hand she extended to him, and it thrilled him. So tiny, so delicate, so soft.

She felt as if her hand had been captured, but she felt safe in that hand.

"Do you speak much English?" he asked.

"A few," she said. "You speak Russian?"

"A few."

He made a circling motion indicating the room. She nodded. He extended an arm for her, but she smiled sadly and shook her head. She didn't think it was a good idea. He understood.

They moved slowly through the crowded rooms. Occasionally, someone would stop to speak with Zoya. Another time, the American major, now obviously drunk, stopped Jack by grabbing his arm. "How you doing, pal?" He gave Jack a leering wink.

"Just fine," Jack said, and was surprised at the coldness he felt toward the man. Hell, he barely knew this woman, or even what she was. Why was he feeling so protective?

They stopped in front of the string quartet. The violinist raised his bow as a salute to Zoya. He turned and said something to the others, and they struck up a melody that she seemed to know. She bowed her head in thanks. She began to sing softly so that only Jack could hear.

He didn't know what the song was about, but he thought her voice was a good one. When she finished, he mimed applause to her. She blushed.

"Spasibo," he said.

Zoya smiled. "You're welcome."

They began to walk again. "Are you a singer?" Jack asked.

"Actress. In cinema."

He looked impressed. Zoya was pleased that he didn't know her. At least, it told her he was interested in the woman, not the motion picture actress.

The trouble with this conversation, Jack thought, is it doesn't allow for subtleties and for damn little small talk. Well, there was nothing to do but plunge right in and hope she was as interested as he was. "Do you live in Moscow?"

She looked puzzled. He rephrased it. "Your home. House. Moscow?"

"*Da.*"

He took a deep breath. They had almost completed the circle of the room, and he didn't feel like going around again. The place was too crowded. "Is your husband here with you? I would like to meet him."

She didn't understand. He made a ring with his fingers around his wedding finger. She laughed. "Not married. You?"

"Separated." She didn't know the word. He tried again. "No good. Divorce when I go home."

She nodded and seemed pleased.

They looked at each other without speaking, knowing they had communicated, that something had begun between them.

Zoya smiled with mock sadness. "I go now."

Jack asked if he could take her home. Zoya shook her head. She needed time to think about this American. That she was attracted she had no doubt, but she had to think about the risk of being seen with him.

Jack walked her to the entrance hall. He helped her on with her coat and boots.

She held out her hand. He took it. They looked deep into each other's eyes. Then she turned to leave.

"Zoya!"

She turned and stopped. Jack took out a pad and his pen. "How do I find you? I want to see you again." She didn't seem to understand.

"Do you have a telephone? What is your number?" Jack

acted out putting a telephone receiver to his ear and dialing.

Zoya smiled as she realized what the pen and pad were for. "Da." She wrote her telephone number for him.

She gave him a last smile and started to leave.

He looked at the number before he put the pad back into his breast pocket. He felt excited at the thought of seeing her again, and he was surprised at himself. Here he was in his middle years feeling the thrills of youth again.

Suddenly, he realized he was hungry, and he remembered that all the time he had been with Zoya he hadn't eaten anything. He walked back into the first room, the one in which Molotov had received his guests. Now there was one long table down the center of the room. He took a plate and heaped it with roast beef and duck, skipping the sturgeon, which he wasn't used to.

As he turned from the table, he stopped and stared. Zoya was back, down at the far end of the table near the entrance. She had her fur coat draped over her shoulders like a cape. As he watched, she opened her purse under cover of her coat and, slipping some slices of beef onto a napkin, stuffed them in. She then left the room.

Jack laughed. "I'll be damned."

The streets were bitter cold and slippery with ice. Zoya barely noticed. She didn't even see the man who recognized her and tipped his hat. She was too busy thinking of the American she had met and humming the song from her film that the musicians had played for her. Every few moments, she would say, "Jackson, Jackson," under her breath. Such a name, but she wanted to remember it if he should telephone. No, she corrected herself. When he telephoned.

Both of her sisters were waiting for her in her apartment as she had told them to. The sight of Alexandra's serious face made Zoya feel giddy. "La-la!" She gave herself a fanfare and spun in a circle.

Both sisters reacted as Zoya knew they would. Maria's little face lighted up, hungry for all the glamor of the evening. And Alexandra frowned. "You are drunk," she said.

Zoya laughed. "In a way."

"Was it wonderful?" Maria asked.

"Very wonderful," Zoya said. She opened her purse and took out the napkin, which was wet and red with beef juice.

"You have ruined your purse," Alexandra said.

Zoya laughed and unfolded the napkin. "Do you mind?" she asked as the thin slices of beef lay before the women. There were five slices. Zoya gave three to Alexandra—after all, she had two children—and two to Maria. "Next time, I will carry a bigger purse."

Alexandra said, "You could be sent away for life for stealing food."

Zoya laughed. "And you for receiving stolen property. If you fear it, dear sister, do not take it."

Alexandra sniffed. She wrapped two of the slices in a piece of newspaper and ate the third. Maria took delicate bites of her slice, as if it were fine chocolate that she wanted to last.

Zoya put the kettle on for tea, talking all the while. It was a performance she was giving and she knew it. She exaggerated her moment with Molotov into a full conversation. She told of the musicians playing one of her songs, and how people had burst into applause for her afterward. But all the while she spoke, she thought of Jackson and tried to decide if she should tell her sisters about him. After all, what was there to say? She had met an American man and there had been a flirtation. That's all there was to it, so why talk about it like some silly school girl with a new love every day? Let there first be something to tell, and then she would share it.

She filled the tea glass. And yet, she thought, even if it was only this one brief meeting, this American had brought her back to life. That was something to share with her sisters. That was news worth telling. Ivan would always be in some part of her heart, but now she was beginning again.

When they were seated around the table sipping their tea, Zoya said very casually, "I met a most attractive American military officer tonight. He asked for my telephone number."

Alexandra's eyes narrowed. "Did you give it to him?"

Maria laughed in excitement. "What does he look like? Is he very tall and thin the way one hears they all are?"

"Not that tall, and I wouldn't call him thin. But a good sturdy build."

Alexandra reached out and grabbed Zoya's wrist. "I said did you give him your telephone number?"

"Yes, of course. I told you I found him attractive."

"Fool!"

I shouldn't have told you, Zoya thought to herself. Now, the happiness is gone from the room. I only did it so that maybe we could smile the way we used to before the war.

She looked at Maria staring down at her tea, her shoulders tensed against the outburst that would come in a minute. Poor Maria, Zoya thought, so like me. She wants to see the joy in life. Only Alexandra sees life seriously, like a continuous punishment. There is enough bad in our lives today without always looking for more.

"And if he calls, will you see him?" Alexandra asked.

Zoya looked straight into her sister's eyes. "Yes. Why not?"

Alexandra leaned forward. "I'll tell you why not in one word. Papa."

"And what has Papa to do with this?"

"Papa asked the German for the address of a doctor, and that question led to his death."

Zoya knew there was truth in what her sister was saying, but she refused to understand. To understand was to go back to that gray world she had lived in until this evening. "You forget, Alexandra, that the Americans are our allies. If he should telephone to ask me out, and if I should go, I would not be consorting with the enemy."

"Who knows for certain who the enemy is in these times? Was the German our enemy when Papa asked him the name of the doctor? We weren't even at war then. Your American has nothing to fear. Only you can lose. Think with your head for once, Zoyatchka. This is not the cinema."

If only Alexandra would stop. There would be time enough to think it all through if he telephoned.

"And what can they do to me?" Zoya said. She held up her hand to silence her sister's answer. "I am not some little nothing farm girl. I may be your little sister, but outside of this room I am Zoya Fyodorova, and that is something. People love me. No one would dare to touch me."

Alexandra said nothing for a moment. "I hope so."

The three women drank their tea in silence. Finally, Zoya said, "Anyway, there is little to worry about. This great romance has problems. My Americanyets and I can barely speak with each other."

Maria giggled. Alexandra smiled. It was over.

Jack Tate sat on the sofa facing Red Square and had a last cigarette before bed. Tired as he was, he didn't think he'd sleep. The evening had shaken him up. How had that little blond creature reached him so immediately? It had been some time since he had been with a woman. Maybe that was part of it, but he didn't think so. After all, he wasn't a horny kid anymore. And it certainly wasn't anything this Zoya said to him. Hell, they could barely reach each other conversationally.

It was just some special something that was more than physical attraction or desire, more than admiration for her mind—not until they could speak could he find out if she even had a mind. It was a warmth that surrounded her like a mist and enveloped him from the moment he saw her. He couldn't really explain it to himself because no woman had ever affected him this way before.

He wanted to see her again, but should he? Though he would never admit it, he felt something akin to fear—just the faintest twinge of it. The years of navy life and the rigorous demands it made on a man had sealed off most of his emotions, and he wasn't certain that he could unblock them, or wanted to. He only knew those few minutes with her made him think of a time when he had heard the far-off roar of a tidal wave approaching long before he saw it.

He butted his cigarette and stood up. Time for bed. He turned and banged his thigh against the sharp edge of the grand piano. He cursed and rubbed at the pain. Why the hell was there a piano in this room anyway, when nobody played?

His last thought before he fell asleep was that he would call Zoya. And he must remember, first thing, to buy a Russian-English dictionary.

Zoya lay in bed. She could hear the occasional rumble of traffic from Gorki Street. The little slice of sky she could see through the window was dark. Snow again, probably. Her thoughts were slowing down. Soon she would be asleep.

Of course, Alexandra was right. There would be some risk in seeing this American, but only maybe. He was an ally of the U.S.S.R., and she was Zoya Fyodorova, at the height of her popularity. But still. . . . She wondered why she always had to fight Alexandra, even when she agreed with her. Alexandra always saw the worst, was night to Zoya's day. They loved each other, but when they were together there were sparks in the air. And Maria was always in the middle, reaching out to both of them.

Jackson. Jackson something Tett. Well, Jackson, anyway. That was enough to remember for now.

She smiled in the darkness remembering their meeting. Zoya had been so flustered she had forgotten most of the English she knew. It would serve her right if he didn't telephone.

Not that she knew that much English, but there were words and phrases she had picked up through the years. Working in films had brought her into contact with people from outside the Soviet Union—newspaper people, magazine writers, diplomats. She had listened and learned. But two words from this man, and almost everything had flown out of her head. Well, at their next meeting, she'd be in better control. Maybe it would be a good idea if tomorrow she called her friend Elizabeth Egan, who was a journalist. She could help Zoya with some American phrases.

Zoya began to sing: "My bonnie lies over the ocean. My bonnie lies over the sea." She smiled into the darkness. She had never found out what a *bonnie* was. And what was the name of the journalist who had taught her the song at that party? Maybe a bonnie was something dirty?

If he telephoned, she would buy a dictionary with both Russian and English in it.

She turned over and fell asleep.

The next day, Jackson spoke with the interpreter who had been assigned to him during the working day. He unfolded a piece of paper on which he had printed "Seven o'clock/ Tomorrow night/ The night after that?/ What is your address?/ I'll come for you." He stuck it on the desk in front of the man. "Give me the Russian for these words. Only phonetically. No Cyrillic."

The man read the phrases. He smiled knowingly up at Jack, then began to print.

That evening Jack dialed her number. "Zoya?"

"Da."

"Jackson Tate, remember me?"

"Jackson, hallo!"

He read the words carefully from his paper and made a date with her for the next night at seven o'clock.

He was surprised that at the end of their conversation she said, "Thank you very much, Jackson."

The next afternoon, his interpreter said to him, "Forgive me, Captain, but those words you asked of me yesterday. They were for a Russian woman?"

Jack looked at him suspiciously. "What's it to you?"

The Russian held up his hands in protest. "Please, sir, I mean friendly."

"So?"

"Only that I would not wear my uniform. Is better for her. No trouble that way."

"What trouble?"

The Russian shrugged and walked away.

Jack wore the blue suit and his cap that evening. When Zoya opened the door for him, she pointed to the suit. "Good," she said, and nodded her head solemnly to indicate he had made a wise decision.

He caught it. "Are you afraid?"

She didn't understand. She held up a finger indicating he should wait a moment. Then she went to a table and picked up the small dictionary she had purchased. She held it up so that he could see what it was.

Jack smiled and fished his dictionary out of his coat pocket. They laughed.

The Tsentralnaya was only a few blocks from Zoya's apartment on Gorki Street. But that wasn't why Jack had chosen it.

He had been told that along one wall there was a row of booths curtained off from the room. Back in the days before the revolution, when the Tsentralnaya had been Filippov's, the grand dukes used to bring their little ballerinas here for discreet suppers. Jack was hoping for one of those booths so he could be alone with Zoya. He had nothing in mind that required discretion, he just hated the fact that in Russia a table for two was almost an impossibility, and the idea of sharing a table with two strangers and two dictionaries was more than he was up to.

When they entered, the woman in charge of seating rushed up to them. She ignored Jack completely. "Welcome, dear Zoya Fyodorova. We are so pleased to have you here."

The curtains were drawn in front of the booths, and before Jack could get around to asking if they were all occupied the woman was leading Zoya into the room that was only half-filled. She was about to seat them at a round table with another couple when Zoya said something. The woman nodded and took them to an empty table in the corner.

When they were seated, Jack asked, "Do you know her?"

Zoya shook her head. "She know me. My movies."

Jack sighed. So this was what it was going to be like, courting a movie star.

Zoya leaned toward him. She spoke softly. "If speak English, speak quiet, yes?"

Jack understood. "Are you afraid?" he asked her again.

"*Nyet.*" But she made a wiggling gesture with her hands to indicate a certain caution. Although she still believed that no one would harm her, she knew there was wisdom in what Alexandra had said. There was always enough trouble in Russia without going out of one's way to ask for it.

A stocky waitress brought a pitcher of kvass to the table and filled their glasses. Then the hostess came over with the zakuska, the traditionally elaborate smorgasbord. It was at best a skimpy plate with two thin slices of sausage on it, and the rest of the plate filled with pickled apple wedges and shredded cabbage. "Forgive the zakuska, Zoya Fyodorova, but it is the war."

Zoya said something in Russian that made the woman smile.

"You want this stuff?" Jack asked. "Would you rather have vodka or champagne?"

Zoya smiled. "You will not get."

She was right. They weren't even brought menus. Instead they took what the restaurant could provide. The meal began with cabbage soup. Jack groaned, thinking of Luba and the daily cabbage soup she prepared at the apartment. But the soup at the Tsentralnaya was less watery and had some sort of herbs in it that helped it.

The main course was *kurnik*, a chicken and rice pie, which ran more heavily to vegetables than to chicken. Again, "the war."

But the food didn't matter to either of them. They were both caught in the throes of discovery and revelation. Jack asked about her movies and didn't understand what a "lyrical heroine" was. Zoya fluttered her hands and batted her eyelashes to show him. He laughed.

He told her that he knew people at M-G-M if she was interested in making films in America.

Zoya smiled at his innocence. She had never been outside of the U.S.S.R. and she didn't think she would ever be allowed out. She thought of Beria and saw that cold smile of his. No, she would never get out while he lived. But she told Jack she would think about it.

She asked about his wife. It was important to her. "I must understand," she said. There had been enough pain in her life without becoming involved with a married man, and an American at that.

"Only the law says we are married," Jack explained. Zoya looked up the word "law" in her dictionary. She still didn't understand. Jack tried again, spacing out the words. "Not—love—each—other." Zoya nodded. "Not—see—long—time." Zoya nodded again.

"Dee—vorss?" she asked.

Jack nodded. "When I get home."

Did that mean he would be leaving soon? Zoya was surprised at the way her breath seemed to catch. Did this man matter so much already? "You go home soon?"

Jack shook his head. "I doubt it." She didn't understand. "I—think—not."

He smiled. It's Tarzan talking to Jane, he thought.

"What?" Zoya asked, seeing him smile.

Jack pointed from himself to her. "You. Me. It is crazy."

Zoya nodded. "But why not?"

Jack toasted her with the kvass. "Why not?"

The hostess threaded her way through the tables that were now all filled. Two men followed her. She seated them at their table. Zoya, pretending to wipe her mouth with the napkin, put a finger to her lips. They finished the meal in silence.

When they were outside, Jack suggested a walk. Zoya pulled the collar of her coat up and they started out. Jack reached for her hand, but Zoya pulled away. She explained that it was considered immodest in Russia to show affection in the streets.

They headed for Red Square. Traffic was sparse, and there were few people in the streets. An old lady, bundled in shabby scarves, was sweeping slush toward a drain. Jack looked and shook his head. The poor old thing should be indoors, somewhere warm.

"What?" Zoya asked. When Jack told her, she said, "But she must eat."

They passed two drunken soldiers. They made grand bows, doffing their caps. "Zoyatchka!"

Zoya stiffened and walked swiftly on. Jack hurried to catch up to her. Had they insulted her?

"Da."

Jack turned, ready to go back to the men. Zoya grabbed at his arm to stop him. She explained that the insult wasn't anything they said, but that they had been familiar with her name. "Zoyatchka is only for family, for a man one cares for."

A biting wind raked their faces as they stepped into the openness of Red Square. The gold domes of the Church of the Assumption gleamed dully in the thin moonlight. Jack pointed to one of the dark shadows. "That is where I live."

Zoya nodded.

Two women carrying *avoskas*, the net shopping bags that seemed almost a part of every woman's wardrobe in Moscow, hurried by. Suddenly, the blacked-out square burst into light and color as the sky was pierced by a shower of Roman candles. From all over the city came the dull, heavy thumps of cannon fire. Zoya grinned. "Good."

It was a "victory salute," the government's way of telling the citizenry to turn on the radio for the announcement of another Red Army triumph. Jack looked at Zoya, her face radiant, bathed in the soft glow of the colored sky. She was at her loveliest, and he wanted to take her in his arms right out in the middle of Red Square and kiss her. But even in this excited moment of victory, he knew it was out of the question.

There were usually two or three victory salutes every night. Sometimes they were announcements of important victories such as a town taken in the Russian march toward Berlin, and sometimes they were meaningless word games that when added up simply meant that a Russian tank brigade had not advanced but it also had not retreated. More times than not, Jack had dismissed the salutes as morale-propaganda, but now looking at Zoya's face he saw the value of them. It had been a long and costly war for the Russians. The people had been depleted by it in every possible way. They lived on hope now, and every skyrocket burst was like a shot of Adrenalin to them.

Jack reached for her hand and took it for a moment. "Soon. Soon it will be over."

"I hope," Zoya said. Then her face saddened. "And you will go home, Jackson."

He shrugged. "There's no one waiting for me."

She was right, of course. He would go back to the United States some time in the future. But where in the States would he go? Florida, California, Texas—he had lived in so many places, but none of them were really home. If he had a home, it was on board the *Altamaha*. That ship had been his home, perhaps more than any place on land.

Home was where someone cared for you. Because of Zoya, home at the moment was Moscow, a place he could never be completely comfortable in. He barely knew her, he admitted to himself, but already an undefined bond existed between them. He felt it, and he was certain she felt it, too.

They turned and left Red Square and started along Gorki Street toward Zoya's apartment.

She invited him up and, once inside, took his coat from him. "I must talk," she said.

He sat down and waited, while she fidgeted with a handkerchief. "Is something wrong?"

She looked up and smiled. "No, I am just . . ." She had to turn to her dictionary. "Embarrass."

"Tell me."

She took a deep breath. "If you will see me again?"

"Is that what's embarrassing you? Asking me that?"

Zoya was looking at her lap again. She nodded her head.

Jack laughed. He reached out and took her hand. "Zoya, look at me." She raised her head. "I want very much to see you again, do you understand?"

She nodded her head. "Then we must talk." In halting English, with several stops for the dictionary, she told him there had to be some rules for their seeing each other. It was not that she was afraid, but it was foolish not to be cautious. Therefore it would really be better if he wore the suit instead of his uniform. But if he was going to wear his uniform, he should please understand if she brought someone along, maybe her sister Maria, so that they did not look like a couple. And when he wore the uniform, he should understand if they walked a few feet apart in the street. And when he wore the suit and the cap it would be better if they did not speak English when other people were around. That way people would think he was a Russian. Even if they met a friend of Zoya's it would be better if he kept silent. Most of her friends she trusted, yes; others, who could say? Since the coming of Stalin, there had been too many stories one heard of friends and even family members who had turned each other in to the NKVD.

"But our countries are allies," Jack said.

Zoya shrugged. "Today, yes. But who knows tomorrow?"

"All right," Jack said. "It's your country, so you're in charge. I guess I'd better bone up on my Russian."

"Bun up? What is?"

He laughed. "Practice."

"Good," Zoya said, "and I bun up on English for when we are alone."

He stood up, and she helped him on with his coat. She followed him to the door. He turned and took her in his arms. She lifted her face to his, and he kissed her. "Zoyatchka." He whispered it into her hair.

She nodded. "Yes, for you, Zoyatchka."

They kissed again.

He called her the next evening. A woman answered. "Zoya?"

"Who is this?"

"It's Jackson. Who is this?"

"Zoya is not here." The telephone went dead.

He waited an hour and dialed again. This time, it was Zoya. When he asked about the other woman, she told him it was her sister Alexandra. "She does not like."

"Doesn't like what? Me? She hasn't even met me."

"Not you, Jackson. You and me. She thinks it is very bad, very much trouble."

"Do you feel that way, too?"

Zoya laughed. "I take chance."

"I'm glad. I want to see you. Tomorrow night?"

"Yes."

"Seven o'clock. I'll come for you."

"You come. I make dinner."

Jack was touched. It was rare for an American to be invited into a Russian home, and even rarer for anyone to get a dinner invitation these days. The rationing had made the sharing of food too much of a luxury. "Tell me what you need, Zoyatchka. I will try to get it for you."

"Nothing," Zoya said. "Just you."

When he hung up, Jack went to the refrigerator in the apartment and took the stick of butter from its dish. He wrapped it in a clean handkerchief and stuck it on the ledge outside of his bedroom window. Let the other guys think it was Luba. They all knew she often took home bits of food, and they had said nothing.

Then he went back to the kitchen and emptied half of the box of salt into a paper bag. Salt was rarer than diamonds in Moscow. He scooped some coffee out into another bag, and then took a can of Spam from the shelf. If anyone accused Luba, he'd confess. He hid it all under his bed, where by the looks of things Luba had never cleaned.

Then he got a piece of paper and printed a note on it: "Will swap American cigarettes for a bottle of wine." He signed his name and apartment number and took it downstairs and tacked it up beside the elevator. He had the wine within an hour from a chain-smoker.

The next day, Zoya thought, I must be falling in love to invite this man for dinner. There is no other explanation, unless I am out of my head.

She could not even plan what she would serve him, until she found out what she could get. Her ration of bread she was certain of, but what else? Too often she had gone to the shops to purchase her meat ration only to find there was none.

She began her shopping early in the morning and found herself standing on line for over an hour to get her ration of bread. Then it meant another line for meat, but when she approached the shop there was no line, and her heart sank. There was only one explanation. There was no meat. The butcher shrugged. "The war, Zoya Fyodorova, the war. What else can I say?"

"Then give me a bone for a decent soup, at least that."

He stretched out his arms. "You may search if you wish. There is nothing. It is all gone. But tomorrow, come early and I promise you meat."

Zoya rushed from the butcher to the vegetable stalls. She was able to buy some beets that were only a little shriveled, and potatoes. At another shop, she got some sprats, which didn't please her, but it was something. Jackson would get a borscht of some sort, and fish that she would do something with. It would not be a meal she would be proud of.

It was a bitter cold night, and Jack decided to take the car that had been assigned to him. Why the Russians referred to this winter as an "orphan's winter," meaning a warm one, was beyond him. He thanked God he hadn't been around for a normal winter.

The food for Zoya was on the front seat beside him. It had been a rough day. The Russians, who were supposed to be cooperating on the building of the Siberian airfield, had been more difficult than ever. Yes, concrete was available, but it was not advisable considering the weather in Siberia. Wouldn't asphalt or tar be better? Were they available? Well, we will have to check on that, but had not the Americans said they wanted concrete? Finally, Jack had walked out of the meeting. He had gone over to the embassy and gotten a canned ham for Zoya, which meant he could return the Spam he had taken from the kitchen.

When he pulled into Zoya's courtyard, the radio in the car was playing the American song that the Russians called

"Coming in on a Wing and a Machine." He clicked it off.

The elevator wasn't working in her building, so he took the stairs. Why did the halls smell of urine? Granted toilet paper was a rare commodity in Moscow, but the toilets still flushed.

He knocked at Zoya's door. When she opened it, he saw that she had been crying. He waited until she had closed and locked the door behind him before he asked, "What is it? Tell me."

"Smell, you will know."

He sniffed. There was a foul burnt smell in the apartment. "What happened?"

"The dinner. I go to fix my hair, and the fish burn up. So dry little things, they go poof! I ashame, Jackson."

He kissed one of her wet eyes. Then he took out the ham. "The U.S. Navy to your rescue, Ma'am."

Zoya put a hand to her breast. "Ham? Is it ham? My God, I cannot even remember ham."

And she obviously had never had a canned ham. Jack had to show her how to open it. When the cover came off, Zoya pressed both hands to her mouth and stared at it as if it were the czar's jewels. She cut off small slices and put them in the borscht. Then Jack took over and fried ham steaks, while Zoya marveled over the other foods he had brought her. "It is a palace here tonight!" she said.

Only the coffee disappointed her. Not that it wasn't better than the stuff they served in Moscow these days, but it was an alien taste to her.

When they finished, Jack insisted on helping her clean up. Zoya washed and he dried. She looked at him shyly. "Is like married," she said and burst out laughing.

"The hell it is," Jack answered. "I never helped my wife with the dishes."

Afterwards, they sat and talked. Zoya asked him to tell her about America. She kept interrupting him with "What that?" when he used a word she didn't understand, and with an awestruck "I don't belief" when he described something that Americans took for granted, but which was unknown in the Soviet Union. What seemed especially to fascinate her was the idea that you could rent or buy an apartment or house wher-

ever you wanted instead of being given one by the government. Didn't it make for confusion? And when Jack told her
that his wife lived with her children all by themselves in an
eight-room house, she accused him of fooling her. The great
Stalin himself only maintained a three-room apartment in the
Kremlin.

Then Zoya told him about her life, and Jack didn't understand. If she was such a well-known movie star, why didn't she
have her own car or a larger apartment or furs? "But I have
fur," Zoya said and got out the karakul coat and hat she wore
the night she met Jack. And she didn't need a car because she
didn't know how to drive. And anyway, automobiles were very
difficult to get. "Much money."

They ended up admitting that although they didn't understand each other's lives, they did like each other. When Jack
kissed her good night, they made a date for the next night. As
he was about to leave, Zoya told him to wait a moment. She
went to the kitchen and brought out the ham that was left. She
couldn't believe that he meant to leave it with her. It was so
rare and so expensive.

Jack refused to take it. "For you, Zoyatchka."

"Jackson," she said and touched his face.

The next evening, Jack took her to the Moskva, which he had
heard was a fine restaurant. There was a line waiting in the
street which Jack found amazing considering the temperature.
He also found it infuriating that reservations were unknown in
Moscow. People in the line turned to stare at Zoya and to greet
her. When they signaled her to go to the front, she shrugged
and winked at Jack and marched grandly to the door, where
they were ushered inside and given a table immediately. Zoya
leaned toward him and whispered, "See? Movie star."

They were seated with a soldier and his fat wife who talked
loudly throughout their meal. It wasn't at all what Jack wanted.
Mentally, he cursed all of Moscow. Didn't the Russians know
anything about intimacy? Didn't they ever crave privacy?

Zoya seemed happy in the room. And she looked triumphant
when they were presented with menus, something they hadn't
received at Tsentralnaya. She pointed to herself indicating she

would order for them. But when the waitress came, almost everything she requested was unavailable—"the war, Zoya Fyodorova."

Jack didn't think the meal was very good, and the sounds of the soldier sucking on chicken bones didn't help.

When they were outside, Zoya said, "Good, no?"

Jack said, "No. I wanted to be alone with you."

Zoya looked surprised. "We alone now."

When they got into Jack's car, Zoya gave the directions. "I have surprise."

She took him to see one of her films, *The Night in September*. While Jack didn't understand what was being said, it was not hard to get the general idea of the film. Loving, virtuous woman, brave, heroic man, both doing their best for the Soviet Union, happy ending. The Russians seemed to love it. And he could see why they loved Zoya. The woman on the screen wasn't the Zoya he knew. His Zoya had fire and life to her, while the woman on the screen seemed completely giving, self-sacrificing, too noble. But she was lovely. The camera and the lights caught a luminous softness to her that made her seem to glow from the screen. A strength came through, but it all seemed coated in velvet. By her talent alone, she made the audience—Jack included—suspend disbelief and accept the woman she played as a valid human being, even when logic told you she couldn't exist.

When they were back in Jack's car, Zoya asked, "You like?"

Jack glanced about. The windows were all covered with frost so that no one could see in. He pulled her to him. "Very much." He kissed her.

Two nights later, he took her to see an American film, *The Thief of Bagdad*. It was the big hit in Moscow. While Zoya laughed and applauded along with the rest of the audience, Jack thought it was second-rate. "The trouble is," he said, "your government won't import any pictures except fluff from us."

"Was pretty," Zoya said.

Jack brushed that aside. "They don't want you to see the way we live."

Zoya thought about that for a moment. "I see Joan Crawford. And Hedy Lamarr. Such clothes. Is that how American women dress to work?"

Jack laughed. "Only if they work in Hollywood."

February turned to March. The victory salutes lit up the night sky almost hourly each night as the Allies fought their way toward Berlin. The Americans had bridged the Rhine at Remagen. The Russians were on the outskirts of Szczecin and Danzig and had taken Oder, only 38 miles east of Berlin.

Outwardly, nothing changed in Moscow. The snow still fell, blanketing the city. Rationing was as tight as ever. Yet there was a feeling of springtime excitement in the streets and people smiled more readily. Victory was coming. V-E Day was talked about everywhere. Soon, very soon.

In terms of the job he had been sent into Russia to do, nothing changed for Jack. While the paperwork inched forward, the Russian red tape and buck-passing always seemed on the verge of burying the Allied project.

But away from his office, Jack felt he was a different man than the one who had come to Moscow two months before. He was younger and happier than he had been in years. It was all because of Zoya. Before he met her, the end of the day found him tense and furious at the Russians he had to deal with. Now he was able to forget them almost immediately. He still wanted that airfield built in Siberia, and he wanted to be in on the war against Japan—it was a matter of personal pride. But now he could lock his office door and say to himself, "Screw them, we can finish Japan off without their help." Perhaps he wasn't getting the job accomplished, but he wasn't wasting his time in Moscow. There was Zoya.

At the beginning, he had tried to figure it out. How could he feel this way about a woman he had difficulty communicating with, a woman whose whole life had been completely different from his? And then somewhere along the way, he stopped asking himself any questions. He only knew that he waited for the time when he would go to her, that he resented any occasion that prevented his seeing her.

It had happened for Zoya, too. She had stopped asking herself why, or trying to figure out how she could have cared so much for Ivan and then found Jack. There was no resemblance between the two men, none at all. But she cared deeply, she knew that, even more deeply than she wanted to care. Where was the future for them? she would ask herself, and although she came up with no answer, she still looked forward to her evenings with him.

She no longer listened to Alexandra, who kept warning her of the risks she was running. Finally she told her firmly, "It is too late for warnings. The only danger I fear now is that I will not see Jackson. If you must speak of him, my dear sister, then speak with happiness for me because he makes me happy. Jackson is a good man. He will do me no harm. I know that, as I know what is in my heart for him."

Alexandra began to wring her hands, and tears came to her eyes. "It is only because I love you, Zoyatchka. . . ."

Zoya kissed her. "I know. Then be happy for me. I know it will be all right."

Maria reacted oppositely from Alexandra. She found Jackson glamorous, his romance with her sister exciting, and she thirsted for every detail Zoya shared with her. "It is like going to the cinema all of the time, only this is real."

While Zoya would never have thought of asking Alexandra, even if she didn't have two children at home, Maria was always ready to drop whatever she was doing to go out with them when Jack called to say he was coming straight from some reception that required him in naval uniform. Maria had always enjoyed walking in the streets with her famous sister, but now it was twice as exciting to link arms with Zoya and share with her the intrigue of the man who walked a few feet behind them as if he wasn't even with them.

And the things they did, things that Maria could rarely afford on her salary. Twice she went with them to the circus to see the weekly bill. Maria would shriek at the clowns and she loved the animals. She only disliked the animal acts when someone cracked a whip at them. If possible, Jack would get a seat behind the two women. Once when the circus was dark except for a spotlight on the man in the ring, she saw Jack lean forward and put his hand on Zoya's arm. Maria pretended not to see.

Another time the three of them went to see the film *Ivan*

the Terrible. Zoya and Maria cried together while Jack fell asleep fifteen minutes after the picture began. As he told them later, "That seems a crazy way to me to begin a picture, with a man dying. And he keeps rearing up and falling back again. That picture wouldn't make ten cents in the United States."

Zoya looked at him. "You know so much about filmmaking, I suppose? If you made this film, Ivan would go running off all over the world, and who would care about him then?"

Now why had she gotten angry, she asked herself? She could have bitten her tongue off. She could see in his face that she had hurt him.

"No one, I guess," he said. He started to turn away.

Zoya put her hand on the sleeve of his jacket. "Well, maybe one woman would," she said softly.

He smiled.

Zoya often had to make appearances at the request of the government as part of the wartime morale campaign. It could be a theater concert or a visit to a hospital ward or a factory. Jack would offer to drive her there and back, but she would refuse. "It is daytime. You wear your uniform. It is not good."

"I won't wear the uniform."

Zoya still didn't like the idea. "What you see, Jackson? I tell jokes you won't understand. I sing a few songs. I can sing for you here."

They were in her apartment. "I just want to be with you. I want to share all of your life."

Zoya was touched. "Maybe," she said.

Finally, one day she gave in. She was to appear before the workers of a shoe factory at nine in the morning. It was the idea of sharing her life that had gotten to her. It was true. She could sing for him in her apartment, but it wouldn't be the same thing. She would just be his Zoyatchka. But performing in front of an audience, then she became Zoya Fyodorova. He should see that part of her, why not? What harm were they doing to anyone by caring for each other? Why should they have to sneak around? What, after all, was the shoe factory? There was no big secret about shoes. And it was a few kilometers out of Moscow. Who would see them?

Jack picked her up in his car at 7:30 in the morning. Before she opened the door, Zoya walked around the car. Satisfied that there were no special markings to say that it belonged to an American, she got in. She looked Jack over. The suit, the boots, the cap—fine. "You must promise me that you will not speak all the time we are there," Zoya said.

"Sure, but what if someone speaks to me?"

"Jackson, not one word. Point to your throat like you are sick. Anything, but do not speak."

At the factory they were directed to the large shed where Zoya would perform. They were joined by a male singer from the Moscow opera and by the man who would play the piano to accompany Zoya. A makeshift stage had been set up at one end of the room with wooden partitions on either side so that the performers could exit and enter. Zoya took Jack to a position behind one of the partitions just off stage from which he could see. There she left him while she spoke with her accompanist and the factory official who would introduce her.

Jack watched her. The delicate little woman he cared for was gone. The Zoya he was now seeing was a professional in action. She never looked back at him, had made no introduction of him to anyone.

At nine sharp, the workers filled the room.

The opera singer was on first. He sang three numbers, then came off and stood beside Jack to watch. Jack didn't understand Zoya's introduction, but the stamping of feet was deafening when she stepped out onto the stage from the partition opposite.

He assumed she was telling jokes or anecdotes and that she was acting out the parts in her stories, all of which met with enthusiastic laughter. Then she introduced her accompanist who began to play the popular Russian favorite, "Blue Handkerchief." Zoya's voice was a clear, light soprano. When she finished, she motioned for the audience to sing with her and began the song again. She finished to wild applause.

She's wonderful, Jack thought, more wonderful than he had imagined even after seeing her in films. Even though she never looked over at him, Jack felt that special warmth that emanated from her and flowed out to capture an audience.

The accompanist came off on Jack's side of the stage while Zoya stood alone, head high, in the applause that seemed to go on and on. "She's good, isn't she?" the man said.

Jack merely smiled.

"You got a cigarette?"

Jack nodded. He reached into his jacket and pulled two cigarettes out without removing the package from his pocket, hoping the man wouldn't notice that they were American. He gave him one and then lit them both. The man thanked him and Jack nodded.

Zoya finished a long story and the accompanist butted his cigarette on the floor and put the stub in his pocket. He went back on stage to work with Zoya on her final number. When they came off, there was a brief conversation between them, with many glances at Jack.

Zoya avoided Jack, walking instead with the accompanist and the factory official to where the car was parked. Jack went directly to the driver's side and got in. He waited while Zoya thanked the accompanist and said good-bye to the official. She did not speak until they were out of the factory gates and on the open road. Then she burst into laughter. "I nearly died when I saw Sasha speaking to you."

"You and me both. What's so funny about it?"

Another wave of laughter swept over Zoya. "Do you know what he said? 'When I asked him for a cigarette, he didn't say a word. At first, I thought he was dumb, a mute. Then I took a good look and I was afraid. The way he stands, so stiff, and with a foreign suit, and he even gave me an Americanski cigarette—I tell you, Zoya Alexyevna, I was afraid to take it. That is a big boss, that one. He is someone high up in the Communist party. I could tell the way he looked at me, and he never said one word. Who is he, Zoya?' " She collapsed into laughter again.

"So what did you tell him?"

Zoya put a silencing finger to her lips and looked about her mysteriously. "I told him I was not allowed to say."

Jack checked in the rearview mirror. There were no cars nearby. "Come here," he said and swung off to the side of the road. They kissed.

She pulled away, nervous. "Please, Jackson, someone might see. We do not do this in the open in this country."

Jack smiled. "It can't be wrong, Zoyatchka. *Yah vahs lyoob-lyoo.*"

She was confused. Her eyes darted about his face. "Do you know what you have said, Jackson?"

"Yes." He repeated it.

Zoya shook her head. "You meant to say I like you. You have said I love you."

"I know what I said. I do love you, Zoya."

She took his hand and kissed it. "And I love you, Jackson."

You could feel the tension in the streets. Victory had to be any day now. How much longer could the Germans fight? It was as if in every street there were invisible electric wires humming with mounting power.

Zoya had a special evening planned. This time she had gotten the meat before she invited Jack to dinner. It was not a large piece of lamb, but it was lamb. This dinner would be a good one.

And she had gotten tickets for the gypsy theater, the Roman—he would like that. They were doing Strauss's *The Gypsy Baron.* Even in Russian, he would understand it, and the music was lovely. She laughed to herself as she thought of poor Jackson at the opera the week before, sneaking little looks at his wristwatch all through *Eugene Onegin.* How he had suffered for her. And he never said he hated it. Of course, he never said he loved it either. And two days later, he had taken her to the Bolshoi to see *Swan Lake.* She was most impressed that he was able to get the tickets. It was not something that a Russian could do easily, though foreigners seemed to have less trouble. She thought he had liked the ballet, but she wasn't certain. He seemed uncomfortable—or was she imagining?— when the male dancers first appeared in their tights?

But tonight would be all for Jackson. She had even learned how to make a lamb stew from her American friend, Elizabeth Egan, though Zoya was not much impressed with the recipe. There were better things that could be done with lamb, but this was his night.

When she tasted the stew, she thought it needed something, but she didn't know what. More meat was her guess, but that was out of the question. And maybe this was how it was supposed to taste. Americanski food, who knew?

Jack laughed when he tasted it. "Where the hell did you learn to make an Irish stew?"

"Irish?" Zoya was startled. "It was from America, no?"

Jack tried to explain how it could be an American dish and an Irish stew, but he didn't have enough Russian and Zoya didn't have enough English. She was satisfied that he was pleased.

He hadn't heard of the gypsy theater—it was not one of the great Moscow theaters—and when she said "Roman," he expected a show with everybody in togas and wondered why she had chosen that to please him. "What is it, *Julius Caesar?*"

They were standing in front of the rundown theater building, while a trickle of people went inside. Zoya was confused. "Why *Julius Caesar?* It is . . ." She had to look up the words in her dictionary. "It is *The Gypsy Baron* by Johann Strauss."

"Then why is it called Roman?"

"Not RO-man. Roh-MONN. It means gypsy." She shook her head. "Americantzis," she said wonderingly.

The snow had begun during the first act. It had already turned the sidewalks white when they came out for the intermission. Most of the audience had stayed inside, so they went out where they could talk. "It is April," Jack said. "Doesn't it ever stop snowing here?"

"Soon, it is beautiful," Zoya said. "You will see."

They both found the story of the Strauss operetta idiotic, though Zoya cried over Saffi's love for Barinkay, but they liked the music. When they were in Jack's car, they began to sing Barinkay's waltz at the top of their voices, with Zoya clapping her hands over her head as if she were beating time on a tambourine. Except for the two half-circles cleared by the windshield wipers, they were blocked from outside view by the snow. It was like a heavy curtain of steady white descending on the city. Jack was grateful that there were few cars on the streets for his tires were not gripping well. But he wasn't worried about making it home. It wasn't that bad yet.

Zoya sang the waltz with the Russian lyrics. "What's it all about?" Jack asked.

Zoya gave him a very rough translation. "He is gypsy who is poor and he is very, very happy."

Jack laughed. "He is idiot."

Zoya pretended to be offended. "Jackson!"

"I'll get us some better words."

Zoya clapped her hands. "Jackson! You write poetry."

He shrugged. "Some. Nothing fancy."

"Jackson! My Americanski Pushkin!"

He pulled into the courtyard of her apartment building. When he helped her out of the car, he waltzed her around in the snow to the music that had become their song. Zoya put her hand over his mouth. She looked nervously up at the building. Who could say who was watching?

In her apartment, he helped her off with her coat. "A coffee?" she asked.

Jack shook his head. "I don't think I should stay. The snow is very bad. I might not get back to my place."

"What will you do then?" Zoya said, very casually. She filled the kettle with water and lit the stove.

"I guess I'll just have to stay in the car all night. I can't leave it out in the middle of the street."

"That is bad, Jackson. You could freeze."

"I suppose I'll have to take that chance."

She stood facing the stove, her back to him. "It might be better to leave the car where it is until morning."

He moved to stand behind her. "I think it would be much better." He put his hands on her shoulders and she turned to slip into his arms. Their kiss was long and intense. He reached behind her and turned off the gas.

He was falling asleep, and he didn't want to. There would never be another time so sweet and precious as this first time and he didn't want to lose it. He could feel her warmth against his side and the softness of her shoulders against his arm. Zoya. Zoyatchka. She moved slightly and he smelled her perfume. It was something Russian and much too sweet, but it was her to him. It would be with him all of his life. It would always bring back this night when they were together in a world gone silent and white.

He heard the waltz music. It was being played by one musician somewhere far up ahead in the darkness. He felt as if he had to go to it. It was calling to him, and he began to walk into the darkness that was growing pale and bright. He was asleep.

Zoya carefully raised herself from his arm. He would get a cramp. She moved the arm to his side. For a moment, there was a break in his sleep rhythm, then it began again, calm and deep. She stared down at his face. There was an innocence to him in sleep that she had never seen before. Gently, she reached out and with her fingertips touched his crew-cut hair. He was starting to gray. Oh, my Jackson, she thought to herself, so many years we have been on this earth without each other. Imagine, it took a world war to bring us together. Good can come even from something horrible. But soon the war will end. . . .

Her thoughts jarred to a halt. Soon the war will end. And what then? Will we be together afterward? Yes, it had to be yes, but how? In which country? His? Mine?

She forced herself to stop. Zoya Fyodorova, she told herself, this night, just this one night, do not be a Russian and turn an occasion of love and joy into unhappiness. Enjoy this night, and the ones that come after, and do not think too far ahead. It will be all right. Somehow, it will come out well. You and Jackson together will see to it.

Gently, so as not to wake him, she lay down again close to him, so that she could feel him next to her. "My American-yets," she whispered, and closed her eyes.

The snow had stopped during the night. From the window they could see it was not deep, and they could hear the traffic moving on Gorki Street. "I guess I could have gone home," Jack said.

Zoya looked at him. He grinned. "But I'm glad I didn't."

Zoya gave a sad little smile. "Do not make the joke with me, Jackson. I do not understand too well."

He kissed her on the nose and went to shave. She sat quietly at the table sipping her morning coffee and watched him out of the corner of her eye. "I'll have to get you some razor blades," he said. "This one is terrible."

How nice, she thought, to have a man with you at breakfast. He makes the room come alive. She watched the way his arm muscle rippled as he moved the razor down his cheek. How lovely. He was humming the waltz from *The Gypsy Baron.*

Suddenly, he turned. "Listen." And he sang in his gravelly voice:

I'm just a Yankee captain.
You're a Russian film star.
And I will always love you
Whether near, whether far!

He waited for her reaction. He expected her to laugh. "Well?"

Her face grew sad. "You write that, Jackson?"

Jack nodded. "I told you I wasn't much of a poet."

"Very nice," she said and turned away from him so that he wouldn't see the tears that were running down her face.

Jack went to her. "What is it? I thought you would laugh."

Zoya shook her head. "Forgive me, maybe I don't understand."

He sat down beside her. There were still spots of soap on his face. "Understand what?"

"The end words. Far. It says you go away."

Jack took her in his arms. "You know I would never go away and leave you, Zoyatchka."

"But you said 'far.' "

Jack wiped the tears from her cheeks and tilted her chin up so that she was forced to look at him. "That was so it would rhyme with 'star.' It means only that I will always love you."

"Make a different rhyme, Jackson."

He thought a moment. "Okay, you like this better? And I will always love you except when you smoke a cigar."

She smiled. "Much better."

Jack kissed her. "You're a foolish woman."

He went back to the sink to wash the soap from his face. As he finished up, he sang the waltz with the new last line. "That is now our song, Zoya. Isn't that pathetic?"

"I like," she said.

When he came back to the table to drink his coffee, Zoya said, "Jackson, tell me truth. What happen to us?"

"What do you mean?"

"When war is finished, you will go away."

Jack thought a moment. "First off, the war is not finished."

"Any day," Zoya said.

Jack took her hand across the table. "Any day, Germany. But there is still Japan. My country is at war with Japan. And your country will be, too."

"But after? Please, Jackson."

He shook his head. "Darling, I just don't know."

Zoya nodded her head and her eyes filled again. "You will go away. You will forget me."

"No, I didn't mean that. I mean I don't know how we're going to work this out because I haven't thought it through yet. You and I, we haven't talked about it at all."

"Do you want to talk about it?" Zoya said. "Tell me truth, Jackson."

He went to her and pulled her to her feet and wrapped her in his arms. "Of course I want to talk about it. I don't want to lose you, Zoya. My biggest worry is not how we are going to be together—there has to be a way—but about my love for you. I don't think I am very good at love. There are two bad marriages behind me and that frightens me. I love you more than I have ever loved any other woman, and I don't want you to be hurt by me."

Zoya pressed her head against his chest. "You cannot hurt me, Jackson. Only by leaving."

He kissed the top of her head. "I won't leave you."

They stayed that way for several minutes. Then he removed her arms from him. "Except to go to work."

She watched as he put on his jacket and coat. "Will you come back tonight?"

"Yes, but after dinnertime. There is some function over at the Embassy I am supposed to show up at. I'll get here between eight and nine, and I'll be in my uniform, so we won't go out."

Zoya saw him to the door. "I make dinner for you?"

He kissed her. "They'll have something there."

When he returned, there was a grin on his face. "Surprise. You're not the only one who can steal food." He took a napkin from his coat pocket and opened it to display an assortment of hors d'oeuvres. Zoya clapped her hands and laughed. She tasted one of the little sandwiches and made a strange face. "What is?"

Jack took a bite. "I think it's Spam with something chopped into it. Piccalilli, maybe."

"What is pick. . . ." She couldn't say the word.

He explained. Zoya looked at the sandwich. "This is what you eat in America?"

"Well, only at parties. But not all parties."

Zoya ate the rest of the sandwich, though she obviously did not like it. "Okay, I will learn."

They began to talk about their future together. "You know," Jack said, "when Germany falls, I may have to leave you for a while. There is still the war in Japan, and I expect to be sent there. I'm still in the navy."

Zoya nodded.

"And I still have a divorce to get. There's no problem there. Helen and I have talked about it and agreed to it. It will happen as soon as I get home, and then we can be married."

Tears came to her eyes. Jack didn't understand. "What's wrong? What did I say?"

Zoya smiled through her tears. "Not wrong. You never say marry before."

Jack kissed her. "See, my Zoyatchka? I told you I was no good at love. Of course, I want to marry you. Will you marry me?"

Zoya touched his face. "Oh, yes, Jackson."

She went to the kitchen shelf and came back with the bottle of wine he had brought the first night he had come to dinner. There was still some left. They toasted each other and drank. The wine had begun to sour. Neither of them said anything but Zoya thought to herself, it is an omen.

"Jackson" she said, "if you go to Japan, maybe you cannot come back to Moscow."

"Then you will come to me in the United States."

Zoya smiled to herself. Americanyets, so innocent. "And if I cannot come to you?"

Jack thought, how Russians love to worry. "Zoya, our countries are allies. It is good between us. Why would they not let us be together? We would be doing nothing that would hurt either of our countries."

They live so free, she thought, that even when they are in a country that is not free they see nothing. "Yes, well . . ." she said.

Jack took her hand and kissed it. "Look, let us not worry about what we don't have to now. If the time comes and there are problems, then we can worry. I know important people in my country, Zoya, and they will help us. Tonight, let us just decide about us."

"All right," she said, but she felt a heaviness in her heart.

"I can't tell you where we'll live in the United States," Jack said. "After all, it depends on where the navy stations me. It could be anywhere from New York to California."

"But I am Russian," Zoya said. "I have career here."

"But you can be an actress in America," Jack said. "I know people in Hollywood who will help you. And as my wife, you will be an American citizen."

"But I love my country. Why can you not live here with me, Jackson?"

"For one thing, because I could not get along at all in your country. I don't even understand your government. And I have a career in the United States Navy. I've devoted my whole life to it, and I just can't throw it away. I couldn't start over in the Russian Navy even if I wanted to, but you could start over in American movies."

Eventually, they agreed that they would live half a year in each country. It was the only solution they could come up with, and it was a solution that neither of them dared to think about, because then they would have to realize that it made no sense whatever. But still, they told each other, who would believe that an American navy man and a Russian actress would meet and fall in love? Did that make sense? Well, if that was possible, then all the rest had to be possible, too. It would work out. It had to work out.

They heard the dull thud of cannon fire. Zoya looked out of the window and saw skyrockets. She turned on the radio. Jack couldn't understand the Russian announcement. All he caught was the name "Roosevelt." Zoya shut off the radio. She looked stricken. "What is it?" he asked.

She sat down beside him and took his hand. "Franklin Roosevelt. He is dead."

She had to repeat it, because he didn't seem to understand. He shook his head violently. "That can't be true. That's some kind of Russian propaganda."

"But they said. . . ."

Jack stood up. Tears were running down his face. "I've got to go, Zoya. I've got to find out for myself."

The streets were strangely quiet as Jack drove through them. Well, of course, Jack told himself. Everyone in Moscow had heard the news and believed it. It was only proper that they react this way. But it just wasn't so. It couldn't be.

A guard at the American Embassy confirmed the news. The president had died at Warm Springs, Georgia, of a massive cerebral hemorrhage.

Jack drove away from the embassy. A block away, he pulled over to the curb and shut off the motor. He put his head down on the steering wheel and cried. It was as if he had lost someone very close to him, as close as the father he could only dimly remember. When he had gotten hold of himself, he tried to think of the name of the new president, but all he could come up with was a hazy picture of a man with glasses.

It was later on, when he was back in his own apartment and almost asleep, that he remembered the name, Harry Truman. But he didn't know much about the man except that he was from Missouri and once had run a men's clothing store. Oh God, he thought, why did Roosevelt have to die when the war was so near to the end? Was the little guy with the glasses capable of finishing the job?

Two weeks later, on April 27, 1945, the American forces met the Red Army. Germany was split in half. The people of Moscow rushed into the streets, while overhead, rockets shot into the sky from the antiaircraft stations throughout the city. Jack was wildly excited. "Any day now!" he told Zoya. "Any day now!"

She was happy, of course, and she tried to share his excitement, but inside of her a voice kept saying, "Any day now, they will send him to Japan."

Finally, it happened. V-E Day in Moscow, May 9, 1945. On the evening before, the streets swarmed with people wandering from square to square in restless excitement. Jack had swapped two cartons of cigarettes for a bottle of French champagne, which he took to Zoya's apartment. They sat together by the window watching the crowds. They laughed when a drunken soldier embraced an elderly woman sweeping the street. She was scandalized and tried to hit him with her broom.

Jack raised his glass to Zoya. "*Yah vahs lyooblyoo.* I love you, Zoya."

"*Yah vahs lyooblyoo,* Jackson."

They kissed. He took her face in his hands. "*Malenkaya devotchka,* that's what you are. My little girl. Did I say it correctly? I just learned the words."

Zoya laughed. "You hot stuff, Jackson. My new words."

He refilled their glasses. "I am happy with you, Zoyatchka. I want to grow old with you."

They sat quietly in the dark room, content with each other.

Later, he told her that he would not stay the night. "There may be special orders for tomorrow. I should be there in case. But I will come for you early tomorrow and we will celebrate this victory together."

Moscow was wild. The sidewalks overflowed into the roadways. The Russians, usually reserved and unemotional in public, were running amok in celebration. It took Jack almost an hour to get his car from Red Square to Zoya's apartment, usually only a matter of minutes. He was continually being stopped by Russians, who, upon seeing his uniform, rushed at the car demanding to shake his hand or who pounded on the sides of the car, grinning at him and shouting "Americanyets!" and "Victory!" He drove at a snail's pace, certain that at any moment he would feel the crunch of a body under his wheels.

Zoya threw herself into his arms when he arrived. He kissed her long and passionately. "What a day!" he shouted. "Victory! Victory! Today, we go out and I wear my uniform."

Zoya laughed. "Of course today."

"Well, let's go!" Jack said. "This is no day to be indoors."

Zoya took his arm and turned him. A little boy was looking at Jack bug-eyed. "Who's that?" Jack asked.

"This is my. . . ." But Zoya didn't know the word. "This is Yuri, Alexandra's boy. He came so he could see the excitement."

Jack said, "Well, let's take him along." He stuck his hand out to the boy, who shrank back against the wall.

Zoya went to him and spoke in Russian. Then she pulled him forward. "He is shy. He has not seen Americanyets before."

Jack squatted down in front of him. "I won't bite you, Yuri."

The boy let Jack take his hand. "That's the fella," Jack said. "Okay, get your coats."

Though it was May, it was still cold enough for Zoya's karakul hat and coat. When they got down to the courtyard, Jack hoisted Yuri up onto his shoulder. At that moment Zoya's sister Maria arrived at the building. She blushed and giggled when Jack kissed her on the cheek. They took her along, too. Zoya sat in front, Yuri and Maria in the back.

As he pulled out into Gorki Street, Jack took off his cap, thinking it would speed their trip if people didn't recognize him so readily as American. It didn't help much, because people flocked to the car when they saw Zoya.

They decided to go from square to square or to as many of them as they could reach. Red Square, where they started, was a sea of people with more pouring in by the minute. The driving was impossible and Jack was tempted to abandon the car, but he didn't think they'd get very far without it. At one point, he was forced to come to a complete stop until the people directly in front of him finished the wild dance they were performing.

Swinging away from Red Square, they inched their way toward Manezch Square. Jack parked as best he could and they got out. They had only walked a few feet before the mob recognized Zoya and surged toward her, shouting her name. She was hoisted onto the shoulders of two soldiers. Jack, too, was hoisted up, and they were carried to the platform used for park entertainments. A man with an accordion struck up a Russian melody and Zoya began to sing to the accompaniment of whistles and stamping feet. On the second chorus everyone joined in. There was pandemonium when she finished. Jack ran from corner to corner of the tiny stage clasping his hands over his head like a prizefighter. "America! Russia! Friendship! Friendship!"

People leaped onto the stage to embrace them both. Then the accordionist was playing again, and Jack and Zoya were caught up in a wild circle dance. He shouted to her, "We'd better get out of here before they tear us apart."

There were embraces for each of them all the way back to the car, where Maria was waiting, holding tightly to Yuri's hand. Two other women, whom Jack did not know, had joined them. Judging by the babushka on one and the fur coat on the other, he decided that one was Russian and the other maybe English or American.

She turned out to be Elizabeth Egan, Zoya's American correspondent friend. The other woman was a costume designer named Marina from Zoya's film studio. "Okay," Jack said, "everybody in the car. We're moving on!"

As the day wore on, the driving became more hazardous. Too many people, drunk either with the victory or with vodka, were running into the streets without looking. It was decided that they should take Yuri back to Alexandra. The little boy was worn out by the excitement and fighting hard to stay awake.

When they got to Alexandra's apartment building, Maria took the boy upstairs to his mother. Zoya said, "I should give kiss for victory to my sister, but I stay with you, Jackson."

Jack laughed. "Maybe I should give her a kiss, too."

Zoya snorted. "Do not spoil her day."

Mayakovsky Square was a repetition of what had occurred at Manezch Square. Again, Zoya sang to the crowd, and once again, Jack shouted to them, "America! Russia! Friendship! Friendship!"

When they had fought their way back to the car, Jack said,

"I don't know about you, Zoya, but I've had it. No more touring around, please."

Zoya agreed. They looked around for Maria and Zoya's two friends but couldn't find them. Jack helped Zoya into the car. He honked the horn several times to let the missing women know they were leaving, but it was unlikely they could even hear it over the crowd.

Jack headed away from the large squares, trying to find some peace and quiet. But it was hopeless. Finally, he pulled to the curb near a hotel. They went into the cocktail bar, which was not filled. Jack ordered drinks for them. "Today is such a day," Zoya said, "that I will drink, too." But she shuddered at the taste of the vodka.

"To victory," Jack toasted. "And to you and me."

Zoya nodded and took a second sip. "And maybe no Japan."

Jack shook his head. "I wouldn't drink to that one, Zoyatchka. I'd say sure as shootin' that's where I'm heading next."

Zoya raised her glass. "Then I drink to your coming back to me."

Jack smiled. "That's one I'll gladly drink to."

The sun was setting when they left the hotel bar. Jack suggested they go over to his apartment so they could see the festivities in Red Square. Zoya had been to his building once or twice, but she was usually nervous about going. Where he lived was American territory. Few Russians went inside unless they worked there. For anyone else it could be asking for trouble. But today was different. She readily agreed and felt no unease about it.

The approaches to Red Square were still as jammed as ever and it was dark by the time they arrived.

Jack switched on the light as they entered the living room. He went to the windows that swung outward onto Red Square and opened them. The square was dark with people moving like a restless tide.

"Peace," Zoya said and looked at the lights on all over Red Square. "So beautiful."

The first victory cannonades sounded, dull cannon thumps from all over the city. Then there were the flamelike streaks as rockets pierced the sky, followed by the shower of firework explosions in the dark night. The sound from the crowd below floated up like a collective sigh.

"There will never be another night like this," Jack said.

Zoya nodded.

"Zoya!" Someone below had spotted her in the window.

They could see heads turning below. As the name was picked up by the crowd there was a rippling movement of heads that fanned out like a current in an ocean.

"Zoya! Zoya!" It became a chant. She stepped to the window and threw double-handed kisses to them.

Jack ran to his bedroom and got out his last carton of cigarettes. He ripped open a pack and poured the cigarettes out on the piano. Then he began throwing them to the people below. "America—Russia! Friendship! Friendship!"

The crowd surged forward, pushing to get beneath the windows, arms outstretched. Jack told Zoya to open the other cigarette packs. "Just save me one."

The noise from below was becoming a wild roar as the crowd grew larger. Two men got into a fistfight over a cigarette. Zoya threw several more their way to try to stop the fight, but other people rushed over to catch them, and the two fighting men were pushed to the ground.

There was a sharp pounding on the apartment door. Jack opened it to an American he didn't know. The man was angry. "What the hell are you two doing?"

"Just having a little fun. A victory celebration."

"Yeah, well stop throwing stuff down. There's going to be a riot out there."

"Oh, come on," Jack said. "It's only cigarettes."

"Well, cut it out."

"Is that an order?"

The man looked grim. "It's a request. From Ambassador Harriman."

"Oops," Jack said.

He told Zoya to stop. He signaled to the crowd that there were no more cigarettes. Zoya blew some more kisses, and they stepped back from the window. Jack turned out the light so that the people below would think they had gone.

They sat on the sofa and watched the fireworks sail into the night sky. Zoya rested in Jack's arms. "Tired?" he asked.

"A little," she said. "But such a night."

"We will remember it always," he said and kissed her.

"Together, I hope," she said.

Jack nodded. "Together."

She fell asleep in his arms, her head on his shoulder. He listened happily to her soft, steady breathing. So this was love, he told himself. Nothing more than the simple pleasure of listening to little sounds from someone who means the world to you. So simple. So uncomplicated.

She stirred for a moment. He brushed her forehead with his lips.

When she awakened, they decided to walk to Zoya's apartment. It was easier than taking the car.

The tanks had begun moving like lumbering elephants down Gorki Street for the victory parade that would take place in Red Square the next day. The line was a long one, as far as the eye could see.

At Zoya's apartment, Jack closed the window, but the sound still came through. They went into her small bedroom and began to undress.

Jack took her into his arms as soon as they were in bed. "My wife," he said.

She smiled into the darkness. "I will become pregnant tonight," she said.

Jack laughed. "How do you know that?"

"I know."

"Then it is only right," Jack said, "that we name our child for our glorious victory. If it is a boy let's call him Victor. If it is a girl, Victoria."

Two weeks later, Jack came to her apartment to pick her up for dinner. He found Zoya in tears. "What is it?"

"I going away."

"Where? When?"

"Tomorrow. I have been told I am to go on tour to the Black Sea. Soldiers. Hospitals. I am to perform."

"For how long?"

"I do not know. Three weeks. Maybe a month."

Jack lifted her wet face and kissed her. "I will miss you terribly, but it is not forever."

She took the handkerchief he handed her. "It will seem that way."

"No," Jack said. "You are an actress and you are being dramatic. You will be very busy, and the time will pass quickly." He didn't know what else to say to help her. For himself, he knew that he was lying. He felt pain at the thought of separation from Zoya, and it was a new sensation to him. It surprised him, because his entire life had been one of separations—from wives, children, friends, places that he called home—but none of them had ever hurt before.

"I miss you very much already," Zoya said.

Jack kissed her again and forced a smile. "And I shall miss you every moment until you come back to me."

He arose the next morning at six and began to dress in the darkness of her bedroom. A car would be coming for her at 7:30, and it didn't seem a good idea for him to be there. He dressed as quietly as possible, but even so, she stirred in her sleep.

When he was ready to go, he bent over her and kissed her. "My wife," he whispered.

No one was awake at his apartment. Jack sat in the living room on the piano bench watching the sun rise over Red Square. This morning the view did not thrill him. Though spring had finally come, the city looked gray and cold to him. Between cigarettes, he looked at his wristwatch. At 7:35, he knew she was gone. Moscow was again a lonely city for him.

From one of the bedrooms he heard one of the two men who shared his apartment whistling to himself as he dressed. Suddenly there was a sharp knock at the door.

Jack ran for it. It was Zoya, he knew it. Something had happened and she wasn't going out on tour. She had come to tell him. But it was a man from the American Embassy. He looked grim. "Captain Jackson R. Tate?"

Jack nodded. The man handed him an envelope. "What is it?"

"Your expulsion orders. You have been declared persona non grata by the Soviet government. You are to leave the Soviet Union within forty-eight hours."

"What?" Jack couldn't believe it. "What have I done?"

The man shook his head. "I don't know, and they didn't say. But the order stands."

"I don't understand."

"Neither do we, but that's it," the man said. "I'd suggest you clean up your affairs here today. The Navy has been notified, and your new orders are being cut now. You should have them tomorrow morning."

The man nodded and left. Jack went into his room and sat down on the bed, stunned. He opened the envelope and read the paper inside. It told him nothing more than the man from the embassy had.

He lit a cigarette and tried to think it out. Even with the Russians, whom he rarely understood, there had to be a logical reason behind this order. But what? Did it have something to do with his job? That made no sense. If they didn't want to build the airfield in Siberia, there was no reason to throw him out of the country. They could just go on passing the buck and dragging their feet, and the damn job never would get done, which was how it looked at the moment.

It had to be something to do with Zoya. It was the only explanation. Send her out on tour, and while she is away throw her boyfriend out of the country. That way the great Russian film star would not be contaminated by association with an Americanyets.

He butted his cigarette. How simple life was inside the Soviet Union, he thought. All you had to do was resign yourself to not wanting, not thinking, not feeling, and everything would be taken care of. Where you lived, how much you got paid, even love—it could all be regulated.

Well, Jackson Rogers Tate wasn't a Russian. They could throw him out, but he'd be back after the war, and one way or another he and Zoya would be together.

If only he could reach Zoya before he left, but there was no way. He got out his stationery and wrote:

My Zoyatchka,
   This morning you left on tour. And this morning I received word that I am ordered out of your country. No reason has been

given, but I must leave within 48 hours. I think it has all been arranged—your tour and my expulsion (you will have to look up that word)—to separate us. I do not believe any harm will come to you. They just do not want us to love each other.

But you and I know that they cannot stop that. I love you. In our hearts we are husband and wife.

As you know, I am in the Navy of the United States, and my country is at war with Japan—as yours soon will be. I must go where my country sends me, just as you went on tour for your country. This has to be.

But the future is ours. So long as we love each other, nothing can keep us apart. Believe in that, *malenkaya devotchka*, as I do. I will come back to you.

> Until. . . . *yah vahs lyooblyoo,*
> I love you.
> Jackson

He was crying when he sealed the letter into its envelope. He got his coat and went out into the street. It startled him that the sun was shining and that there were people laughing and rushing about as usual. It was obscene for any of this to be when his world had fallen in.

Jack walked to her apartment house. Just on the off chance, he went up to Zoya's apartment and knocked on the door. There was no answer. He was going to slip the letter under the door, but he decided against it. What if Alexandra found it and destroyed it? No, it would be safer in her mailbox.

He went downstairs and folded the envelope lengthwise so he could slip it into the slot of the locked metal box.

BOOK
III

ZOYA

Yalta, Simferopol, Sevastopol, Sochi—the tour was in its third week with at least another full week to go, and there were mornings when Zoya would awaken to look at the strange walls around her and not be able to place where she was. It was a grueling tour and her throat felt raw. Her pianist complained that the dampness from the Black Sea was causing his hands to swell and ache. But except for missing Jackson, Zoya did not mind. When she saw the men in the hospital beds missing arms and legs and eyes, some with injuries too horrible to imagine, she knew she had no right to complain. If a few songs and some silly stories from her made any difference to them, how could she refuse? She smiled. Even if she could refuse.

But oh, Jackson, my Americanyets, how I miss you. I want your arms around me. I want to feel that rough spot on your face that you always miss with your razor. If ever I needed you, it is now.

She could picture his face and the look of astonishment that would come over it. And then he would smile. And then there would be tears in his eyes. She loved that most about him. He was a man, and he could cry without shame. And all this would happen when she told him that they were going to have a child.

Oh, he would laugh, too, and call her a Russian witch, because she had said on V-E Night that she would become pregnant. And now she was.

She should have had her period over two weeks ago, and it still had not come. All her life, Zoya Fyodorova had been regular, right on time. Others could say that it was the strain of this tour, but she knew better. Nothing had ever thrown her off schedule. Not her father's death, not Ivan's. Not even the fear when the Germans were approaching Moscow.

When she got back to Moscow she would see a doctor and it would be official. That was just a formality. She knew. Even this early, she felt it. Let others say this was nonsense. She knew better. She knew with a mother's heart.

Whenever she thought of the life within her, no matter where she was, she would gently touch at her stomach. "Victor," she would whisper. "Victoria."

Soon, Jackson, soon. Eight days, maybe ten days, and you will know.

Jack Tate was flown to Washington for reassignment. The more he thought of Zoya, the more he worried. Suppose she hadn't gone on a theatrical tour, but had been arrested? That could be, even though she had told him often that her popularity was such that she was safe. But what if she had been wrong?

He told himself time and again that he was torturing himself for no reason. If Zoya had been arrested, she would simply disappear and no one would ever see her until she was allowed to come back from wherever they put her. There would be no need to order him out of the country, because he'd never find her. No, the fact that he was expelled from the Soviet Union meant that Zoya was on tour and was coming back to Moscow, and they didn't want them to be together again.

He had hoped the top brass in Washington would be able to tell him what had happened in Moscow, but they asked him before he could ask them. The issue was closed as far as Washington was concerned. "What orders do you want?" was the next question.

"Just what I have been trained for all my life. I want to go to the forward area."

Jack was assigned to the Fifth Fleet under Admiral Halsey for reassignment to a carrier. His first stop was Pearl Harbor, where he spent approximately ten days in commanding officer's school being brought up-to-date on the latest matériel of war. New facts and data about new equipment were hammered at him every day for ten hours each day.

Each morning he would awake and think of Zoya and promise himself he would write to her. But at the end of each day, he would collapse on his bed and fall into a deep, exhausted sleep. It wasn't until his last day that he wrote to Zoya on V-mail:

> You have gotten the letter I left for you, so you know as much as I do about what has happened. I am far away now, and I am not allowed to tell you where, but the Navy knows, and if you write to me at this address I give you, the letter will be forwarded to me.
>
> You must not worry about me, because I promise you that nothing will happen to me. I am protected by your love. And though I worry about you, I know you are wrapped in my love. There is only distance between us, *malenkaya devotchka,* my little girl. Our hearts are still together.

Jack flew out to Admiral Halsey and was assigned to take over the *Randolph,* some 250 miles off Tokyo, as captain.

It was while he was on the *Randolph* that Jack learned that his wife, Helen, had died. He was a free man.

As soon as she had taken off her hat and coat, Zoya called Jackson. It wasn't quite noon, so she dialed the number where he worked. But the man who answered said he didn't know any Jackson Tett. Zoya spelled it for him. "Tett. T-A-T-E." The man said he wasn't there anymore.

Zoya was puzzled. She dialed his apartment. It was Luba who answered, but she knew nothing. Only that he was gone.

Something was wrong. Fear, like a hand, squeezed her heart. She wanted to call the American Embassy, but she didn't dare. Who could say who might be listening to her telephone?

Zoya dialed her American friend, Elizabeth Egan. The minute she said her name and heard Elizabeth's "Oh," Zoya knew that something bad had happened.

"Tell me!" Zoya said through clenched teeth. There was a scream rising in her throat and she had to fight it back.

"He was ordered out of the country. They gave him 48 hours notice."

Zoya felt as if a rock had been slammed into her back. She had to put her free hand on the table to support herself. "But he will come back?"

"Zoyatchka, you know better," Elizabeth said. "You will never see him again."

Zoya put the phone back on the hook and sat down. Suddenly she was numb. She didn't scream or cry. She just sat very still. Her body was dead. Only her mind stayed alive. Not see Jackson ever again. How could that be? She was carrying his baby. He would come back. It had to be.

It was well over an hour that she sat there. The afternoon sun was coming in her window. It caught at her eyes and she moved.

Suddenly she was on her feet. If Jackson had gone, he would have left a letter for her. He was a thoughtful man. Zoya ran from her apartment and down the stairs to where the mailboxes were. She stopped.

The door to her mailbox had been ripped open. It hung by one hinge. She looked, but she had no hope. The mailbox was empty. They had come for Jackson's letter and taken it away.

The tears that would not come when she had hung up the telephone came now, hard and heavy. Zoya put her head against the cool metal of the mailboxes and sobbed. Her body shook with her tears.

"My poor baby. We are alone."

Jack never received an answer to his letter from Zoya. Did she get his letter? Possibly, he thought, but not very likely. And if she had, had she answered? And what had happened to her letter?

He wrote her several times from the *Randolph*, but with each letter he sent, the conviction grew that he would never hear from her or see her again.

The war ended, and finally the *Randolph* headed for home.

From Baltimore Jack wrote to Zoya again. He was certain now that his letters weren't getting through. Perhaps if he wrote an innocuous letter:

> Dear Zoya,
> At last the war is over, a glorious victory for both our countries. I have returned home and am well, and hope you are the same. I still remember Moscow with great love. If you get a chance, I would enjoy hearing from you.

Would that fool whoever was intercepting his letters? Would Zoya understand that the love for Moscow was his love for her?

Zoya thought about abortion and rejected the idea. She wanted this baby. To kill it would be to kill all that she had left of Jackson. Let the little petty people say what they would, she would carry her child with pride.

After all, she was more than old enough to have a child. Soon, in fact, she would be too old. And even if love should come again while there was still time for a child, how could there ever be another baby made with a love such as the one she shared with her Jackson?

Zoya was pleased at the attitude of her friends. One or two made nasty comments and drifted away, but most of them gathered around to help her. And above all, there was Sasha.

He was tall and so thin he looked like a weed. Sasha was a pianist, often her accompanist, and a composer, forever wandering absentmindedly through the streets of Moscow, listening to the music he was playing in his head. He was perfectly capable of showing up at a formal function in trousers and an open shirt with a pencil sticking in his hair. Or in formal clothes and the pencil still in his hair. But he was one of the kindest men Zoya ever knew.

When he first learned of Zoya's pregnancy, he came to her and offered to marry her for the sake of the child. Zoya was touched. She refused. "We are close like friends, but not like a man and woman. It would not be right to tie you to me legally. But if you would agree to say you are the father. . . ."

He kissed her hand. "Gladly, Zoya Alexyevna. With pride."

* * *

Zoya thought it was foolishness, but so many people said that an expectant mother must only look at beautiful things and hold beautiful thoughts if she hopes to have a beautiful child that perhaps it was so? Why take chances?

Throughout the summer of her pregnancy she kept fresh flowers in her apartment. The moment they began to droop she would replace them with fresh lest her child be marked by the dying flowers. She tried, whenever possible, to see happy films and to attend concerts rich with the great classics.

But it became difficult to hold beauty within her.

Zoya became aware that she was being watched one morning in August, when she woke near dawn feeling thirsty. She got herself a drink of water, then went to the window facing the courtyard to open it wider. There were two men standing at the far end looking up at her window. She was convinced it was her window they were watching because they turned away when she looked out.

Zoya went back to bed, but sleep was impossible. Why was she being spied on? It could not be because of Jackson. He was gone several months now. Then why?

Perhaps it was not she they were watching. But three days later she knew for certain. It had been a difficult day's filming at the studio and she was tired. Her feet had begun to swell, and her back was bothering her.

She was grateful for the break while the cameras were being moved. Zoya sat down in a corner of the sound stage to wait for her next call. She glanced at her wristwatch. It would be at least two more hours before she could go home. She yawned.

A man at the studio who was a member of the Communist Party saw it. "Tired, Zoya Fyodorova?"

"A little," she said.

The man smiled. "If one is going to make films, it is not a good idea to stay out past midnight at parties."

Zoya felt as if she had been struck with a sword. "How do you know that?"

The man walked away.

That evening, she set her clock for 5 A.M. The sun was just coming up when the alarm rang. Zoya got out of bed and peeked out the window from behind a curtain. Two men were in the courtyard again, though she did not think it was the same two men as on the other morning.

Zoya showed herself in the window. "Hello!" she called.

The men turned their backs and pretended to be busy with something. "Yes, you two," Zoya called. "It is not sunrise yet, and you are already here!"

They hurried off.

But she knew they would be back.

Why? Why? The question kept repeating itself in her brain as she lay in bed trying to sleep, and there was no answer she could come up with. There was only Jackson, but he had been put out of the country, so to watch her now made no sense. If the NKVD knew everything, as people said they did, they knew she was pregnant. What harm could she possibly do, or even try to do, in her current condition? And surely they knew she was an actress, and nothing more. She was not a political person, nor were any of her friends.

No, it made no sense, and yet she was being watched. She smiled to herself. They couldn't possibly think she would try to escape to Jackson. A pregnant woman? She didn't even know where he was. His letters, if he had written any, had not reached her.

Beria!

She thought about him for a moment. No. How many years ago was that incident with him? If he had wanted revenge, surely he would have taken it by now. No, there had to be some explanation that she had not thought of. Or some crime that they mistakenly thought she had committed. Like the time her father had asked the German for a doctor's name, and they thought he had become a spy.

Well, there was nothing she could do about it. To complain or to ask why she was being watched would accomplish nothing, except to call attention to herself, and that was not wise. Only time would reveal what this was about. Until then, she could wait and worry, or she could wait and try to hold onto the beautiful things so that her baby would not be marked.

She closed her eyes and forced herself to think of a carpet of flowers flowing down to a river's edge.

* * *

Zoya was lucky that Maria was with her when her water broke. Maria immediately took charge.

She made Zoya lie down on the bed and covered her with a blanket. Then she unfastened Zoya's wristwatch and put it in her hand. "You will time your contractions. It is important to know how far apart they come."

Maria went to the telephone and called the Kremlin Hospital. Thanks to Zoya's importance in films, a bed had been promised to her when her time came.

"No, I cannot bring her," Zoya heard her sister say. "The labor has already begun, and her water has broken."

Pain, like lightning, tore through Zoya. She grabbed the bars at the head of her bed and squeezed as hard as she could to keep from screaming. It left her limp, her face drenched with perspiration.

She heard Maria give the apartment number and address and hang up. She came to the bed with a damp cloth with which she wiped her face. "You must tell me what to pack for you."

Zoya told her. "And as soon as I am at the hospital, call Sasha."

Maria nodded.

It was early evening when the ambulance took her to the hospital. She was taken directly to the delivery room, where six other women lay, already in labor. The attendants placed her on a hard table, a nurse undressed her, covered her with a sheet, and she was alone. And her contractions stopped.

She kept waiting for them to begin again. But nothing happened. And no one came for what seemed like hours. The doctor acted angry at her for not being in labor. He called some attendants, and Zoya was taken to an empty room. Something was injected into her arm. The doctor said it would start labor again.

At 8:32 A.M., January 18, 1946, Zoya gave birth. "A girl," a nurse said dryly.

The baby weighed 7 pounds 2 ounces and was 1 foot 8½ inches in length with deep blue eyes—"They will change," the nurse said with the same indifference—a head heavy with dark straight hair, and long eyelashes.

"Victoria," Zoya said. She fell asleep.

Later, when the baby was brought to her, tears ran down her cheeks as she studied the little face. The dark hair and something about the eyes, even closed, reminded her of Jackson. If only he could be here now to see the miracle they had made together. Victoria.

She lowered her head to the little bundle pressed against her breast. "Oh, Victoria, my Vikka," she whispered. "Forgive me for the life I will give you. It will be hard, but I will love you enough for two parents. I promise you this."

By the next day the red birth-blotches had begun to fade. Yes, she is beautiful, Zoya thought. She put the baby to her breast and felt its lips begin to suck. At last, she thought, someone I can give everything to who will not leave me as Ivan and Jackson did.

When the nurse came to take Victoria away, Zoya said, "You have seen many babies. Tell me, is mine beautiful or am I just being a mother?"

The nurse looked at Zoya with eyes of gray steel. "She's beautiful. And all things considered, she'll need to be."

Before Zoya could say anything, the woman scooped up the baby and left the room.

The nine days in the hospital seemed an eternity. Only the moments when Victoria was brought in were joyous. The rest of the time, Zoya felt a tension in the air. The nurses were all polite, but decidedly cold to her. When she asked one of them why, the woman looked at her in astonishment. "I don't know what you are talking about. It must be that actresses have great imagination."

But one day another nurse came into the room and leaned close to Zoya as if to straighten her pillow. "Do you know that there are men who come to watch you?"

"Who?" Zoya asked.

"I do not know for certain, but I think NKVD."

Zoya felt her heart stop a moment. "Where are they?"

"Outside your room, but no one is there now. But there was one all last night."

The woman stood up and turned to leave. "Thank you," Zoya said.

Zoya lay back and stared up at the ceiling. "Forgive me, Vikka," she said.

When she left the hospital with the baby, Sasha was waiting in the lobby as he had promised. Zoya had hoped that he would think to wear a suit and tie so that the nurses would see what a fine father Victoria had, but she should have known better. He wore an overcoat that was ragged at the elbows over a sweater and shirt. The bouquet of flowers he carried was a small one of cheap flowers. But he had come, and he played the father role well, with loud regrets about having to be out of town while Zoya was in the hospital.

Zoya introduced Sasha to a nurse she knew from her floor. "This is my husband. He is a musician."

A thin smile crossed the nurse's lips. "A musician? I thought he might be a pencil sharpener!"

Sasha touched his head and sheepishly removed the pencil.

When the nurse left them, Sasha said, "What is wrong, Zoyatchka? Why do they speak to us this way?"

Zoya shrugged. "I think there has been gossip about me and my baby. Perhaps your coming has put an end to it. It doesn't matter. I will never see any of them again."

"Shall we go? If you will take the flowers, I will happily carry the baby."

Zoya said, "The flowers are very pretty and I thank you." She spoke softly. "Come close as if to kiss me, but keep your face blocking my mouth from view."

Sasha brushed her cheek with his lips. "What is it?" He held his face against the side of her face.

"Perhaps you should leave me. I am being watched."

"Why?"

"It must be because of Jackson. It makes no sense."

"What does? Anyway, I have already been seen with you, and I will not leave you."

Sasha took the baby from her. "What a beautiful daughter you have presented me with, my darling wife!" He looked around the lobby to see if anyone was listening to them.

"Come," Zoya said. "You are a dear friend, Sasha, but a terrible actor."

*   *   *

The birth was recorded in the civil register of births for the year 1946. The certificate listed the female child as Victoria Fyodorova, with the patronymic Yakovlena for Jackson. The mother was Zoya Alexyevna Fyodorova. Where the father's name should have appeared there was a blank space. Zoya couldn't bring herself to lie. It wasn't fair to Jackson. And by the time her Vikula might see the certificate, she would be old enough to know the truth. And old enough to understand. Somehow, when the time came, Zoya would know how to tell her.

As soon as she felt strong enough, Zoya began a new film. Again, she played the lyrical heroine, the noble woman who loved her man and her country with equal devotion. Zoya cannot remember the name of the picture today. She was always a conscientious actress, but at this time her career was secondary to the baby whom she left each day in the care of Shura, the maid she had hired. Victoria completely filled the void in Zoya's life that Jackson had left.

At first Zoya saw resemblances in her daughter to Jackson. It was the dark hair and the eyes that she shared with him, and maybe the firm chin, though she admitted that perhaps she imagined the chin. In time, her memory of Jackson began to change so that he looked more and more like Victoria.

It was sad, Zoya admitted to herself, but Jackson was fading away. It was easier to remember now the fact of their love than the emotions of it. The way his arms felt around her was gone, and she could no longer smell his after-shave or really hear his voice. It was rough, she remembered, and it had a funny Americanski accent, but that was all.

I suppose I am fading for him, too, Zoya thought. Had he tried to write, she wondered? There had not been one word from him. Well at least I have his child, and that is a great deal. I regret none of it.

Jackson Rogers Tate was assigned to the naval air station at Terminal Island off San Pedro, California. His job was to put the station out of commission.

Whenever he thought of Zoya, it was to wonder what had become of her. Had she received any of the letters he had

written? Had she tried to reply? How foolish we were, he
thought, to believe that we ever had a future together, that
we'd be allowed to have one.

He had lost track of the number of letters he had written to
her, or ones he had sent to prominent Russian names he
thought might help them. None of them had been answered.
And the letters to his own government had brought back nothing but a lot of phraseology that added up to "forget it."

With the passage of time, the pain of losing her had eased.
But he still wanted to know that she was safe within Russia.
Just because she had said that no one would touch her didn't
necessarily make it so. He wanted to know.

The answer came to him one bright sunny day through the
morning mail that was always neatly stacked at the right-hand
corner of his desk. It was in a cheap envelope postmarked from
Sweden with his name and address printed on it in ink. Now,
who the hell could be writing him from Sweden?

He slit the envelope open, unfolded the coarse white paper,
and looked at the signature. He didn't recognize it. It was only
an initial and a last name. It could have been masculine or fem-
inine, as could be the note which was printed in ink:

> Why do you keep annoying Zoya with your letters? She has
> married a composer some time ago. They have two children, a
> boy and a girl, and are very happy. She is upset by your continu-
> ous efforts to reach her. Please stop.

Jack read the letter several times. At first he didn't believe
it. The Zoya he knew wouldn't forget so quickly. Zoya didn't
fall in love that easily. And even if the letter were true and she
had met and married someone within days after he had left
Moscow, there still wasn't time for her to have had two children.

But then again, she could have given birth once to twins.
There was time enough for that. Or the composer could be
a widower with two children. And it made sense for Zoya to
marry someone in the arts. Whoever he was, he was probably
more right for Zoya than Jack would have been.

Probably the letter was from some journalist friend of
Zoya's—she knew lots of them—whom she had asked to write
Jack as soon as he or she had left Russia.

Jack read the letter once more, then tore it up and dropped it in his wastebasket.

He wouldn't write her anymore. He owed her that. Goodbye, Zoyatchka. Be happy.

(Since Zoya never knew of the letter, and Jack never knew of Sasha, neither could have been aware of the grain of truth contained in it. Sasha, who occasionally accompanied Zoya when she appeared in concerts, was a composer, though never a famous or successful one. There is a strong possibility that whoever wrote the letter knew of Zoya's arrangement with Sasha to be what she called "a pretend father." Certainly the NKVD knew that Zoya was not married to or pregnant by Sasha. Whether the writer's choice of Zoya's "husband" as a composer was coincidence or based on knowledge of Zoya's arrangement with Sasha remains unknown. But the purpose was obvious: to cut off all attempts by Jack to reach Zoya.)

The filming was going well. Zoya had always been able to stand apart from her work and evaluate herself, and she knew she was doing well. Not that the part made any new demands on her. The character was like so many she had played before. Still, she gave it her best.

It was not the happiest of times for her, however. Each day, when she dressed to go to the studio, it was a wrench to tear herself away from the baby—Victoria, Vikula, Vikka, Vikotchka, so many love-names for her. But worst of all was the continuous watching—sometimes it was one man, sometimes a woman, more often two men. They were always outside her apartment, and she was followed when she took the baby out to the park for the spring air. And she saw strangers lurking in corners of the set watching her, or she thought they were watching her. Once, when her nerves were raw, she went up to a man. "What is it you want? Why do you keep staring at me?"

The man was flustered. "Forgive me, Zoya Fyodorova, but you are a famous film star. I did not think you could see me. I merely wanted to watch you act so I could tell everyone when I went home."

A very good story, Zoya thought. She didn't believe him for a moment. "Then by all means, tell them, and tell them that

Zoya Fyodorova is not afraid of them. I have done nothing wrong."

The man seemed even more confused. "A thousand pardons, Zoya Fyodorova, but I do not know to whom you refer."

"Really? Am I to believe that? Do you know that we do not have visitors when a film is being made? Of course if the man is a member of the NKVD, exceptions would be made."

"You mistake me, great lady. I am here with a construction crew. Have you not seen the building that is going on next door?"

Zoya felt foolish and paranoid. She was beginning to see spies everywhere. Maybe that was what they wanted. But why? What were they looking for? And if they were going to do something, when would they do it?

She was several weeks into the film when suddenly she was told that her part was to be given to another actress. "What do you mean?" Zoya demanded of her superior at the studio. "Are you not satisfied with my work?"

The man busied himself with his cigarette lighter. "I am not at liberty to discuss the matter."

"I want to discuss it. Are you displeased with my acting?"

"No."

"Then why are you doing this to me? I know this woman you are giving my role to. She is not as good an actress."

"Maybe not, but the feeling now is that she is more right for this part than you."

"I do not believe that."

"I cannot help what you do or do not believe. It is done. We will call you when we have more work for you."

The man left the room. Zoya sat for a few moments to compose herself. This had never happened to her before. It wasn't her work, she was certain of that. Then what? Was it tied in with the people spying on her, or was she again being paranoid?

She went to the room where she dressed and got her things together. A woman she had thought of as a friend started to come in, saw Zoya, and said, "Oh, I'm sorry," and darted out again, her face flaming red.

It was the same in the halls. A typist who always had a smile for Zoya was now too busy to look up from her typewriter. The old man who swept the corridors pushed his broom around the corner as she approached. They all know, Zoya thought. I have some terrible disease and they are all afraid to come too close.

She forced her head high and walked from the building. She felt the beginning of nausea. Please, dear God, do not let me be sick where they can see.

When she came to a park, she sat down on a bench. She felt weak and she was trembling. It was coming now, and it was close. Whatever the spying had been about was now going into its final phase.

Zoya was associated with the Theater of Film Performers. It was an adjunct of her studio, a place where the film actors could appear in live theater when they were between films. The lobby was decorated with large portraits of all the film stars who appeared there. Zoya's portrait had hung in a place of prominence for a long time. But now, suddenly, it had been removed.

When Zoya heard of it, she went to look for herself. It was gone. She was frightened. Looking at the place where her picture had been and now finding a stranger's face in its place was like seeing herself disappear. She was beginning not to exist. First her picture, and in time—when they were ready—Zoya herself. And no one would ever know that she was gone.

She came out of the theater and looked around. She saw no one, but they were somewhere watching her. In a doorway, around a corner—somewhere. And there was nothing she could do about it. There was no place to run, no place to hide. For the first time she accepted what she could never believe before: she was going to be arrested.

December 27, 1946. It had been a lovely Christmas party at the home of the English newspaperman Alexander Vert and his wife, Maria. It was such a good time with so many interesting people, people who were familiar with and had worked in countries outside of the Soviet Union.

Zoya decided to walk to her apartment. It was less than ten blocks away, and even if it was one in the morning, the streets of Moscow were safe. She pulled her fur coat tight about her—

there was still warmth in it, though it was beginning to show wear badly—and started out.

The cold air felt good. It cleared the heavy cigarette smoke from her head. She looked around for her "watchers," as she had come to call them, but she saw no one. She laughed to herself. Perhaps they had frozen to death waiting for her to leave the party.

When she entered the apartment, there was silence. Shura was already asleep. Zoya took off her coat and hat and went in to the baby. Victoria was asleep on her stomach. Zoya tucked the blanket around the baby and leaned over to kiss the back of her head. She breathed deeply. The powdery smell of a baby— it was the loveliest perfume in the whole world.

Zoya watched her sleeping. Imagine, almost one year old. Oh, what a birthday party you are going to have, my darling Vikka. I will shower you with presents no matter what it costs.

She leaned over and kissed her again, then tiptoed from the room. Poor Jackson—she could think of him now without pain—what you are missing!

She went to get herself some fruit juice. Champagne never sat well with her, not even the little bit she had drunk at Alexander's party. It always produced a dull headache and left a dryness in her mouth. She had her hand on the cupboard door where the glasses were kept when there was a sharp pounding at the door to the apartment.

Zoya froze. She couldn't move, her terror was so great. She knew who it was. All of Moscow knew of the knocks that came in the middle of the night when there was no one awake to see.

She didn't move until the second knocking came, harder, more insistent. She had to answer, or they would hammer down the door.

She went to the door and opened it. Six men and one woman pushed inside. Zoya recognized only one of them—a yard-cleaner from the building. He didn't look directly at her. He shouldn't, Zoya thought to herself. He should be ashamed of himself to be a witness against those who thought of him as a friend and neighbor.

Zoya felt as if she were in a dream, and there were two Zoyas, one to whom this was happening, and another one standing aside observing it all and noting little things: the woman wearing a fur coat and the men in dark green uniforms. One had red epaulets on his. These things are unimportant, one Zoya told the other. You must stop this. Pay attention and think. Your life is at stake at this moment.

The man with the red epaulets took out a paper and held it in front of her face. She caught only the words "crime" and "arrest."

Zoya shook her head violently. "It is a mistake. I am an innocent person. I have committed no crimes."

The man's expression didn't change. "If you are innocent, there is nothing for you to worry about. You will come with us and we will look into your case. If you are innocent, it will all be straightened out and you will be brought back. You do not need to take anything with you."

There were men on either side of her taking her arms. "I must get my coat," Zoya said.

The man with the red epaulets nodded to the men holding her arms. They released her. Zoya went to the front closet, where the woman was removing everything and tossing it all on the floor. Zoya had to rummage through the clothing on the floor to find her coat. She put it on. The woman paid no attention to her.

Zoya saw Shura standing against the wall in her nightgown, her hands over her breasts, her eyes wide with fright. The room was already a shambles. One man was removing the drawers from a bureau and dumping everything onto the floor. Another had removed the drawer from the dining table and had emptied everything on top of the table and was poking through it, examining each item. "Why are you doing this?" Zoya asked.

The man with the epaulets said, "If you are innocent, what does it matter? It is time to go."

The men had taken her arms again. Zoya flung them from her. "My baby! She is only 11 months old. She cannot be left alone."

"You have a maid who is here. She will notify your sister. If your sister wants to take the child, fine. If not, the child will be cared for in a house of orphans. Come!"

"I want to see my baby once more."

The man shook his head. "No."

"I must see my baby or I will not go."

The man looked bored. "You do not have rights to say what you will or will not do."

Zoya put her head back and began to scream. One of the men holding her arms put his gloved hand over her mouth. The man with the epaulets seemed shaken. "Very well, you may look at her, but do not touch the child."

They followed Zoya into the baby's room and stood in the doorway watching her. Zoya ran to the crib and dropped to her knees. Thank God, the baby had turned so that she was on her back and Zoya could see her face. One little hand was clenched into a fist and lay beside the face.

Zoya wanted desperately to reach out and touch that little hand, to stroke the cheek, to kiss the face. Her tears were blurring her vision so that she wiped her eyes. She must study the face, memorize it so that it would be with her forever. This might be the last time she would ever see her baby.

Her crying was coming now in great ugly sobs. The baby reacted to the sounds and turned her head away from Zoya. Don't turn away from me, Zoya begged silently.

From the doorway, the man said, "Come. It is time to go."

Zoya leaned as close to the child as she dared. "Good-bye, my Vikka. I will never see you again."

They had to lift her to her feet and take her from the room.

The car was waiting outside the building with the motor running. Three men went with Zoya. The other three and the woman stayed behind in the apartment. Zoya was crowded into the middle of the back seat with a man on either side of her and the third facing her from the jump seat. The man on the jump seat rapped on the glass partition and the driver started the car.

"Where are you taking me?" Zoya asked.

The man in charge said, "Lubyanka."

"But why? What is my crime? Why are you taking me there?"

"Lubyanka does not necessarily have to be a prison. If you are innocent, you will just answer some questions and you will go home. That is all I can say."

Not necessarily a prison. Perhaps, Zoya thought, but while she had heard of people who had gone into Lubyanka, she had not heard of any who had come out.

The car moved silently like a black shadow through the deserted streets of Moscow. This is insane, Zoya thought. I am wearing a fancy gown and party shoes and I am going to prison.

The driver turned into Dzershinki Square, and there was Lubyanka in front of her, a huge gray stone shadow with a darker shadow in it that was the iron gate. Even on bright sunny days there was a grim darkness about Lubyanka that even the trees in their summer greenery could not brighten. Now the naked branches thrashing in the night wind looked to Zoya like hands reaching out for her. Guards opened the iron gate to admit the car. I am being swallowed up, Zoya thought.

No one spoke to her. She was walked down to a room where a fat woman in a guard's uniform was waiting. She stood up as Zoya entered and came to her. Her voice was dry, bored. It was all routine to her. "I will take your clothes now—they will be kept for you until you leave—and you will take a shower."

Zoya shook her head. "I do not want a shower. I want to see someone. This is a great mistake."

The woman looked at her indifferently. "You will remove your clothes and give them to me. Things will go better with you if you do as you are told."

Zoya undressed. She was given a towel that was rough and thin. It barely covered her nakedness. The guard unlocked the door and pushed Zoya out ahead of her.

Zoya found herself moving at a brisk pace through corridors that turned right and left, and all looked the same. When they reached the shower room, she was completely disoriented. The shower was a boxlike room. There were no knobs to control the water, only a little window through which the female guard looked. When Zoya was inside, the water was turned on. It came down hot and hard, hotter than Zoya liked. She gasped and pushed back against the wall until her body adjusted to it. She looked about but there was no soap.

It didn't matter. After a few minutes, the water was turned off. The door opened and the guard tossed Zoya's towel in to her. It was too worn to absorb much water. Zoya used it to rub at her hair, which had been done for the party and was now completely ruined. She wrapped the towel around her, clutching at the side to keep it from opening, and they marched back to the room from which they had come.

Zoya looked for her clothes, but they were gone. The guard handed her a skirt, a military-style blouse, and a pair of underdrawers. They were all a dark, drab green, and they were threadbare from too many years of wear. Zoya felt her skin cringe against the feel of them. They reeked of the strong laundry soap they had been boiled in, and they obviously had not been ironed.

Tears came to her eyes, but she fought them back. They were prison clothes. She no longer felt like Zoya Fyodorova, but someone anonymous, from whom all identifying marks had been removed.

The woman signaled her to the door, unlocked it, and opened it. A male guard was waiting. The woman motioned to Zoya to follow him.

He took her to an elevator and they rode to the second floor, where there was another corridor. At the end, the guard knocked on a door and opened it. He closed the door behind her.

It was a large office dominated by a desk covered with many papers. Behind it on the wall was a picture of Stalin. Seated at the desk was a man in a civilian suit. There were two other men seated along one wall, wearing NKVD uniforms. Obviously, the man in the suit was also NKVD, since Lubyanka was an NKVD prison and he was clearly their superior.

His name, she would learn, was Abumokov, a stout man with dark brown hair and a pockmarked face in which there was no sign of warmth. His eyes moved over her as if he were studying a curiosity.

At first no one spoke. All three men simply stared at her until she wanted to scream. She was not used to being studied as if she carried a disease. Finally it began with the men sitting against the wall. One of them laughed. "Look at her in her wrinkled clothes and her terrible hair. Do you find her at all attractive?"

The other man said, "I had heard that people once considered her pretty, but how could that be? She is so ugly."

Zoya wanted to touch at her hair and to fix a button that had come undone, but she didn't dare to move. They are trying to humiliate me. It is their game, but I will not listen.

"Someone said that she was once in films, but how could that be?"

"That one, impossible. Unless it was a long, long time ago."

The first one laughed again. "I think it will be a long, long time before she ever sees a film studio again, when one considers her crimes."

It went on that way for what seemed like hours. All the time, Abumokov said nothing. He merely studied her.

Zoya was tired. Surely it must be near dawn, though no light showed as yet through the second-floor window. If only they would let her sit down. Though there was an empty chair directly in front of her, she didn't dare to take it.

Finally Abumokov spoke. His voice had a roughness to it. A peasant's voice, Zoya thought, and the voice of a dangerous man. "I think now it is time for you to talk with us. If you will be completely honest with us, and tell us the entire truth, reveal to us everything about your crimes, then perhaps there is hope for you."

Zoya looked from man to man. "I don't know what you are talking about. There has been some terrible mistake. What crimes? I am an innocent woman."

Abumokov shook his head sadly. "I am trying to help you. Tell the truth. Confess. If you try to hide things from us, I can assure you it will go much worse with you."

Zoya stretched her arms out to him. "I swear it, I am guilty of nothing. How can I confess what I do not even know?"

Abumokov nodded. "Very well, if this is how you wish it, I assure you we can wait. We can wait your whole lifetime if we have to. But you will tell your crimes to your interrogator, you will see. This is no motion picture with happy endings guaranteed. If you are to have a happy ending, you will have to confess your crimes."

This is madness, Zoya thought, complete madness in which some horrible game is being played with my life. "If you wish me to confess, tell me what I am accused of. If what you say is so, I will admit it. But you must tell me first what you think I am guilty of."

Abumokov stood up and prepared to leave. "Your visit is

now over. Good-bye, and I suggest you think over your life most carefully. I think you will discover your crimes."

He rang a bell, and a guard came in. "Take this prisoner to her cell."

After marching through several corridors, they stood in front of a door to what turned out to be Zoya's cell. The door had a small, barred window in it. The guard ran her hands over Zoya's body, then opened the door and motioned her to go in.

It was a small room. There were no windows other than the little one in the door, through which she could see the guard's eyes watching her. A naked light bulb hung down from the ceiling. Zoya looked for a switch to turn it off, but there was none.

There was little to see in the room: a wooden parquet floor— somehow she had never imagined that a prison cell would contain such a floor—a chair, a small table, and a bed on which there was a thin, rolled-up mattress, a shabby blanket, and a pillow. Zoya looked around for a toilet or a sink, but there was nothing. At that moment the door was unlocked and a woman guard came in. "I would suggest you rest. It is almost five o'clock in the morning. We get up here at five-thirty."

"Where is the toilet?" Zoya asked.

The woman shook her head. "Prisoners are taken to the bathroom twice a day. You had better learn to adjust yourself." She left.

Zoya unrolled the mattress and lay down. The light overhead was directly in her eyes. She pulled the thin, smelly blanket over her eyes. She was exhausted, but sleep would not come. You must sleep, she told herself. Soon the questions will begin again, and they will drive you mad if you do not get every bit of rest you can.

Then she thought of Victoria and she began to cry. Surely, Shura would go to Alexandra or Maria and one of them would take the baby. Dear God, she prayed, even if I can never see my baby again, let me know that she is with my sisters who will care for her and tell her how much her mother loves her.

She didn't know that she had fallen asleep until she heard a voice bark, "Get up!" and felt something sharp jab her in the side. It was the guard poking her with her key. Zoya sat up in terror, frightened by the strange voice. Then she realized where she was.

The guard placed a small piece of black bread, a cup of watery tea, and a spoon that had a bit of sugar in it on the table, and walked out.

Zoya dragged herself to the table. Her body ached and her eyes burned. If only she could sleep. She looked at the door, and the eyes were there watching her. No, they wouldn't let her sleep.

She brought the wooden chair to the table and sat down. Whatever was in the cup was so weak that she couldn't be certain whether it was tea or water. All she could taste was the faint sweetness of the bit of sugar. The bread was stale, but she softened it in the warmish water and forced it down. Who knew when they would feed her again?

She became aware of the silence, and she remembered that all the corridors she had walked down were carpeted. No sound of life came to her. Only the eyes at the door told her she wasn't all alone.

Zoya had eaten her breakfast and now there was nothing to do but sit and wait for whatever was to happen next. Again she thought of Victoria, but she pushed the baby's face from her mind. They will not see me cry! Never! I will think instead of the terrible mistake they have made and of how soon they will realize that I am only an actress, and nothing more. How could I commit so serious a crime as to bring me here? They have to realize their mistake. It will be today, and tonight I will be home with Victoria again.

The door opened and the guard stepped in, her pistol in her hand. "You will go to the washrooms now. You will be told this only once, and mistakes will not be tolerated. Whenever you pass another person in the corridors—a prisoner, a guard, anyone—you will turn your head to the wall away from that person and look only there until the person has passed. You understand?"

Zoya nodded. They started down the corridor again.

In time Zoya was to discover that all the corridors at Lubyanka looked the same. There was carpeting to dull any sound, and some nondescript color on the walls, unidentifiable in the dim lighting. She quickly lost her orientation, never knowing for certain even on what floor her cell was. A guard told her that her interrogation took place on the seventh floor. "That is the floor for questioning of extremely dangerous political prisoners."

There was no privacy in the toilets and for some time she was constipated because of the watching eyes. Her human dignity was being stripped away. She needed sympathetic human voices to say some kind word, but all she got were questions day after day, and when she was alone, silence. As time dragged on—how long, she would wonder, days, months, how long?—the memory of herself as a film star began to seem unreal. Perhaps that had been a dream she had had. More and more, Lubyanka seemed like her life, and such things as sunlight and laughter became inventions of her mind.

Zoya knew that her confusions were what they wanted. They were cultivating them in her, she knew, but she was too tired to fight her way out of them. The only thing she could do, had to do, was refuse to confess. How could you confess what you did not know?

Colonel Lihachov was questioning her. Zoya had trouble keeping track of her interrogators. There were four main ones who rotated the daily sessions. Lihachov, Samarin, Sokolov, Gnevashev—Zoya would never forget their names or their faces. Different men, yes, but they were all the same. They all wanted the same thing from her. But this day, this blessed day, Lihachov made a mistake, a glorious mistake. He said, "I do not understand. How could *you*, such a great actress, fall down to such a big and terrible crime?"

He had referred to her as an actress! It was as if windows had opened somewhere and cool fresh air had blown in on her, tearing from her mind the fogs that they had been pouring in daily. Zoya Fyodorova, the film star, was not a fantasy, but the reality of what she was before this nightmare began. Everything she had begun to doubt about herself was real. Only this nightmare of Lubyanka was unreal. God bless you for this, Colonel Lihachov, I am alive again.

"Why are you smiling? I said nothing funny."

What was it he had said? Crime? "I have never committed a crime, or even thought of committing one."

He laughed. "You are not a fool. You know your crimes. I do not know what you think you will accomplish by lying when all of Moscow has seen you."

At last a clue to what this was all about. "Do you call love a crime? If that is so, then yes, I committed a crime. I met an American and I fell in love with him. And I was with him, I do not regret it. If there are other crimes, you will have to tell me them."

The colonel shook his head sadly. "No, you will tell us. As for falling in love, you could do that whenever you wanted. That is no crime. But to fall in love stupidly, that is a crime. And to give birth to a potential enemy of the country instead of having an abortion, that is a crime. You cannot pretend you did not know that your fine American was a spy. Oh, yes. We know that."

"I don't believe that," Zoya said.

"Perhaps you did not know about it, but that seems unlikely. You were his victim, but you helped him with information."

"Impossible!"

"He had his microphone concealed in his buttons on his sleeves, and he took many pictures of you when you were naked, did you know that?"

"Hah!" Zoya flared at him. "And if I was naked, why was he wearing his jacket? If I must tell you anything, I will tell you this. I am a very shy and modest woman. It is one of my problems. I do not flaunt myself when I am naked."

The colonel reached into his jacket pocket and took out five or six snapshot-sized pictures and threw them on the desk in front of Zoya. "Then perhaps you can tell me how these pictures of you came to be?"

Zoya reached out to pick them up and examine them, but Lihachov slammed his fist down on her hand so that she cried out with pain. Quickly, he scooped up the pictures and put them away. "Oh, no. They are not for you. They are our evidence."

The pain in her hand slowly diminished. Zoya moved her

fingers to see if anything had been broken. It was all right. The pictures were obviously fakes. Otherwise, he would let her see them. In any case, she never made a display of herself when she was nude. And Jackson would never take such pictures.

"So you see how much your Americanyets cared for you? At this minute, you are being disgraced and laughed at all over the United States. You have helped a spy. You have been used by a spy, and for what? He has shamed you."

This is ridiculous, Zoya thought. But she said nothing. She was thinking of the enormity of the crime she was being charged with. She was being accused of being a spy, an enemy of the state. It was worse than she had imagined.

"Therefore," the colonel said, "I again advise you to tell the truth. Tell us everything. We know your crimes, but it will go better with you if you confess them freely."

This is all a terrible game they are playing, Zoya thought, and I cannot stop it. But I will not help them. "And I must tell you again that I have committed no crimes."

He rang the bell for the guard. "Take her away. She has more thinking to do."

The days took on a routine, each one the same. The questioning would begin around eight in the morning, though Zoya only guessed at the time because her wristwatch had been taken away with all of her belongings. But if she was awakened each morning at 5:30, then it had to be about eight when she was taken to her interrogator. It lasted for at least six hours before she was returned to her cell. There was time for a rest, but she was not allowed to lie on the bed. She would fall asleep sitting straight up in her chair.

The second session would begin around nine in the evening and go until four or five in the morning. She would get only the briefest of naps before the five-thirty wake-up. The burning in her eyes, the aches in her body, the headaches, were continual now, as her body hungered for sleep.

And she was losing weight, but that was no surprise. A little warmish tea and a piece of stale bread for breakfast, a tasteless cereal with more weak tea at midday, then a watery soup with a few limp vegetables for dinner. She ate it all—though at times she gagged at the sight and smell of vegetables that had begun to rot—because she wanted to stay alive.

Once during one of her brief sleeps before five-thirty in the morning, she was in a large, strange courtroom. Everyone there had horrible faces and they were all surrounding Zoya, hammering questions at her more quickly than she could answer them. And they hit her with tree branches when she did not reply quickly enough. "Why do you want to live?" one of them shouted at her, and slashed at her.

She awoke with the question still in her mind. Why do I want to live? Was it only that they should not have the pleasure of her death? No. Then why? Victoria. My Vikka.

Yes, the child was a reason to live. The only reason. Zoya thought of the baby as she was the last time she had seen her. Your first birthday, and I was not there. And there will never be another first birthday.

Zoya began to cry. She turned her back to the little window in her cell, so the guard could not see her tears. How many more birthdays of yours will I miss, my little one? Will I ever be with you again?

Zoya forced her mind away from Victoria. Any minute now the guard would come in with her tea and bread Another day, the same as all the other days, would begin, and she needed her strength. What good would self-pity do her?

But today was different. The guard came to take her for her shower. Zoya was surprised. She was allowed a shower a week and by the little record of scratches on the wall she had begun to keep, a week had not gone by since the last shower. Was today special for some reason? Or was her mind going so, that even the simplest of things, such as making a tiny scratch on a wall once a day, was beginning to be too complicated for her?

It always embarrassed Zoya to have to strip in front of a strange guard, but there was no alternative. She would turn her back and try to hide her body as she uncovered it beneath the skimpy towel. Her face would burn as she pictured the guard standing behind her looking at her.

But worse than this was the walk through the endless corridors with guards saying terrible things about her and laughing as she passed, clutching her towel over her body.

This time, when the water came on, Zoya screamed. It was boiling hot. Zoya pressed back against the wall, but she could not avoid the burning water. It felt like a million electric wires cutting into her. The room was alive with steam, and each drop of water was a touch of agony on her bare flesh. She fainted.

When she came to, she was lying on the bed in her cell. She was still naked, but the blanket had been put over her. Zoya touched her face and breasts. There were blisters. When she took her hand away, it felt sticky. Someone, perhaps a doctor, had put salve on her burned skin.

Zoya began to tremble and to cry in choking sobs. "I cannot take much more. I cannot."

That evening, she was taken to Colonel Lihachov's office again. He said, "I heard you had an unfortunate accident in the shower this morning."

"I do not believe it was an accident," Zoya said.

The colonel laughed. "My good woman, we are not monsters here who torture helpless women."

Zoya remained silent.

He reached behind him and brought forth a thick folder crammed with papers. On top of it, there was a small American flag. "Do you know what this is?"

Zoya said, "Papers, an American flag, what else?"

He leaned forward and his voice snapped at her. "This is a dossier of your many crimes. Now do you still want to protest your ignorance of them?"

"I cannot imagine what they are."

He held up the flag. "And this? You do not recognize this? It came from your apartment."

Zoya had to think. Did it really come from her apartment or was this manufactured evidence? Then she remembered. It was one of the flags that had been on the front fenders of Jackson's car. He had given it to her as a souvenir, a love token. Zoya told Lihachov about the flag.

He smiled. "And was it love that made you keep this flag or was it some proof of your allegiance to a foreign power?"

Zoya felt her anger rising. "That is too silly to answer. I put it away in a drawer and forgot about it. How could I have allegiance to a country I have never seen?"

The colonel opened her dossier and took out a photograph and placed it in front of her. "And this? The uniform is not Russian you will notice."

It was a head-and-shoulders portrait of Zoya wearing an American military hat and military jacket. She wasn't even certain what branch of service it was. "You are joking," she said. "If you know everything, then you know that was a picture taken at a party."

"Really? It goes well with the flag. And this picture?"

He placed another picture in front of her. It showed her dancing with Averell Harriman at some embassy function. "Yes, I was invited to the American Embassy on some occasion, and the ambassador asked me to dance, that is all. This was at least a year before I met Jackson. What does it prove?"

Lihachov lit a cigarette. He blew the smoke toward the ceiling and watched it curl upward. "By itself, perhaps nothing. But when you put it together with the other pieces of evidence I have shown you, it creates a picture of a very foolish woman who seems to have spent too much of her life with non-Soviets, people whose interests are contrary to the interests of the Soviet."

Zoya leaned toward him across the desk. "You know that is not so. I am an actress, and so I meet many people of the world. The Soviet itself invites me to the functions that these people attend. Do you think I would have been at the American Embassy if I were a factory worker? Should I have said to the ambassador, 'Thank you for having me to this grand affair, but no, I cannot dance with you because you are an American?' Should I have thrown away the flag which is one of the few memories I have of the father of my child, because it is an American flag? Should I have told my film studio that . . ."

The colonel had opened his desk drawer. He placed a pistol on the table. "And what about this?"

It stopped Zoya. "I know nothing about guns."

"Oh?" He smiled. "This came from your apartment, too."

Zoya was startled. She stared at it without recognition. The colonel said, "You may pick it up. It is not loaded."

As Zoya lifted it, she recognized it by the weight. It was just the hollow shell of a pistol. It had no internal workings. "Yes, I remember. A pilot gave it to me when I performed a concert on the front lines. He said it had been taken from the Germans."

The colonel smiled. "It is a Browning. I believe that is American."

"I told you, I know nothing of guns. I only know what the pilot said who gave it to me. If it is American, then the pilot took it from a German who had taken it from an American. What do I know? I said I was afraid of such things, and the pilot showed me that it would not shoot. There is nothing inside."

"Really? Even an empty gun could come in most handy if one wanted to get in somewhere, such as perhaps the Kremlin."

"Madness! Madness!" Zoya screamed the words at him. "Can you honestly see me pushing my way into the Kremlin with a fake gun? And what would I want in the Kremlin?"

The words came at Zoya like a thunderclap. "What any enemy of the Soviet would want. To assassinate our glorious leader, Joseph Stalin."

Zoya put her hand to her mouth. At last she knew the enormity of the charges against her. She began to shake her head violently from side to side. Her body shook, too, and she fell back into the chair. All the fear she had fought down since she had been taken to Lubyanka rose in her. My God, help me, she begged. I will have a stroke. I will faint. For what he was accusing her of, she could be shot.

The colonel smiled. "At last, you are frightened? I would think so. I told you we knew all."

"No! No, no," Zoya said. "I have never thought to kill anyone. I do not even know how to fire a gun. I swear it!"

"Do you know that you have no legal right to keep a gun? And only a fool—and I do not believe you are one—would keep a gun unless he knew how to use it."

"I swear I do not know. And this one will not fire. It is a case only, a souvenir."

The colonel slammed his hand onto the desk. "This is enough! We are going in circles now with your lies. We have your statement. It is written down. The statement you made to your group. You stated, 'I want to free the world from the tyrant.' You remember now?"

Zoya said, "I am not an assassin."

"You thought everyone in your little cell was loyal to you, eh? Well, you were wrong. There was one decent Soviet citizen in there who has told us of your treachery."

But the moment of her panic had passed. All right, Zoya told herself, I will be shot. It is all right. I cannot take much more of this. Even to be shot will be better than this day after day. Let it end. They want my death. Let them have it. But I will not help them to achieve it. "I never made such a statement. As for a cell, the only cell I know of is the one you have given me in this place."

"Really? Would you like me to tell you the names of the people with whom you plotted your crime?"

"You may tell me names, I cannot stop you. They will probably be names you have made up, as you have made up my revolutionary group."

He shook his head. "I think you know every one of these traitors. Do you know a Marina Vigoshina, a costume designer at your studio? Sasha Mirshoff, a composer? Sinitzyn, the singer? Pitacova, a correspondent who has gone so far as to translate her name to the English, Nickel? And Ilene Terashovitz, I believe an old friend of yours?"

"I have not seen her since my school days!"

"And one more name. Maria Fyodorova, or do you also deny knowing your own sister?"

Zoya felt as if she were going to be sick. "I know every one of these people, and I swear, on the head of my daughter, they are all innocent."

"We will find that out, because they have all been arrested. They will confess, as you will confess, and they will be punished for their foolishness in joining with you in your scheme."

Tears came to Zoya's eyes. Let him see them, she thought. They are his shame and my sorrow. "I do not know why you are doing this to me, and I no longer care. But to arrest people whose only crime is that they are dear to me is horrible beyond imagination."

"And your crime against Stalin? That is not beyond imagination?"

"I have never met Stalin! I wouldn't know where to find him. And with a gun that has no insides, what would I do to him?"

The colonel motioned her to be silent. "I want only one thing from you. Tell us your name!"

Zoya looked at him as if he had lost his mind. Her name? "Zoya Alexyevna Fyodorova. You know my name."

"You know what name I mean. The name you used in your treachery. What name did your fellow plotters call you by? What name did your lover take back with him to the United States? What name did they contact you by?"

It is hopeless, Zoya thought. I cannot get through to this man. He knows the truth and he will not accept it. "My name is Fyodorova. It is the only name I have ever had."

The colonel stood up. "I advise you to rethink your position. You know your crimes now. They are numbers 58/10, 58/11, 58 1/a, 58 8/17, and 182. The punishment is most severe, but if you will tell us your real name, perhaps the punishment will be a little less. Think about it. Think most seriously about it!"

He rang for the guard to take her back to her cell.

Zoya lay down on her bed and felt the stings of her burns start up again. Soon it would be the guard with the bread and tea, and another day of questioning. She needed sleep, but there was no hope of it. She kept seeing sister Maria's little face. Why Maria, always so happy and laughing? Her health would not stand harsh treatment. And poor Sasha. She could see his confused eyes. He wouldn't even understand what they were talking about.

Zoya saw each face that had been named, and if it wasn't so sad, so horrible, it would be laughable. Her cell! All of them together couldn't plot the assassination of a mouse.

Zoya sat on the hard wooden chair and waited for the guard to come for her. She sat there all day but no one came. Her only sense of time came from the bringing of the noon meal, the dinner of thin soup, and the evening trip to the bathroom.

She spent the long day and evening thinking of the people who had been arrested, thinking of Victoria. She did not think about herself or what would become of her. That no longer seemed like her problem. She had no say in her life anymore. Whatever would be, would be. They would decide, and she would accept. She did not wish to die, but she was tired, and death seemed so inevitable now, that it would be a relief when it came.

Finally the guard stuck her head in the door and told her she could lie on the bed. Zoya lay down and closed her eyes against the naked light bulb overhead. If they left her alone this evening as they had all day, it would be the first full night's sleep she would have since she had entered Lubyanka.

But she couldn't sleep. The number 58 stayed in front of her closed eyes. An anti-Soviet person, a traitor, an enemy of the state, a plotter, a spy, a would-be assassin—the words kept coming at her. She would surely die. When evidence could be manufactured, when they could hold someone until they got the confession they wanted from them, what hope did she have?

She would die, and no one would know. She would disappear the way her picture had from the lobby. Suddenly, and with no explanation. And her child would grow up calling someone else mother.

Zoya shook her head to clear it of the thoughts that could drive her into madness. If I am to die anyway, then at least let me sleep. But sleep wouldn't come for what seemed like several hours.

It was the beginning of the insomnia that was to torture her for years.

The days passed and then the weeks. Zoya saw no one but the guard who brought the food or took her to the bathroom, and the guard was under strict orders not to speak to her. The continued silence day after day became as much a danger to her as the interrogation sessions had been. She began to imagine sounds. There was a faint scratching sound as if a little animal was running up and down the wall somewhere behind her. But whenever she turned, there was nothing.

Another time, she thought she heard someone in her cell clear his or her throat—she couldn't be certain whether it was a man or a woman—as if preparing to speak. Again, no one.

And if she listened intently, she could hear a faint electrical hum as if a wire was thrumming somewhere. All of it frightened Zoya, because she knew that none of these sounds could be. They were signs to her that her mind was weakening.

But most frightening of all were the trips to the shower, what should have been a high point because they broke the monotony of her days. She was terrified that they would turn on the boiling water again. The first time after she had been scalded, she walked bravely through the halls clutching her towel about her. She told herself she wasn't afraid. After all, if one is to die, does it really matter which way death comes?

But when she was about to enter the shower stall, she froze. She couldn't move. Her body began to tremble and her knees locked. It took two guards to force her into the stall while she screamed and clawed against the door. The water came on, and it was only warm.

Later, back in her cell, Zoya wondered at herself. She had thought she had resigned herself to her death. Then why had she fought the shower stall? Obviously, she still wanted to live.

She spent her days reciting scenes she could remember from her films. It was something to do, and at least she heard a human voice, even if it was only her own. The eyes that were always at the slit window in the door became her audience. She played to them, tried to manipulate their emotions. Could she make those eyes laugh or fill up with tears? There was never any reaction.

The next time Zoya was taken to the shower, she began to tremble again, but she was able to enter, and the temperature was bearable again.

But the third time, the water came out boiling and steaming. Zoya screamed until it was turned off. She was hysterical when the door was opened.

There were large watery blisters all over her body that night, and no doctor visited her cell. Sleep was impossible.

The next morning the guard came for her. The prison clothes hurt as she walked through the corridors. The material rubbed against her blisters and made them burn with pain.

When Zoya entered the interrogation room, she saw Abumokov, the man who had questioned her the first night, behind the desk. He didn't look up, but continued reading a paper on his desk. Zoya stood and waited.

Finally, he looked up. "And now are you ready to talk with us?"

Zoya said, "I have always been willing to talk with you. It is just that I have nothing to tell."

"Your name. Have you decided to tell us the name you used?"

Zoya looked at the eyes in the pockmarked face. Was there any intelligence there? Did Abumokov really believe the charges against her or was he in on the manufacturing of them? There was no way to know. "There is no name," Zoya said, "because I was never a spy or a plotter or any of the other things I am accused of being. I do not know at how high a level these charges against me are coming from, but if you are a highly placed man, then you know they are all false. You know it as well as I do!"

Abumokov looked at her with contempt. "We do not need your acting talents and great speeches here. We need only one thing. The name you used."

"How many times must I tell you, I had no code name, because I was never. . . ."

Abumokov stood up and leaned over his desk toward her. "Do you fully realize the stupid game you are playing? You are a traitor. You can be shot! I am offering you a slight hope."

Zoya nodded. "And I would take it if I could. But there is no name, so I cannot."

He sat down again. "Then remember, before you die, remember this. It is your own doing."

"I think I will die in any case," Zoya said, "but at least I know I will not die a liar."

Abumokov rang for the guard.

Judging by the little secret scratches, it had been two weeks since she had been taken to Abumokov. The perpetual silence, the inability to sleep, had taken its toll on her nerves. That was the only explanation Zoya was able to come up with in later years for what she suddenly decided to do.

It was sometime in mid-morning when she went to the door

and banged on it until the guard opened it. "I want to see my interrogator," Zoya said.

The guard shook her head. "You will be sent for when they want to see you."

"No!" Zoya shouted with such force that the guard stopped in the middle of closing the door. "Tell him I have something to say to him. Something he wants to hear."

The guard came back in a few minutes. Zoya was taken to Lihachov's office. He nodded to her." Do you want to tell me something?"

"Yes."

"The name?"

"Yes, the name. Only get a stenographer in here to write it down. Let it be on the record that I told you what you wanted to know."

The colonel rang for the guard and sent her for the stenographer. When the man came in and was seated, Lihachov nodded to Zoya. "Begin."

Zoya took a deep breath. "The name by which all the spies knew me was Chiang Kaishek. There, now you know."

Lihachov looked at her. "Do you take me for a fool?"

"What do you mean? I told you the name. Don't you believe me? Did you expect me to say Mata Hari?"

"I did not expect a stupid lie."

Zoya smiled. "Then you know my name if you call this one a lie. Then you tell it to me."

He was angry now. "I have just about run out of patience and sympathy with you. You are begging to be shot."

Zoya was suddenly tired. The threat of being shot no longer frightened her. She had lived with it for so long now that it had become meaningless.

She looked straight at the colonel, and suddenly she didn't care what happened. The game was over as far as she was concerned. "You can shoot me. You have this power. But know this one thing: everyone will die some day. If I die in this place, I will die as your victim. And when you die, you will die as my assassin. And some day, the whole truth will come out. Everybody will know what you have done, and—"

Lihachov raised his hand to stop her. He was smiling. "A great speech, but you should have more of an audience."

He rang for the guard, whom he motioned to his desk. The guard went out and returned a few minutes later with two men, one of whom Zoya thought she recognized from her first questioning session with Abumokov. The colonel said to the men, "I think you should hear this. We are about to be accused of crimes by this traitor."

He turned to Zoya. "Now you may proceed."

Zoya was stung. "You think this is funny, don't you, to play with lives?"

The colonel shook his head. "No, I think it is most serious. Please go ahead."

"Well, I don't care what you think. I said that one day all of Russia will know how you treated people like me, all of you. We are innocent victims, and you are our persecutors. I am the victim of this regime, and you are my executioners!"

The men looked at each other. Zoya knew that she had said too much. She had probably signed her death warrant, but she didn't feel fear. Surprisingly, she felt lightheaded, almost giddy, as if she had rid herself of something rotting inside her system.

Colonel Lihachov stood up. "I will say this for you. You are a brave woman. You are also incredibly stupid to say such things, unless you truly want to die."

He rang for the guard to take her back.

The next day, she was brought to Abumokov. He was seated, as usual, behind his desk. Zoya saw her dossier with the American flag still on top, in one corner. Abumokov nodded to her curtly and picked up a sheet of paper. "You know, of course, that we have enough evidence to shoot you? But our government is a humane one. Therefore you will live to think of your crimes. You have been sentenced to 25 years in prison."

The guard took Zoya back to her cell. She felt numb inside. Only later did it occur to her that there had been no trial and she had not signed a confession. All she could think of was that she would be old when she came out of prison, and Victoria would be a grown woman, one who no longer needed a mother.

A guard came to her cell with the clothes she was wearing

the night of her arrest. "You will get your things together. You are being transferred."

When Zoya put on her own clothing, the softness of the materials felt strange to her. She ran a gentle hand along the silk of her dress and the fur of her coat. It brought tears of memory to her eyes. How sweet and easy life had been then, and she hadn't even known it.

It was night when they took her out into the prison courtyard. The air was cold. It was winter. Then she had been in Lubyanka for a year! A whole year had been taken from her life that she would never have back again.

But she would think of that later. At this moment, she was caught by the incredible smell of the air, the feel of the winter wind on her skin, the dazzling sight of the night sky. Had the world always been this beautiful?

The guard prodded her in the back. "Move!"

Ahead of her, Zoya could see a line of about seven or eight people standing in front of a prison truck, the one they call "The Black Crow." The other prisoners moved in slowly. When it came Zoya's turn to step from the ramp into the back of the truck, she had to feel her way. It was pitch-black inside. A narrow central corridor ran between thick bars.

Zoya stumbled forward as the guard kept prodding her. Finally he said, "Stop!" Zoya heard, rather than saw, a door of bars open. She was pushed inside. Something hit against her knees and she pitched forward, striking more bars. She felt near her knees and found a narrow seat. She turned and sat down. By putting out her hands, she could feel the bars all around her. She was in a narrow cage.

When the door closed and the van started up, Zoya could see nothing. She knew there were other people in the cages surrounding hers, but she couldn't see them, and no one dared to speak.

By the time the van stopped, Zoya's eyes had adjusted enough so that when the door was opened, she could make out shadows of people and guards. It was another prison courtyard.

Again the routine was the same. She was marched into the prison in silence, ordered to strip, taken to the showers, and then given clothes to put on. Then she was taken to her cell.

Zoya shrank back when the door was opened and the damp,

sour smell of a cellar in which something had died came toward her. The guard shoved her inside and slammed the door behind her. The cell was smaller than the one at Lubyanka, and it was dimly lit by a naked blue bulb hanging from the ceiling. There was a narrow barred window high up in one wall. From the damp smell that clogged the air, she doubted that sunlight ever came through. There was a toilet bucket in one corner, a wooden table and chair, and a narrow metal bed with a dirty mattress rolled up on top of it. The door to the cell had a round, glass-covered peephole.

Zoya looked at the filthy bucket and was repelled. She walked over to the bed and slapped at the mattress. Even in the dim light she could see the dust that rose from it, and when she smelled her hand, her throat tightened with revulsion.

She went back to the chair and sat down. She knew she couldn't sit there forever. At some point she would have to use the bed and the toilet, but she was not ready yet for either. They had not yet reduced her to the animal level.

Zoya dozed on and off. Sometimes she heard sounds of crying or screaming from other cells. Once it was a woman shouting, "You're wrong! You're wrong! I am innocent!"

Poor fool, Zoya thought. Hadn't she learned yet that no one would listen to her? We are all innocent and no one listens.

There was light, grayish and dull, coming through the little window high up on the wall, when the guard unlocked her cell and brought her breakfast. It was a piece of bread, not thoroughly baked. There was still raw dough at the center. The cup contained hot water, but there was no spoon with sugar to flavor it.

The guard had turned to go. Zoya put out her hand. "Wait! Tell me where I am."

"Lifortovo," she said and slammed the door behind her. The key turned in the lock.

Lifortovo. On the east side of Moscow.

By midday, Zoya's back ached from the wooden chair. She longed to unroll the smelly mattress and lie down, but she knew she was not allowed to until night. Finally, when her back screamed with pain, she was given permission.

When she unfolded the mattress, Zoya saw that there was a

large gash in it and grayish, dirty stuffing was coming out. It was no better on the other side. Well, she would have to accept it. There was no choice.

She was almost asleep when she felt a sensation along her leg as if something were crawling on her. Then the same sensation was on her arm.

Suddenly, her whole body itched and stung with a hundred pinpricks. Zoya sat bolt upright and screamed. Small reddish-brown bedbugs crawled all over her. She leaped to her feet and beat herself. Angry welts began appearing all over her. She rushed to the toilet and vomited the little food that was in her stomach. When she straightened up, she could see the guard's eyes at the peephole.

Zoya went to the door and pounded on it. "Open! Open!"

The guard opened the door. "What do you want?"

Zoya stuck out her arm so she could see the bites. "Look at this! And here, and here! Kill me, but don't torture me! This place is crawling with bedbugs."

The guard shrugged. "Tomorrow morning, our boss will come to you, and you can tell him. It will be taken care of. There is nothing I can do." She slammed and locked the door.

Zoya shuddered. Could she live until tomorrow morning in this place?

The light in the window had faded and it was impossible to see the dark floor clearly. Were there creatures moving along the floor, or was she imagining them? No, there was one. She stepped down hard, but there was nothing. Another, and nothing. Her mind was playing tricks on her.

She went to the chair, brushed the seat, and moved it away from the table. She sat down but kept stamping her feet up and down, in case the bedbugs were crawling over the floor to her.

Finally, exhausted, she fell asleep. She was awakened by the guard with the evening meal. It was some sort of soup that smelled rancid and a piece of stale black bread. Zoya forced herself to eat. It was revolting and she gagged several times, but she got it down.

When the guard came for the spoon and cup, she looked at her and smiled. "So where are your bedbugs now?"

Zoya stuck her arm out again. "Do you think I made these up?"

The guard shrugged and left.

Zoya wondered about what she had said. Yes, where *were* the bedbugs? Could they just be in the mattress? Couldn't they smell living flesh? Wouldn't they leave the mattress to come find her?

Or had the bedbugs been fed into her cell to torture her? She still had not signed a confession. But if they had been fed in, how were they withdrawn?

That struck her as funny. Were there such things as bedbugs who were loyal to the Soviet, who worked for the NKVD? No. Only people submitted to them, not bedbugs.

She slept on and off through the night. Twice she was awakened by being bitten, but each time it was only by one bug. One bug she could stand. But each time she brushed the creature to the floor and felt its shell crack under her shoe she shuddered. She would stand up then and walk the floor, waiting to hear other crackling sounds beneath her shoes, but there was nothing. She would return to her chair and doze again.

In the morning, the guard's superior officer came. "Now what is this nonsense about bedbugs?"

Zoya showed him the bites. "Nonsense? You call these nonsense? This is torture!"

The man took a quick look about the cell. "They are gone now."

"Examine the mattress, please," Zoya said. "I think you will find thousands there."

The man went over to the mattress. He dug his hand into the opening and pulled out a chunk of the gray stuffing. He rubbed it through his fingers. "There is nothing."

He turned to leave. Zoya stepped in front of him to block his way. "Then what are these bites? Did I bite myself?"

The guard pushed her aside. "Stranger things have been done in Lifortovo."

Zoya was alone again. She went over to the bed. Steeling herself, she stuck her hand inside the mattress and examined the stuffing. There was nothing. She poked around, then beat at the mattress. Not one bedbug appeared.

Then she went along the wall around the entire cell. There were many cracks and holes. They could easily feed the bedbugs into the cell through any of them. And if they could do that, then could they not find some way to draw them out again? This is crazy thinking, Zoya told herself, but she could think of no other explanation.

Nervously, she lay down on the bed. But each time she was near sleep, she awakened, imagining she felt something crawling on her body.

Finally she gave up and went back to the chair. I cannot take much more of this, she thought, or I will go mad.

All roads were leading to madness: sounds only from outside the cell; inside, nothing but the change of light from the dull gray of day to the dim light of night. And always the eyes at the little window watching her. Except one pair. A gray-green, and they appeared in the morning and stayed until after daylight had faded. But not continuously as the others did. They would disappear for minutes at a time, and Zoya would hear the muffled sounds of voices.

To think was certain madness. She didn't dare think of her baby, who would be talking and walking and would have no memory of her mother, or she knew her heart would burst.

Nor could she think of Maria and Sasha and all the others. God only knew what had happened to them. The only thing Zoya dared to think of was herself, because it produced a nothingness in her. Her future was all determined and was beyond her imagination. And her past, except for Victoria, was just a blur somewhere far back. The faces that mattered then had all grown vague in her exhausted mind. The life she had once led was more like a story one remembered than a reality.

Could one sit in this cell day after day for 25 years and come out alive or even sane? She doubted it, but then her mind couldn't really grasp how long 25 years would be, taken day by day by day. This, too, was something not to think about.

When the guard brought her supper that evening, Zoya scooped out the uncooked dough from the bread and added it to the other pieces she was saving. It was not good to eat, but it must contain some nourishment, and who knew when she might need it? She took a deep breath and held it so that she wouldn't smell the soup as she drank it. It made it easier to keep down.

The gray-green eyes had been replaced by brown eyes that

never left the peephole. Zoya couldn't face another night of sitting up. Hadn't she examined the mattress? It was safe.

She lay down and for once fell asleep almost immediately. How long she slept she didn't know, but it was black outside the window when she woke up. There was no sound from outside the cell. At this hour, the criers and the screamers had all quieted down. What had awakened her? she wondered.

Then she felt a faint tingling moving along her lips. She moved her hand to brush at whatever it was, and felt the crawling body.

She jumped to her feet, violently slapping at herself. She was swarming with bedbugs. They were under her dress and in her hair. The floor was moving with them. Zoya began to scream and dance around the floor. With each step, she felt the bugs crack beneath her feet.

The guard unlocked the door and rushed in. Zoya threw herself at her. "Get me out of here!"

The guard slapped her across the face with the full force of the back of her hand so that she fell against the wall and struck her head. Bolts of light shot across her eyes. She felt herself slipping to the floor.

No, she mustn't pass out. The bugs would eat her up. She shook her head and pushed with her hands against the wall. The flashes of light faded away. She touched her face and felt where she had been struck. The skin felt hot but there was no wetness. She wasn't bleeding.

"If you scream again, you will be beaten," the guard said.

"The bugs," Zoya sobbed. "Please, the bugs." But the guard was already locking the door.

Zoya brushed herself until she was certain she was rid of the bugs. Then she climbed on top of the table, after making sure there were none up there.

She stayed on top of the table all night, running her hands along the edges every few minutes to knock down those that had climbed up the table legs.

Zoya made her decision then. She would die. And she decided how. It would be with her silk stockings, which somehow they had not taken away from her when she came to Lifortovo.

She would do it in the morning when the gray-green eyes came on duty. She would be through with this nightmare.

Victoria wouldn't be hurt by her death. She didn't even know Zoya existed. Surely, if God were watching, the child was with Alexandra, who would raise her as her own.

Pale light began to filter into the room. Zoya looked around. The bedbugs were gone. Only the dead ones were there, crushed into the floor.

When breakfast came, Zoya again carefully scooped out the doughy part of the bread, planning to add it to the other pieces, but they had already hardened. She threw them under the bed, keeping only the soft piece. Then she drank the hot water.

When gray-green eyes left the window, Zoya moved the table and chair, a few inches at a time each time the eyes turned away so as not to cause attention, until they were under the window. Then she pretended to doze while she waited for the eyes to leave again. In her hand was the dough, which she kept kneading to make it as soft and sticky as possible. Pretending to cough, she brought her hand to her mouth and spit into it to make the dough more moist.

Finally, gray-green eyes left the peephole. Zoya ran to it, and smeared the bread dough over it.

Quickly, she pulled off her stockings and knotted them together. Then she put the chair on top of the table and pulled herself up. She knotted one end of the stockings to one of the window bars and tied the other end around her neck.

Zoya forced her mind to conjure up Victoria's face for one last time. Then she leaped from the chair, knocking it to the ground. The silk knot tightened around her neck and she heard gargling noises that must have been her own. Her feet kept hitting against the end of the table. The room began to spin, and she saw pinwheels in front of her eyes. She felt the knot beginning to slip. Let it hold, she prayed, let this be the end.

The next thing she knew, a guard was on either side of her and they were taking her down. The silk was gone from her neck. She had failed.

They carried her to the cot and threw her down. While one held Zoya's arms, the other began cursing and struck her across her breasts and face. Zoya screamed and jerked her face from side to side, but there was no escaping the blows. Then pain, like white-hot fire, shot up her arms from her wrists and she passed out.

When she came to, she could barely open her eyes. She started to raise her hand to see what was wrong, but there was a stab of pain and she gave up trying.

She was in a different cell. And then she remembered what had happened. The flesh of her face and upper body was so puffed up that she could barely open her eyes. Gritting her teeth, she forced herself to raise her hands enough to see. Her fingers were in splints. The guard had dislocated all of her fingers.

It was several days before the swelling went down. When the splints were taken off her fingers, a man handed Zoya her confession. She merely glanced at it. Whatever they had written was a lie. It didn't interest her, and she knew it was senseless to fight them any further. She said, "This is all you wrote? These few pages? It is hardly enough."

"It will do," he said.

Zoya signed.

The man took the confession from her. "We are here to sentence you. Stand up."

"In front of you, never."

"Silence. You have no right to say anything. You are hereby sentenced to 25 years in a hard-labor camp."

Zoya nodded. A hard-labor camp. What did it matter? They would kill her off as they had her father. She looked at the man who had read her sentence. Obviously he was waiting for something. Did he expect her to faint, or to weep and beg for mercy? He would not have that pleasure. "What day is this?" Zoya asked.

The man was surprised. "It is the twenty-first day of February."

"Really?" Zoya said. "With all this nonsense, I thought it was the first of April."

The man smiled. "I salute your humor. But I think you will soon stop laughing."

On her tenth day in Lifortovo her clothes and fur coat were brought to her again. "You are being transferred. Get dressed."

They moved her again when it was dark. The Black Crow took her to a train station. She was placed with 24 other men and women in a compartment designed to hold four people. The windows were sealed shut, and the smell of bodies was strong. They were a mixed bag: prostitutes, criminals, political prisoners. When Zoya arrived, the few seats in the compartment were already taken.

Someone called out, "Zoya!"

She looked around. The voice was familiar. And suddenly there was Marina, the designer from the studio. The two women embraced. Zoya said, "They gave me 25 years. What did you get?"

Marina said, "Only ten." She laughed. "Well, after all, you were our leader."

An unshaven man suddenly stood up. He glared about him. "Do you not recognize her? Move, and let our favorite actress sit down. Her friend, too."

Another man reluctantly stood up.

Their destination was Potyma, a labor camp 300 kilometers north of Moscow, where Zoya was held for two months and then given a new sentence: 25 years in a hard-labor camp, confiscation of all of her personal property and moneys, and exile for her family. That meant that Alexandra, her children, and Victoria, if she was with them as Zoya prayed, would be sent out of Moscow. Zoya wept for her child.

Again Zoya was transferred, this time to the prison in Chelyabinsk, in Siberia, 300 kilometers south of Sverdlovsk. Why do they keep moving me about, she wondered? It is as if they are trying to lose me.

Zoya had assumed that Chelyabinsk was her ultimate destination, but she was wrong. She was there only briefly. Again her sentence was changed. This time it was to be 25 years in prison, not a hard-labor camp, and as before, confiscation of all her property and exile for her family. The man who read her sentence smiled as he said, "You are being sent to Vladimirskaya to serve your sentence. You leave tonight."

Vladimir! Zoya gasped. Who had not heard of Vladimir? It was located 185 kilometers east of Moscow and was a feared prison. If a work camp was to be dreaded, a prison, and Vladimir especially, was worse. In the work camp if one could survive the work, there was still some semblance of humanity. One could walk around, talk with people. That was something. But in prison, there was nothing. A terrible, empty, day-after-day nothingness that rotted the mind and killed the body. Perhaps one could survive 25 years in a work camp, Zoya thought, though she doubted it, but in the living tomb that was Vladimir it was hopeless.

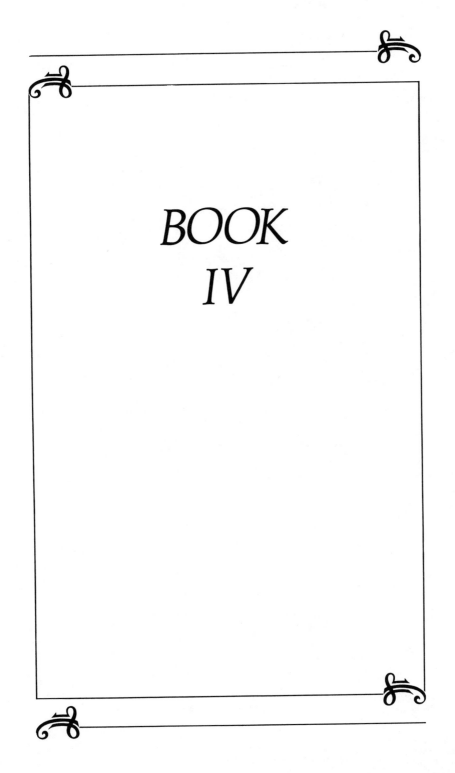

BOOK
IV

VICTORIA

Memory for me begins at the age of three or four in Poludino, a village in North Kazakhstan. It was there that my Aunt Alexandra, who I thought was my mother, was sent when her sisters, Zoya and Maria, were arrested. Years later, I was told that it was her disapproval of Zoya's foreign friends, especially the American Jackson Tate, that had saved her from imprisonment. She had never gone out with the couple as Maria had.

When Zoya was arrested, the maid Shura had quickly gone to Alexandra, who came to collect me. Shortly afterward, Alexandra, twice divorced and the mother of two, was ordered out of Moscow to Poludino—not Siberia but not much different. Since memory began for me in this village of only a few hundred people scraping a sparse living from the steppes, I did not find it hard. I knew no other life. I thought I had a complete family—a mother named Alexandra, a brother named Yuri, ten years older than I, and a sister named Nina, five years older. I didn't miss what I didn't have, because I did not even know it existed. You don't miss dolls or other toys if you have never seen them. And you do not crave meat to eat if you have never tasted it.

For all I knew, Poludino was the world, and like every other place in the world, not that I even thought about it. Poludino was not much more than a cluster of houses set out in the middle of the steppes. As far as you could see the land was flat and open to the weather. In winter, which came early, we scavenged continuously for wood, but the stove never warmed our tiny house enough to melt the ice that formed on the inside walls of the room that was both our living room and bedroom. The little kitchen off it was no better. Outdoor temperatures of 40 below were common, and the wind roaring across the open countryside easily crept in under the door, around the windows, and under the walls that stood on naked ground. Because our toilet was behind the house, we kept a pot indoors for times when the cold was too biting or the snow was too high.

In summer the sun baked us with temperatures that often climbed to 105 degrees. The streams dried into cracked mud and Poludino stank from the waste people emptied into holes they dug outside their houses.

Mama—I called my Aunt Alexandra that until the day she died—worked as a bookkeeper at the local Office of Economic Planning. The job paid only enough to keep us alive, and the hours were long, six days a week. Each winter morning she would wake us long before it was light. We would run across the wet, cold dirt floor to huddle around the stove. Breakfast was always the same: a piece of bread and a cup of very weak tea, more boiling water than tea. And then I was alone all day, until Nina and Yuri came back from school.

Maybe that's where I learned to be comfortable alone, to need people but to be shy around them. And maybe that's where my career as an actress began, because with nothing to do all day except eat my lunch, just a piece of bread, I had time for fantasies. I didn't go outside much when I was alone. Sometimes, it was because of the weather, but most of the time it was because of the people.

Mama had to report twice a week to the police, so that they would know we were still in Poludino. Everyone knew that. And word spread through the village that Mama was a relative of an enemy of the people, and therefore she and her children were enemies of the people. If I went outside, I would see people draw back and pull their children close to them. The population was largely Kazakhs, a leathery-skinned people with an Oriental cast to the eyes, nomadic in nature, moving through Kazakhstan with their horses and sheep. They were largely illiterate, and they did not trust outsiders, and certainly not enemies of the people. The local government encouraged the idea that we were garbage. The people treated us that way, and they often called us that.

I mentioned fantasies, yet thinking back, I cannot remember what they were. There was no television then, and we had no radio, so I wonder where my fantasies came from. I would guess that they were about things like warmth and love and food, but I am not certain.

The sun set early in the winter months, and it was dark before Nina and Yuri came home from school. Yuri would leave right away to look for work. He would go from yard to yard offering to cut wood. Though he was considered trash like the rest of us, he would occasionally be hired for woodcutting if the man of the house was ill or off somewhere with his horses. He was paid terribly, but we needed every coin he brought home. Or if the weather was at all decent, he and Nina would go off to the forest in search of wood.

If Nina and I were alone, we played a game that makes me shudder today. There was a large hole under the table in the center of the room. Huge hairy tarantulas lived deep down in this hole. Nina and I would heat water in the teakettle and pour it down the hole, then run as far away as we could and watch the tarantulas come popping up. The water was never hot enough to kill them and they would stalk around the room looking—we decided—for what had disturbed their winter sleep. We didn't dare move until they had gone back down. Once, Yuri filled in the hole, but in a few days, there was another.

We had two beds. Nina and I shared one, and Yuri and Mama the other. There was only one good blanket. It was made of camel's hair, a light tan color with green flowers on it. Each night before we went to sleep, Mama would heat the iron on the stove and then run it over the sheets. Nina and I would hop in and Mama would wrap the blanket around us, but even so, we would shiver for hours, our bodies pressed close together against the winter cold.

I remember one night, when the weather had turned warm enough so that we were comfortable under our blanket, waking up to see something huge and dark moving over the blanket. It was a tarantula, with a baby on its back. I touched Nina ever so lightly and then put a hand on her arm so that she wouldn't move. We watched, goggle-eyed with horror, barely daring to breathe, as the creature slowly moved across our bodies and dropped to the floor.

It was a day in spring. The nights were still cold, but there was enough warmth in the air during the days so that the ice on the clay walls began to drip. I went to sit outside by the front door to get the warm sun on my face.

There were still large patches of snow over the ground, but here and there were muddy bare spots where little green shoots were popping up. The snow was gone from our roof, and the wet straw gleamed. I thought spring was a wondrous thing.

I saw two little boys playing some sort of game in the muddy road. They hopped about a great deal, splashing mud and shrieking with laughter. I envied them. It would have been nice to have a friend.

Suddenly they stopped and one boy pointed to me. They both stared, then the boy who pointed picked up a stone and threw it at me. He missed, and the stone clunked against the house. I got up to run inside, when a man shouted to the boys and they ran away.

I was about to go in, afraid that the boys might come back, when around the corner of our house came a dog. He was large and brown, and he looked like a wolf. He was painfully thin.

At first, I wanted to run. There were many stories in Poludino about hungry wolves coming out of the forest to attack and kill people. The howl of the wolves at night were as much a part of Poludino as the winter wind crying around our house.

But this animal came to me, nudged my body, and made little whimpering sounds. Carefully, I reached out and patted his head, then I ran my hand down his back. I could feel his ribs beneath his rough coat. He licked my hand, and I fell in love with him. "Who are you?" I asked him. "Where do you come from? Who do you belong to?"

But there was no rope or anything to show he belonged to anybody. He was probably abandoned, left behind by some family that had moved on. He kept pushing at me and licking my hand. He was hungry.

I took the dog inside the house and found a small piece of bread which he gobbled up. He stared at me with eyes that seemed as if they could cry. I decided to call him Rex. He was so big, a king to me. Rex was a perfect name. "I have no more food for you, Rex. We must wait for Mama."

When my brother and sister came home, Nina was delighted, but Yuri frowned. "You'll not be able to keep him. How can we feed him?"

I stood up to him. "I will share my food with him."

Yuri laughed. "You barely have enough to keep yourself alive as it is."

"I don't care," I said. "I love him, and I will take care of him."

"And what will you feed him? Tea? Bread? Cabbage soup? Potato soup? That is all we ever have. A dog cannot live on that."

"He will! He will!" I shouted and began to cry.

Mama was furious when she saw Rex. She immediately said the dog had to go. Looking back now, I can understand. For her it was a miracle that each day the four of us were alive on what she could provide, and here I was confronting her with a fifth mouth—and a giant one at that—to feed. But at the time I thought she was terribly cruel, and I screamed my childish logic at her: I would die if she sent Rex away, or I would run away with him and we would live in the forest.

Finally when I had worked myself into near hysteria, Mama took me on her lap. "All right," she said, "Rex can stay, but we cannot feed him, you understand. Even if he starves to death in front of our eyes. The dog must see to his own food. We have none to spare. He knows how, I am sure. However he has stayed alive this long, he must go on that way. Do you understand, Vikka?"

I nodded and hugged her. It was hard at the beginning to sit down to our bowls of potato soup and see Rex, with his moist, sad eyes, watching us, his mouth open and saliva running down his tongue, and to have to turn away from him.

But soon I learned to let him out early in the morning. He would look about, confused for a moment, as if he were uncertain whether or not he was being abandoned, and then run off across the open fields toward the forest. Late in the afternoon there would be a scratching at the door, and Rex was back. He must have found something to eat, because he would be content to curl up in a corner and sleep while we had our soup.

It was a summer morning. I think Nina and Yuri had gone off somewhere to look for berries. I let Rex out and watched him run for the forest.

In Poludino in summer you could step out of the house and know how hot a day it would be even before you felt the heat. All you had to do was breathe deeply. The smell from the swampy slop holes told you. Today was going to be a very hot day. I went back inside and took my piece of bread for lunch and wrapped it in my handkerchief. I wasn't supposed to leave our house, but I was restless and I did not like to be indoors in the summer, because the tarantulas would come out of their holes with their young.

I decided to walk just to the end of Poludino, to the place where a little stream ran. In spring when the snow melted, it was a rushing torrent, but in summer there was gentleness to the water. It would be nice to take off my shoes and cool my feet.

But the stream was gone. There was only a ditch of cracked mud. I sat down under a scrawny tree that only partly shaded me from the burning sun. I thought about Rex and what he did in the forest. Did he have friends there? Maybe he had wolf relatives he visited and he told them about us.

The heat made me sleepy. I remember thinking about Moscow. Mama had described it to us, and I pictured a place with high buildings that looked like castles, the castles from the folk tales Mama told me, and bright lights of all different colors. Imagine such a place! I fell asleep.

When I woke up, the sun stood high and hot in the sky. I ate my piece of bread and then I started down the dusty dirt road for home.

I was about four houses away from ours when suddenly I heard feet running behind me. I turned and saw three boys and a girl with clumps of mud in their hands. I began to run. "Filth!" one shouted at me. The others took it up. "Enemy!" "Scum!"

A clump of mud hit me in the back. Tears blinded my eyes so that I couldn't see the road clearly, and I stumbled in a wheel rut. Another clump of mud rushed past the side of my head. My legs were too short to carry me out of their range.

I cut off the road to the side toward our house. Suddenly I felt my feet slipping. I flailed my arms about me, but I couldn't stop myself. The stench told me that I was falling into the waste hole. I screamed as I splashed into the hot, wet filth.

I sank until the mud reached the bottom of my rib cage. I could feel no ground beneath my feet, and the more I struggled to reach out beyond the muddy rim for solid ground, the more I sank.

I heard a door slam and somebody call out. I couldn't stop screaming, but I did stop struggling so that I wouldn't sink out of sight before someone pulled me out.

But no one came. The street was deserted. I looked wildly from house to house and saw only drawn curtains. The curtains at one window moved slightly and I knew there were faces behind them watching me drown. At another house, the door was open a crack and I knew there was another pair of eyes there. "Help me! Help me!" I shouted. "Please help me!"

Wherever I looked, there was only emptiness. Suddenly I saw a brown spot moving across the fields. It was Rex. I do not know why he chose to come home early this one time. It couldn't have been my screams that brought him. The forest was too far away for a child's voice to reach him.

He ran around the hole, barking at me to come out to him. Then he pressed his body close to the ground and inched forward to reach me. The slime was almost to my collarbone. I struggled and managed to free an arm, which I stretched out to the dog. The movement sank me into filth over my collarbone.

I stretched my arm as far as I could. Rex, barking continu-

ously, moved to another position and inched out into the mud.
I felt his breath on my fingertips. He moved a bit farther out
and sank his teeth into the sleeve of my dress. Then he began
to pull. I felt my body rise an inch or two through the mud.

I was drawn out another few inches, half expecting that at
any moment my sleeve would tear and I would sink back, or
that my muddy weight would pull Rex in to die with me.

But it was a day for miracles. The flimsy material held, and
suddenly I could free my other arm and throw myself forward.
I felt wet but solid ground beneath my fingers. With Rex still
tugging and growling, I pulled myself up and out.

That night Rex was given a full bowl of potato soup. He was
so used to not being fed at our house that he looked from one
to another of us before he went to the bowl.

The story had a happy ending for me, but not for Rex. Less
than a month later he did not come home from his daily run to
the forest. I called and called. Then I went out to search for
him, certain that he was somewhere nearby with perhaps a
bone or some little animal that he had caught. I found him
three or four houses away, out by the side of the road, writhing
in agony. There was a half-eaten chunk of meat near his head,
and he was rolling in his own vomit. Someone had given him
poisoned meat. I looked around for someone who might help,
but there was no one outdoors, and all the houses were closed
against me.

I decided to run to where Mama worked. She would do
something. But before I could go, Rex was suddenly still. He
was dead.

Another summer day, late afternoon. What I liked best
about summer is that I was not alone all day. Nina did not have
to go to school and so she could be with me. Not only was she
my sister, but she was also the only friend I had in the world. I
could not count Yuri as my friend, because he was ten years
older than I and a boy. He was my brother, yes, but he was
something else, something so wonderful that I could not define
my feelings. It wouldn't have mattered if I could, because in
Yuri's eyes I was a girl and a child, something you paid attention to only when you had time.

Nina and I were seated out on the little patch of grass in front of our house, eating "rolls," our word for the field flower seeds we gathered and ate, pretending they were some great delicacy fit only for important guests who came to our make-believe home in Moscow. The seeds had a sourish taste, but we ate them anyway. They were the closest thing to a toy, and "rolls" was the closest thing to a game that we had. It helped to pass the time until Mama came home.

The dirt street that ran through Poludino was quiet. The women were already indoors preparing the evening meal. The worst of the midday heat was past and there was a faint breeze of the coming evening.

Suddenly, we heard a motor. In Poludino you looked up if you heard an automobile engine, they were that rare. The few that existed belonged mostly to the village government officials and to the police, who were almost all NKVD. A jeep was coming toward us, a cloud of dust rising behind it.

To our amazement the jeep stopped near us, and two men, a Kazakh and a Russian, both in ordinary suits, got out and came toward us. They were smiling and one said, "Hello, girls."

We both nodded, too astonished to speak. Neither of us was used to strangers speaking to us, much less in a friendly fashion.

The other one said, "We just saw your mother. She asked that we tell you she will be delayed in her work, and you are not to worry."

We nodded again. The first man squatted down in front of us. "Have you ever ridden in a car? Would you like a ride in this one?"

It was like the heavens opening up and God smiling down on us! A ride in a real car! Nina and I were on our feet immediately and running for the car before the men changed their minds. Nina climbed in by herself, but the step was high for me. One of the men lifted me up and put me on the side bench beside Nina.

The Kazakh got behind the wheel, and the Russian seated himself on the soft passenger seat, and we were off.

As the jeep moved down the rutted street of the town, everything seemed so different from my position high up on the bench. We called and waved to anyone we saw, just so they could see that it was us—in a car!

Every sensation was a new one, from the cloud of dust that wiped out the town behind us, to the feel of the wind tugging at our dresses and braids. We passed the two stores that made up the shopping center of Poludino, and then the houses began to thin out. I giggled. "This is a real trip."

Nina nodded. "But it is the end of the village. In a minute they will turn back."

But they didn't. We were now out in the open steppes and still bumping over the rutted road. When we looked back, the houses of Poludino were only specks. All around us was the high wormwood grass with bright splashes of yellow field flowers stabbing up through it. The car showed no sign of slowing. We began to get frightened. "Where are we going?" Nina asked. "I think we should be getting back."

But the men didn't even turn their heads. The sun had turned a deep red and the clouds were taking on sunset colors. Nina and I moved close together as if to protect each other.

Without warning, the jeep swung off the road and into the high grass. We shrank back against the front seat to protect ourselves. Then the jeep stopped, and the Russian leaped out. Before we knew what was happening, he had both of us out of the jeep and into the grass that was over my head. He got back into the jeep. "I hope you enjoyed your ride. Good-bye!"

Neither of us said a word. We just watched the Kazakh turn the steering wheel and shift a stick, and they were gone. We were alone, two stupid little girls who in one moment had forgotten everything their mother had told them about the ways of strangers in Poludino—and all for a ride in a car.

The only thing we could hear was the grass rustling in the breeze. The sound of the motor had disappeared. We were alone and night was coming on. Nina began to panic. "What should we do? Which way should we go? Where is the village?"

She was five years older than I, and she was asking me. I tried to think. There had to be something we could do but what? Then it came to me. Of course. "We must follow where the wheels crushed down the grass. That will take us back to the road."

We began to walk. We seemed to be going through an endless wall of green and yellow, and it was growing darker all the time. We never spoke of it, but we were both thinking of the wolves. We heard their cries every night, and there were so many stories of hunger-crazed wolves throwing themselves through windows and dragging away children that people put metal grating or wooden lattice over their windows. And now we were alone, and no matter how fast we ran, the wolves would smell us and reach us long before we got to the village.

We were both crying, and Nina was shouting "Mama! Help us, Mama!" when suddenly we stepped out onto the dirt road. It stopped our tears. But when we looked in the direction we were certain we had come from, there was no sign of the village.

We began to cry again. We heard a wolf howl from far away. We clasped hands and began to run.

There was a faint rumbling sound that seemed to be coming toward us. We saw nothing at first, but then we saw dust and then, the jeep. It was coming back.

It was the same two men, but they were not smiling now. The Kazakh slammed his foot on the brake, and the jeep skidded to a stop in front of us. "Get in!" the Russian ordered.

We scrambled in, and the jeep turned around even before we were seated. My shoulder slammed into the rear of the front seat, but I barely felt the pain. We were saved!

Only later did I wonder about these men—why they had taken us, and why they had come back? In my child's mind, I at first thought they had been playing a game with us, just to scare us. But when I was older, I decided they had taken it upon themselves to rid the Soviet of two enemies of the state as a public service. But then fear set in, and they were afraid that they might be held responsible for what they had done. Getting rid of us was a good act, but they had not been given orders to do it, so their good action could be deemed a crime. I cannot swear that this is what happened, but it is the only explanation that seems logical.

When we told Mama what had happened, her face went white. I expected her to rush off to the police and demand that the two men be caught and punished, but it was Nina and I who were punished. She smacked us both, and then hugged us to her breast and the three of us cried together. She made us swear on our lives that if men came with an airplane or a train, we would not go with them.

The climax of our life in Poludino came on a morning that started off like any other. Mama had gone to work and Yuri was doing his daily exercises. I used to watch him as he would grunt and strain to lift a makeshift barbell, a heavy metal clothes iron, over and over again, his face shining with perspiration. Once, I asked him why he did it, since, judging by the sounds he made, it seemed to hurt him. He laughed. "Little one, you have to be strong to survive. We all must, and I, as the only man, must be even stronger. Do you understand?"

I nodded, but I didn't really understand. It was enough that Yuri wanted to do this difficult thing every morning and I enjoyed watching him do it.

On this day I said to Yuri, "I want to do that, too."

He smiled. "It is too heavy for you."

I shook my head. "You said we should all be strong. I want to be strong, too."

I could be very stubborn. Finally, Yuri put the barbell down in front of me. "Go ahead, but if you can't lift it, give up before you break something inside."

In my stubbornness all I needed was the hint that I could not do what my idol, Yuri, was doing. I was determined to lift it to show him I could.

I grabbed the iron firmly and squatted as I had seen my brother do. And then I strained with all my might. I did lift it a few inches, but when I tried to change my grasp so I could raise it further, it slipped from my sweaty palms and crashed to the ground, crushing the tip of my shoe. I shrieked with pain.

Yuri ran to me. "Are you all right? Sit down."

I could feel my big toe swelling and I screamed when Yuri tried to remove the shoe. The screams turned to hysteria as I saw blood spurt through the little perforated design in the shoe tip.

Yuri leaped to his feet. "Sit still, Vikka. Don't move. I must get Mama."

It seemed hours, though it was probably less than 15 minutes, before he returned with Mama. She took one look at my shoe and told Yuri to pick me up. He scooped me into his arms and they took me to the town's hospital, a small building where there was one doctor and two nurses.

My mother's shouts for help brought the doctor, a stocky woman with a brown bun of hair streaked with steel-gray. Her mouth turned down at the corners. "Silence yourself, woman," she said to Mama. "This is a hospital."

Even in my pain I was frightened. Mama was not. "This child is badly hurt. You must help her."

The doctor merely glanced at my shoe. "The blood will stop. The child will live."

Mama went right up close to her. "You will help her, and right away, or I will report you. You and the whole village knows that the NKVD is very interested in my family. They know me, and therefore they will listen to me."

That worked. The doctor signaled to a nurse, who told Yuri what room to carry me into. The doctor gave me something to ease the pain, then cut off my shoe. My big toe blew up like a balloon. It was smashed. The doctor put it in splints and bandaged it and told Mama it would take time, but the toe would be all right.

Yuri carried me home.

This incident was the breaking point for Mama. She had had all she was going to take of Poludino, of being treated like an outcast. When she had me settled in bed, she told Yuri to stay with me until she got back.

Later that night Mama told us what she'd done. She had marched straight to the office of the man she had to report to twice each week, and confronted him. "I have had enough!" she thundered at him. "More than enough!"

And then she told him what had happened at the hospital, about the two men with the jeep, about the time I had nearly drowned, and about Rex being poisoned. The man never said a word, and as Mama told it, she never gave him a chance. She had ended her tirade with: "If you people think it makes sense to arrest my sisters for I do not know what, that is one thing. To punish me, that is also one thing. But to make innocent children suffer, that I will not stand for."

To her amazement the official agreed with her. He said it might take a little time, but he would see what could be done. But he made her swear that she'd tell no one because he could lose his job.

"Imagine!" Mama said. "A kindness." There were tears in her eyes, something I had never seen before.

A little over a month later, we received permission to move to Petropavlovsk. When Mama told us the news, I danced around the room shouting, "I'm going to Petropavlovsk! I'm going to Petropavlovsk!" I was a very emotional child.

Of course, I had no idea where Petropavlovsk was. "Is it near Moscow?" I asked.

Mama held up two fingers pinched together. "Only that much nearer, Vikka."

"Will I be able to see Moscow from Petropavlovsk?"

She laughed. "Not with the greatest eyes in the world. It is still in Kazakhstan, but it is on a river called the Ishim, and the Trans-Siberian Railroad crosses the river right at Petropavlovsk. And that is something you can see."

I truly expected Petropavlovsk to look like Mama's description of Moscow. Of course, it didn't, though it was ten times the size of Poludino. The buildings were all wooden with very few over one story high. The roads were unpaved, but one saw automobiles with some frequency. There were factories with smoke that belched up into the sky, and there were even several movie theaters, though none of us ever had the money to go.

I looked forward to life in Petropavlovsk from the moment I saw it. Mama had said I would begin school, and that meant children of my own age. I would have friends.

Mama rented a room for us in the house of a woman named Olympiada, a large-busted woman who loved her house and her possessions far more than she did any of the people she rented six rooms to. She liked children least of all. She was always glaring at me if I skipped down the hall, and pushing my fingers away if they touched her walls.

For furniture we had the same two beds we'd had in Poludino, with two tables and four chairs. The larger table was where we ate, and my chair had a missing leg, so we propped it

Jackson Rogers Tate, 1927. (National Archives)

Zoya Fyodorova, 1934.

As a popular film star, Zoya often visited the front during the war to boost the morale of the Soviet troops. (Wide World)

Zoya in some of her roles.

Captain Tate about the time
he went to Moscow, 1945.
(Wide World)

Red Square, V-E Day, 1945. Jack at center stands in back and to one side
of Zoya, who links arms with her friend, Elizabeth Egan, so she and Jack
will not be too obviously together. At right, next to Zoya, is her sister Maria,
and in the forefront at left, Marina Vigoshina, a designer from Zoya's studio.

Zoya with baby Victoria.

Zoya's sister Alexandra, who raised Victoria as her own child.

Part of the "evidence" the NKVD had against Zoya.

Zoya after her release from
prison in 1955.

Victoria when she was about
ten years old, soon after she
was reunited with her mother.

Zoya and Victoria in their Moscow apartment, 1958.

A studio portrait of Zoya taken around 1958.

At the United States Trade Exhibition in Moscow in 1959. Irina Kirk is in the foreground at right, greeting Nikita Khruschev. At left, Vice-President Richard M. Nixon, and Leonid Brezhnev, holding paper cup.

Victoria, age thirteen, at about the time Irina Kirk first met her.

Zoya and Victoria outside the Ukraina Hotel.

Victoria in the film *About Love*, 1971.

Zoya and Victoria in 1970.

Zoya with a group of schoolchildren in 1972.

The picture of himself taken in 1947 that Admiral Tate sent Victoria in 1973.

January 1975. Zoya and Victoria tell their story to the press, and the world learns of Victoria's desire to visit her American father. (UPI)

Jack sits at his desk beneath a photo of himself as he looked when he knew Zoya. (Wide World)

Admiral Tate and his daughter hold their first news conference in Florida on April 10, 1975. (UPI)

Victoria and her husband, Frederick Pouy, at Cape Canaveral.

Three generations—Zoya, Victoria, and day-old Christopher Alexander Pouy, born May 7, 1976. (Wide World)

Victoria Fyodorova begins her career as a model, 1977. (Photo by Christopher Little)

Victoria, Fred, Zoya, and young Christopher in Connecticut, 1978. (Ing-John Studio)

up at one corner with a box. There was a communal kitchen where all the tenants fought to prepare their meals at the same time. The toilet was, of course, in the backyard.

Life was still hard for us. Mama was given another book-keeping job, and she worked from nine in the morning until seven at night, six days a week and more if she could get any extra work. I was not too aware of what things cost, but I remember a few things. Mama earned 700 rubles a month, and our room cost 250 rubles a month, which left 450 rubles for four people to live on. I remember a half kilo of butter cost 50 rubles at the bazaar, a marketplace where farmers sold their produce. Needless to say, we did not have butter or meat at our table.

But there were little luxuries. Once Mama bought us some dried pears. They were black and shriveled, but they tasted marvelously good. And we had milk on Sundays. Mama would go to the marketplace where the farmers brought in milk frozen in soup plates. They would turn the plates over on the wooden tables to free the frozen milk. Mama always bought a big enough plate so that we could have a meal of milk. And she would buy some sugar, too, which we were allowed to put on our black bread. That was our cake.

Best of all was the package of hard candies. Twice a month she would take the package down from a shelf and give us each one. It made the day a holiday. The candies had very little taste, just an undefined and faint sweetness, but I loved them. I would put the piece in my mouth as carefully as if it were a jewel, and I would try to remember not to suck at it so that it would last a long time.

When the candy was gone, we never asked for another one. We just waited, counting the days until it was time again. We never asked Mama for anything, though we were always hungry. Even to ask for a crust of bread was unthinkable. Once Mama gathered all three of us together. We had just finished our evening meal. It was a soup, hot water with only the faintest smell of cabbage to it, and there was no bread. "I am sorry," she said, "but there is only enough bread for tomorrow morning. If I give it to you now, you will have nothing to eat in the morning."

None of us said a word. Mama looked into each of our faces.

"I am sorry," she said again. "If I could, I would give you the world for a dinner, but I cannot, and you must not ask. Do you know what it does to me to see six eyes, all hungry, looking at me?"

We all remembered that time and we never asked for anything.

But once I climbed up on a chair and took down Mama's bag of candies. I took three pieces, one for each of the three children who were playing out in the street in front of Olympiada's house. I knew it was wrong, but I thought if I gave them candy they would play with me. Instead, they took the candy and ran away, and I got a severe spanking when Mama came home.

I was very excited the first day I went to kindergarten. There were so many children, and I knew that there would be friends for me at last. When the first day was over, I went to a group of little girls who were giggling together. Before I could say my name, one of them glared at me. "Stay away, you stupid enemy idiot!"

The other girls stuck their tongues out at me, and they ran off. I cried all the way home. Petropavlovsk was no different from Poludino. Yuri and Nina had friends, and so did Mama, because they were older. They could look around Petropavlovsk for other "enemies" in positions like their own. But I was not allowed to go wandering. My world was the distance between school and where we lived.

I don't know how Mama knew I was lonely, because she was away at work so much, but she did. It is the only explanation I have for her sending me to Moscow to visit Aunt Klava and Uncle Ivan Grigoryev. They were cousins of Mama's and had two children, Igor and Lucia, both older than I.

Somehow Mama got the money for my train trip. I went alone, a distance of 2,500 miles, which took three days and three nights. All I took with me was a paper bag of food, and two changes of underwear. I wore the only dress I owned.

I was not the least bit frightened. After all, I was finally going to see Moscow, and when a child has been alone for a long time, he is either very shy or very self-sufficient. I was self-sufficient. I was five years old, too young for the government to worry about keeping in the city of our exile, and just old enough to travel across Russia.

It was in Moscow that I first heard about my real mother, though I didn't really understand much at the time.

Six families shared the six-room apartment in which my Moscow relatives lived, one family to a room. The bathroom, the foyer, and the kitchen were all communal. The man who had the room next to the bathroom was insane.

I do not use this word carelessly. Gorbunov was truly insane, and in time his way became his wife's way, too. He lived locked in his room, newspapers pasted over the windows to protect himself from the people outside, all of whom he believed were trying to poison him. Every day at mealtimes, he would come out and we would watch him in the kitchen, standing over the stove burning his bread on a stick to get rid of the poison in it. Each morning, he would rise at five and fasten a leash around his wife's waist and take her for a walk. She didn't seem to mind, and when she finally went mad, she slept under his bed as if she were his dog.

For some reason Gorbunov liked me from the minute I arrived. He often came out of his room when he heard my footsteps, and he would pat my head and warn me about eating poisoned food. Sometimes he would throw his arms wide and scream out that the Soviet authorities were terrible people. Everybody ran to their rooms when he did that, certain that they would all be arrested, but nothing ever happened.

A bathtub within an apartment was a very new thing to me. In Kazakhstan you took your soap and your little washtub and went to the public bathhouse. The only thing I liked about the bathhouses was that you didn't have to go too often. But with a bathtub right where you lived, you were expected to bathe every week. Aunt Klava insisted on it. I would fight her all the way.

I think I bit her once. I know I screamed. The first time Gorbunov heard me screaming, he rushed out into the foyer and shouted: "This child is a victim, and they are trying to kill her. They have already killed her mother. Now they want to kill the child!"

Uncle Ivan ran down the hall and told him to shut up. What

Gorbunov said didn't mean much to me. I knew he was insane, and I knew that Mama was alive, waiting for me in Petropavlovsk.

There was a portrait of a blond, pretty woman on the wall over the alcove in which I slept. It was my real mother, but I did not know it. I only knew that I liked the face. One day I asked Aunt Klava about the picture. She smiled sadly and said, "It is the picture of a good actress, that is all."

One afternoon my cousin Lucia said, "Come. Let us go out. I will show you something."

We went out into the busy streets and walked several blocks to the section called Arbat. Lucia stopped in front of a movie theater. There was a poster with a large picture of the same pretty woman in the picture in Aunt Klava's apartment. Lucia laughed and said, "There is your mother."

Something happened to me then, perhaps because I was homesick for Mama—I would cry myself to sleep each night when Aunt Klava tucked me in my bed. I began to look around for Mama, to run all over the lobby, staring up at women's faces. None of them were Mama, yet Lucia said she was there. I ran into the street, growing hysterical, pushing my way between people until I was exhausted. Lucia found me slumped against a wall.

And something else happened that afternoon. I was suddenly terrified of my shadow. It became something or someone who followed me everywhere. I held tightly to Lucia's hand all the way home, walking in the shade whenever possible so that my shadow wouldn't be there. From that point on I tried to avoid going out into the sunlight. This little madness of mine lasted until I returned to Petropavlovsk and Mama.

All the remaining days that I stayed with Aunt Klava and Uncle Ivan, I studied the picture of the pretty lady over the sleeping alcove. There was something about the face that had some meaning for me, but I did not know what it was.

When it was time to go back to Mama, all four members of my Moscow family took me to the station. I had another paper bag of food for the trip. I also had two more dresses than I had come with, dresses Lucia had outgrown, and a winter coat. And best of all, I had my first doll, a gift from my aunt and uncle. She was a stuffed cloth one with a painted face, wearing a little dress that I could take off.

I hugged the doll, which I named Tanya, all the way back to Petropavlovsk. Tanya was more than a doll. She was my friend.

Tanya was so special to me that I couldn't bear to share her with anyone. She was the first thing that truly belonged to me. I knew if I took her into our room, Nina would want to play with her, and I couldn't stand the idea.

As soon as we got back to Olympiada's house, I sneaked Tanya into the backyard where each family had its own woodpile. I dug deep into our woodpile and hid Tanya there. I never took her out. I decided it was better to leave her there than risk someone seeing I had her.

Unfortunately the day came when Mama found her, ruined by rain and snow. I was punished for my selfishness.

In time, we moved from Olympiada's house. Mama had had enough of "my house this" and "my house that," of never feeling welcome. We moved to a room in the house of a woman named Shaposhnikova. She was very different from Olympiada. She was a warm and tender woman who made you feel at home.

I suppose I remember her particularly because I was so hungry for any kindness or affection. I remember well the day in kindergarten when a little boy cut his finger on a toy. He was crying and I saw the teacher put her arms around him. She took him to the medical room, and when he came back, he had a bandage on his finger, and all day long the teacher was especially kind to him. I watched with greedy eyes, and I thought to myself, if someone would treat me that way, I would give them my whole finger.

What I did then strikes me as insane today. When we were allowed outside, I went to a garden nearby where there was a path made of pebbles. I took off my shoes and ran along the path, hoping to cut my feet so that I would be hugged when the teacher saw the blood. But nothing happened.

So I found a thin, sharp stone and shoved it under the nail of my big toe and ripped the nail off. The pain made me gasp, and it started to bleed. Then I did the same thing with the other big toe. I hobbled in agony back to the classroom.

"Help me, please!" I said to the teacher. "Feel sorry for me."

The pain was excruciating, but it was worth it. In a moment I would be hugged and fussed over. But my teacher just glared at me. "You should be put in a crazy house!" she shouted at me, her face red with anger. "Why did you do that?"

I burst into tears. "It hurts. Please! It was an accident!"

"One toe maybe, but two toes on two different feet, never! If you become a cripple on top of everything else, it will serve you right."

"Help me!" I begged.

The teacher shrugged. "Well, the woman in the medical room has left. There is no one to help you here. Go home."

Another teacher came into the room. "What is the matter?" she asked.

My teacher pointed to my feet. "Can you believe what she has done to herself?"

The other teacher was a little kinder. "You shouldn't scream at her. After all, she doesn't have a mother or father to teach her anything."

I looked up at my teacher. For a moment, my pain was forgotten. "What does she mean? I have a mother, and she is the best mother in the whole world."

The woman smiled. "Good, then go home to her and see how pleased she is with you."

I hobbled home in agony. I could not put on my shoes for several days, so returning to kindergarten was out of the question. When Mama asked why I had done this terrible thing to myself, I couldn't answer. How could I hurt her by saying I wanted someone to pay attention to me?

Then Mama asked me if I was happy in kindergarten. I hung my head. "Say yes or no, Vikka. This school costs money."

I said no. Mama nodded. "Then you will not go back. You will stay home until you are seven, when you will go to the regular school."

I was relieved. To be alone was better than to be hated.

That summer of my sixth year, my world became the little shed behind the house in which we lived. It had a wooden door with a little glass window in it, and down near the bottom of the door there was a hole cut out for Shaposhnikova's gray cat, who shared the shed with me.

It was fiercely hot inside during the summer, but I didn't mind. With the door closed, I was in a private world where no one could hurt me or say cruel things. I could make up a better world where everyone loved me.

There was an old metal trough in the shed that became my favorite plaything. I would fetch cold water and pour it into the trough. Then I would take off all my clothes and climb in. I imagined I was in a boat on a river and by paddling with my hands I could go all over the world. I went to Africa and to all the strange and wonderful places that Nina and Yuri told me about from their school studies. It was dark in the shed except for one little shaft of light that came through the window in mid-afternoon. The shadowy shapes of Shaposhnikova's junk became anything I wanted them to be, from tall buildings to jungle huts.

In my secret world I was always a queen. Sometimes a queen in danger (always rescued by loving subjects), but more often a queen who sailed on a beautiful boat to beautiful places where everyone was nice to her.

Fall came, and Nina and Yuri returned to school. It became too chilly for games in the shed. Life became dull and lonely again for me.

But then one day everything changed. One of my fantasies came to life. It was near four o'clock. Darkness was coming on. I was sitting on the little bench down the street from where we lived, waiting for Nina and Yuri to come home, when I saw a woman coming along the street. Even from far away, there was something special about her. She was tall and she walked with an easy stride, and her carriage was regal. She wore a babushka over her head like all of the women, but there was a radiance to her face that made it stand out from all the gray, frightened faces of Petropavlovsk. She was the most beautiful woman I had ever seen.

As she came closer I saw her coat, and I gasped. She must be a true queen, the kind I had only imagined in my trough-boat. Her coat was stylishly cut of some good dark cloth, but the collar which she had up around her face was of fur—I found out later that it was silver fox. I had never seen a woman wearing fur before.

I immediately fell in love with her. I knew she had to be the richest woman in the world with a coat like that. And surely the most beautiful. And the happiest, too, because she seemed to be smiling to herself as she walked past me. I prayed she would see me, maybe even stop and speak with me. But she walked by without a glance.

It became a ritual for me. Every afternoon at four o'clock I had to be at the bench when the lady walked by. I had to see her. She made the days full for me. Just to know there was someone so rich and beautiful—and above all, happy—living in the same world as I, made life possible.

I planned my day around four o'clock. Though I was only six, as the only member of my family who did not go to school or to work, I had to take charge of our room. Cleaning up, washing the floor, bringing in wood for the fire in the evening, cooking the cabbage soup and the potatoes—these were my jobs, and they all had to be done so that there was time to get my coat and be waiting at the bench when the beautiful lady went by.

Each day I tried to imagine where she was coming from and where she was going. It seemed likely, since she passed each day at the same hour, that she was coming from work. But I rejected that. Mama worked, and she and this splendid woman were nothing alike.

When I ask myself what this woman in the fur collar represented to me, I can think of only one word: beauty. That was something I saw only in her, and obviously, it was something I hungered for.

One day four o'clock came, and the woman was not there. Where was she? Had she come by earlier, before I had reached my bench? I searched the faces coming down the street, but I couldn't see her. Then I climbed up on the bench so that I could see better. I stood on tiptoe, and I slipped and fell into the muddy road. When I stood up, my coat was filthy. I started to cry. Mama would be furious.

And suddenly the beautiful-fur lady was in front of me, looking directly at me! "What happened to you, little girl?"

I said, "I was looking for you, and I fell in the puddle."

"What do you mean, 'I was looking for you'?" Her voice was soft and refined, and she was truly beautiful.

"I wait for you every day. Just to see you," I said through my tears. "My coat is dirty, and Mama will be mad at me."

She took out her handkerchief and wiped my face. "Don't cry. I will tell your mother that it was an accident, and it wasn't your fault. I'm sure she will understand. And your coat will clean."

"But," she went on, "you mustn't wait for me. It is getting cold out. And I will not be coming this way anymore."

My heart sank. "Why?"

"Because I am going to have a baby soon, so I shall be staying in my house. Do you understand?"

I nodded, but I didn't understand. Why did you have to stay in the house to have a baby? Why couldn't she walk outside every day so I could see her? I hated the baby that would not let me see the lady.

She never did speak to Mama, and I never saw her again, but the memory of her has always stayed with me.

When I got home, I waited in fear for Mama's return, certain she would be furious about my dirty coat. When she saw it and asked what happened, I burst into tears. "There's no need to cry. Just tell me what happened."

I told her that I fell in the street. I did not mention the lady. Mama examined the coat. "I think it will wash clean. But you will not be able to go outdoors until it dries."

That didn't bother me. There was no reason to go outside anymore. The beautiful lady wouldn't be coming.

I watched Mama scrubbing my coat. I loved her very much, and I was sorry she had to wash my coat after working so hard all day.

In the back of my mind, there was another thought and I was ashamed of it. I wished Mama were beautiful like the lady in the street. I wished she had a fur coat and looked special like a queen.

I didn't know it then, but all my wishes would come true. The first time I saw my real mother she was wearing a fur coat, and she was very beautiful—like a queen.

ZOYA

It was not that she trusted Olga; she *had* to trust her. Lubyanka and the other places had taught Zoya to trust no one,
but now it was different. She might not live to come out of
Vladimir, and Olga was being released and going directly to
Moscow. What good would the fur coat and those silly little
party shoes that she had been wearing when she was arrested
do her in Vladimir, stuffed into a locker? And if Olga really did
as she swore she would—"On the head of my son, Zoya Alexyevna!"—and took the coat and shoes to Alexandra in Moscow,
it would be a wonderful thing. Alexandra could sell them and
the money would help her and Victoria.

So Zoya gave her the coat and shoes.

It was the last she ever heard of them or of Olga. Later on,
when Zoya learned that Alexandra was in Kazakhstan, it
crossed her mind that possibly Olga had tried to deliver the
coat, but she knew she was kidding herself. Olga had cheated
her.

In Vladimir there was no point in making the little marks
that would tell her how many days and weeks had passed.
Twenty-five years was an endless sentence. There would not
be enough wall space for 25 years of marks even if they put her

into the largest cell in the prison. And what did it matter how many days had passed and how many more were still to come when every day was the same?

Up at five in the morning for breakfast. Always a slice of bread that had to last for the entire day, and very weak tea with the faintest touch of sugar. The only thing that broke up the morning was a 20-minute walk outside in a walled cement yard about 20 feet long and 14 feet wide.

Prisoners were then returned to their cells for the rest of the day. The midday meal on the best of days was a little millet gruel and some of the flat, rotten, bony fish that were called "funny fellows." The evening meal was bread and tea, if there was any of one's bread left. Then to bed at 9 P.M. And the next day was just the same.

If there was more than one prisoner in a cell, they could talk among themselves, so long as it was done quietly. Prisoners could also take books from the prison library.

The torture in Vladimir was monotony. The only change in the day-to-day routine was the trip to the shower, once every ten days. But it was hardly a pleasant change. It always occurred in the middle of the night.

For her first six weeks in Vladimir, Zoya was alone in a cell for two people. Day after day she sat in the shabby gray-and-white striped jacket and skirt she had been issued, doing nothing. During this period, which she was told was the standard "quarantine" time, she was not even allowed the morning walks.

Her first cellmate was an elderly woman with bright blue eyes. The moment the guard closed the door behind her, she fell to her knees and began praying.

Zoya never found out her name, only that she was from the Ukraine, and that her sentence was five years. Why? The woman began cautiously, "You must understand, it was a very bad time where we were, and we were starving."

Little by little, the story came out. Unknowingly, the old woman had eaten her seven-year-old granddaughter, who had been killed by her parents. They each received ten-year sentences.

"And I have been given twenty-five years!" Zoya thought.

One night Zoya awoke to find the old woman staring at her. The woman smiled. "Do you know, you have a very beautiful nose?"

Zoya shuddered. What was the old woman thinking? Did eating human flesh once create a craving for it?

From that moment on Zoya was nervous every time she caught the old woman staring at her. That she was insane, there was no doubt, but as long as she was considered harmless she stayed in the cell with Zoya.

When Zoya was transferred to another cell, it was almost a relief, although transfers were a part of life in Vladimir, designed to break up any friendships.

In her next cell were five other women. Two spent their days praying. The third was an Austrian countess, or claimed to be, named Renata. The fourth woman, Ada, was missing her right arm all the way to the shoulder. A woman of great charm and prodigious memory, she passed the time reciting the poetry of Pushkin. The fifth woman, Masha, was a thief and a murderess who fell in love with Ada.

The two kissed openly whenever there was no guard's eye at the peephole, and often at night they would lie together beneath the blankets. Their relationship made Zoya uncomfortable because it was alien to her, but she understood their need for human affection.

Zoya's hair had begun falling out. If she so much as ran her fingers through her hair, she came away with large handfuls. Obviously it was the diet. It was little wonder, considering how little she was given to eat, and how often she could not stomach what was given her. When she complained, to her amazement, she was given cod liver oil, a small sign of humanity on the part of her jailers. She also had her head shaved, and in spite of all the indignities she had experienced, it made her feel ridiculous. Even the little cap that was part of her prison uniform couldn't hide her baldness entirely. But in time, her hair grew back.

Changing cells, and the different types of women she was put with, provided the only variety in Zoya's routine as the days and weeks slipped by. The women were a mixed lot. Anna was an intelligent woman who had left Russia in 1912, just before the revolution. Her father, who had been a colonel in the czar's army, had taken his family to China where Anna had grown up and married. She, along with the rest of her family, had been branded a traitor for not returning to the Soviet Union. But years later when Anna was a widow and homesick for her own people, she was told that she would be allowed to return. She remembered a banner that hung over the railroad tracks where she crossed the border into the Soviet Union. It read WELCOME HOME. She was immediately arrested.

The peasant woman who horded her daily slice of bread would, each day, to the disgust of her cellmates, place the bread beneath her and break wind on it. When she was asked why, the woman smiled and said, "If I do not spoil it, someone will take it from me and eat it. Now, it is mine."

There was the wife of a member of the Communist Party with a high position in Leningrad until he was shot. She had gone mad when she was arrested. Each night when she got ready for bed, she would talk to her husband. "Did you brush your teeth? Oh, by the way, there was a call for you while you were out. I wrote it down." Her bed was next to Zoya's, and the conversation sometimes went on for two and three hours.

Another cellmate, Leda Ruslanova, finally went to the door and banged for the guard. "Listen," she said in her most imperious tone, "I have my sentence. It is for prison, not for a madhouse. You must do something about this woman. Don't you have any other Russians you can give us as a substitute?"

Ruslanova became one of Zoya's two closest friends in Vladimir. She was known throughout the Soviet Union as one of its greatest folksingers. When her husband, General Krukov, right-hand man to Marshal Zhukov, was arrested, she was sent to prison for six years. Since they were both in the arts, it was natural that Zoya and Ruslanova would have met in Moscow at various functions, but they had never been friendly. Vladimir brought them close together.

Zoya's second friend, Yosh Gruschevskaya, had been a secretary-typist in the Academy of Science. Her crime was that she and her husband were Trotskyites. Zoya liked her from the moment she entered the cell. Yosh was tiny, slender, no more than 5 feet 2 inches tall, with brown hair and eyes. There was something in the way she held her head that made her appear to be shy, but her eyes always sparkled.

When the door was locked behind her, she raised her hands and clapped them. "Hello, ladies! Do not be upset, my dears, the Americans will save us!"

It was a ridiculously theatrical entrance. Zoya whooped with laughter and went to her. "I should like to introduce you to everyone here, and then I must leave you to go on a holiday."

When she had met everyone, extending her hand to each as if she were the queen of England on a receiving line, Yosh said, "A pleasure, my friends."

Because Ruslanova had some money, there were occasional treats from the little prison store. She shared them with her friends. And on January 18, the date of Victoria's fourth birthday, Ruslanova presented Zoya with a cake that she and Yosh had constructed. It was very tiny, made by crumbling cookies— which Ruslanova had bought—and mixing them with water to hold them together. There was one candle made from the wax on the outside of a piece of cheese.

Zoya wept when the cake was presented to her. She tried to envision her child at the age of four, but her only memory was of the baby in the crib the last time she had seen her.

"Do you hear from your sister?" Ruslanova asked.

Zoya looked at her as if she were mad. "I have had no letters."

"Surely, you are allowed. I am. I can send out two letters a year, and I am allowed two in return. You must find out your rights."

"You must ask," Yosh said. "If you do not get a satisfactory answer, I will write to the United Nations."

When Zoya inquired, she was told that because of the serious nature of her crimes, she was only allowed one letter each way in a year. "Then why have I not received one?" Zoya demanded.

The guard glared at her. "An enemy of the people does not make demands. You should be happy you were not shot."

Zoya glared back at her. "I am happy about nothing in this place. I want to send a letter. It is my right."

The guard just looked at her. "I will see that you get your rights."

Later the same day Ruslanova made a scene. In her imperious manner, she strode over to the door and banged on it until the guard paid attention to her. "Do you know that I cannot read in this place? The light is terrible. Something must be done."

The next day Zoya and Ruslanova were taken to punishment cells. They were narrow cells, at best four feet wide by seven feet in length. There was no furniture, only what looked like radiator pipes against one wall. There was no window either—the only light came from a weak bulb hanging far above. The temperature was chilly and damp.

Zoya felt the pipes. They were ice cold, which accounted for the chill that was all-pervading.

There was a sudden banging on the wall. Zoya went to it and banged back. She heard Ruslanova's voice from the next cell. "Zoya?"

"Leda? Are you all right?"

Ruslanova shouted back. "We must tell Yosh to write to the U.N. about this."

Zoya began to pace the cell. She was afraid to stop for fear of freezing to death. In reexamining the room, she found a metal shelf among the pipes which folded down into a slab that she could sit on. But it was too cold.

She began to pace again, slapping at herself to try to keep warm. In time she had to sit down. She chose the floor rather than the cold metal slab. She felt sleepy, but was afraid to close her eyes. What if it was not tiredness she felt, but the drowsiness that she had heard comes when one is freezing to death? But surely, she thought, they did not want her to freeze to death. What punishment would that be? It would be a release, and they were not that kind. If she had learned nothing else since the night she first entered Lubyanka, she had learned that these people were clever in their punishments. There was no doubt that they had experimented with how cold a cell could be without a person freezing to death.

Finally, a guard unlocked her cell and brought in her supper—a cup of warm water. "Do you expect me to live on this?" Zoya asked.

The guard smiled. "Do you know it is that big mouth of yours that got you in here? I see you have learned nothing yet." She turned to go.

"Wait," Zoya said, and added, "please," when she looked at her.

"How many days will I be in here?"

"It is your first time. Four days." Zoya shook her head and tears came to her eyes. "I will die."

The guard shrugged. "Perhaps."

"Please," Zoya said. "I have to go to the toilet."

"I will come for you later this evening. Prisoners in punishment cells are allowed to use the toilets twice every twenty-four hours. In between times, hold yourself in or use your cell floor if you cannot."

When the time came, the trip to the toilet was heaven itself. The corridor and the washroom were warm. Zoya delayed as long as she could, until the guard forced her to return to her cell.

Several hours later her door was unlocked. There were two guards. One ordered her to sit on the metal slab and raise her feet. Zoya did as she was told. A long, narrow, red-painted wooden platform was shoved in. It almost completely filled the cell floor. "What is that?" Zoya asked.

"It is your bed."

"How can a person sleep on that?"

"Then do not sleep on it," the guard said and locked the door behind her.

Zoya thought, they will find me dead on it in the morning. She slipped off the metal ledge and stood on the box. The wood wasn't warm, but it was warmer than the bare floor. She knocked on the wall and shouted to Ruslanova, "Did you get your bed?"

"Quiet, please. I am going to sleep."

"Very funny."

"I am feeling warm. I think I am getting a fever."

"You should call the guards and tell them."

"When I am certain, but not before. If it is my imagination, they will keep me in this hole even longer."

Zoya lay down on the box. She wrapped her arms around her chest and drew her knees up to her stomach. For a few minutes she felt some warmth, but it drained away. She lay shivering until they came to take the box out.

For breakfast she received another cup of warm water, but this time she was given a small piece of bread as well. There was no midday meal. In the evening she was given another cup of hot water and a half slice of bread.

Ruslanova was certain now that she had a fever. She had told the guards, but they had done nothing.

On the third day Zoya was given some pills—she assumed they were some sort of vitamins—along with her warm water and bread. She called to Ruslanova. When there was no answer, she called again and put her ear to the wall. She could hear Ruslanova's voice, but she couldn't make out the words. Zoya went to her cell door and pounded until the guard came. "The woman in the next cell. I think she is very sick."

"That has nothing to do with you," she said.

Between the hunger and the cold, Zoya found her mind drifting. She thought she saw her father come into her cell. He held out his fingerless hands to her. Zoya was sitting in the corner of her cell on the floor. "Papa? What is it?" she said aloud and started to get up. He disappeared, and she sank down again. She shook her head to clear it. Of course it couldn't have been her father. He was dead.

She tried slapping her body to speed up her circulation, but she had to stop. Her shoulders ached from the cold dampness.

On the fourth day, when the guard opened her cell, she told her she could come out. Two guards passed her carrying Ruslanova. Her face was shiny with perspiration. Zoya was sent along with her to the hospital to take care of her. She had pneumonia.

When Ruslanova could sit up and talk, Zoya told her she was thinking of going on a hunger strike until they let her have her letter privileges. "My sister must have written to me. Alexandra would have found out where I am. She knows how to do these things. I must have her letter."

Ruslanova shrugged. "It is a risk. They will put you back in the punishment cell. You could die of starvation."

Zoya shrugged. "And what have I got to lose? Twenty years or more in this place?"

Ruslanova took her hand. "I would miss you terribly if any-thing should happen to you. But I, too, would do what you talk of doing."

When they were moved out of the hospital and returned to their cell, Yosh made a big fuss. "Attention, ladies, attention! Our two heroines have returned from their lovely vacation. See how suntanned they are."

The next morning, when the guard brought in their tea and bread, Zoya asked again for her mail privileges. "It has been reported," the guard said, "and it is being considered."

"That is not good enough," Zoya told her. "From this mo-ment on, I will not eat until you bring me the letter from my sister that I know you have, and you let me write a letter to her."

The guard shrugged. "If you are stupid enough not to eat, it is not my affair."

She took her cup and bread out of the cell.

Yosh announced, "This is a brave woman, ladies. I trust you appreciate that you are in the presence of one of the great fighters for human dignity."

"Be quiet, Yosh," Zoya said. "Everything is not a joke." She was frightened. She had committed herself to a hunger strike in front of the women in her cell. She had to go through with it now, but what if she were already too weak? Maybe there was nothing left to live for, but she was not ready to die.

It took effort to refuse the midday meal and by mid-after-noon Zoya was feeling hunger pains. They faded away late in the afternoon.

An hour after she turned back her evening tea, the cell door opened to admit an officer of the prison. "That one," the guard said, pointing to Zoya.

"You are the fool who refuses to eat?" the officer said.

Zoya nodded. "I would like very much to eat, I assure you. But it is more important to be allowed to write a letter as my sentence says I can, and to receive letters, too."

"It is we who decide what you are entitled to, not you. If you do not eat tomorrow, you will be fed. I assure you it is not pleasant."

No one spoke when the officer left.

As the women were getting ready to go outside for their morning exercise period the next day, two guards and a man Zoya had never seen before entered the cell. The guards were carrying a small table. A cloth covered some things on it. One of the guards pointed out Zoya to the man, who nodded and said, "Get the others out."

The other women were lined up and marched out. The man turned to Zoya. "You would not accept your morning meal?"

Zoya shook her head. He said, "Your punishment is that you will live for 25 years. If you will not eat, you will be fed."

He motioned to the guards, who stepped to either side of Zoya and grabbed her. She tried to struggle, but she was too weak. They pulled her over to the bed and just before they forced her down onto it, she saw the man—a doctor, she later learned—remove the cloth from the table. He picked up a length of tubing.

She clamped her jaws shut, even as she felt the bile rising in her throat. Then she fainted.

When she came to, her throat ached. So they had fed her, she thought.

After she refused the noon meal, she tensed herself for what she thought would happen, but the doctor did not come. Nor did he come in the evening. But she knew he would come again the next morning.

But when the guard came in with the morning tea and bread, before Zoya could refuse it, she was handed a letter. "Here. For you. It has only come."

She had won!

Zoya said nothing to the guard. Let her jailers save face if they want, she thought. She looked at the envelope for a postmark, but it had been obliterated.

As soon as the cell door was closed, Yosh leaped up. "A victory toast, my friends, to this gallant woman who has defeated all of Vladimir!"

Zoya turned on her. "Be quiet! I am grateful. Do not grind their shame into their faces."

The door opened again, and the guard signaled to Yosh. "You are going to the punishment cell."

Yosh saluted. "I have seen the victory. I will bear the pain for such joy."

When she was gone, Ruslanova said, "She will not make jokes again for some time."

Zoya sat down on her bed. The letter was from Alexandra. She knew the handwriting. It was a short note, but that was no surprise. Alexandra knew enough not to write too much; they would only confiscate such a letter.

Dear Sister,

I hope all is well with you as it is with me and my children. Victoria is growing up into a lovely child with long, straight brown hair and beautiful eyes. She calls me Mama, and she obeys. She is very polite and a little shy.

Your sister,
Alexandra

At last Zoya knew where her child was. She read the letter over and over again. Polite and shy, my Vikka.

"She calls me Mama"—that hurt, but Zoya understood what Alexandra was saying. She had decided not to tell the child about her real mother in case they were never reunited. Zoya had to agree. It was a wise decision.

A lovely child. Long, straight brown hair. Beautiful eyes. Zoya tried to put the details together to create a face, but she could come up with nothing that satisfied her craving to see her daughter.

Ruslanova gave Zoya a piece of her writing paper and a pencil. Zoya wrote to Alexandra:

Dearest Alexandra,

What joy to receive your letter and to learn the good news of my Vikka! It is right that she know you as her mother. Let it stay that way, since I may never see her again in this life. That I live only for her is true, but what can that mean to a child? But please, I beg you with all my heart, talk to her of her Aunt Zoya who lives far away and loves her very much. And sometimes give her kisses and say they were sent to her by Aunt Zoya. When she has learned how to write, ask her to send a letter to Aunt Zoya and to draw a picture for me.

There are no words to express my feelings to you for what you are doing for my Vikka. I can only send you my love, and to your Yuri and Nina, too.

Zoya

She reread the letter several times. It said so little when there was so much more she wanted to say. But, of course, Alexandra would see beyond her words, into the pain in Zoya's heart. Alexandra was a mother, too.

She checked the letter one more time before putting it in the envelope. Was there anything that the authorities would object to? No, she didn't think so. She left the envelope open. They would seal it after they read it. And now there was nothing to do but live through the year ahead, when she would be allowed to receive her next letter. If it was God's will, the letter would be from Victoria, and there would be a drawing in it.

VICTORIA

After waiting what seemed like forever, I was finally seven years old and could enter school. I even had the proper uniform—a black apron over a brown dress with a white collar. Of course, it wasn't new. It had been Nina's and then put aside for me.

Maybe all children at the age of seven are impossible optimists, or maybe it was just me. But once again, I expected everything to be different. This time I would have friends.

But the only friendly face I encountered was that of the teacher, Anastasia Lyukyanovna. She was fat and very short, with gray hair. She was in her 70s, which may explain why she could afford to be kind to me and to even go so far as to invite Mama and me to her home for tea. I think because of her age she understood that in our country one could be an enemy one day and a trusted citizen the next. In her time she had seen regimes come and go.

But a teacher for a friend was not what I really wanted. I wanted someone my own age. But there was no one among the little girls. They had all been taught by their parents not to trust me, that it was dangerous to know me.

Right away, they saw I was different. They had come to school knowing nothing, having to learn to read, write, and count. I could already do all of that. Mama and Yuri had taught me at home. I saw the girls looking at me and rolling their eyes, and whispering to each other. I was hurt, of course, but I sat up straighter to show my superiority. It didn't help when the teacher praised me in front of my classmates.

After school, I found myself surrounded by seven girls from my class. "Shame on you to put pencil on your eyebrows and lashes!" one of them said, and the others all agreed.

Back then my hair was a light brown, but my brows and eyelashes—which were quite long—were very dark. "It is not true. This is the way I was born."

The girls all laughed. "You are a bad, bad girl. Only bad girls make up their faces."

I dipped my handkerchief into a puddle and rubbed at my eyes and brows. "See? It does not come off. It is natural."

One of them shoved me so that I fell to the ground. "You are a bad girl, and a liar besides."

That night I asked Mama if there was some way I could have another color for my eyebrows and eyelashes. She smiled. "When you are a woman, you can do something if you wish, but I do not think you will want to. Right now, what you have is natural, and it is good. You are a sweet-looking girl."

I didn't want to be sweet-looking, I wanted to be liked. After another day of teasing at school, I came home and took action. While Nina watched, I put a nail in the stove until it was very hot. Holding the nail with a piece of cloth, carefully, so as not to burn my flesh, I moved it across the tops of my eyelashes and my brows. Then I rubbed at them with my fingers. My work was uneven. My lashes were short stubs, and there were patches of bare skin in the line of my brows. In any case, the hairs were charred, which, I felt, erased the offensive color.

Nina approved. "It is good. Now, it will all grow in much bigger." She was referring to her own thin hair which Mama shaved off every summer in the hope that it would grow in thicker by the fall.

Mama was shocked when she saw me. "Vikka, what has possessed you? Do you know what you look like?"

I didn't care. I felt I had improved my appearance. Nina, however, got a good spanking from Mama for allowing me to do this to myself. She was older and should have known better.

It changed nothing at school. Now the girls laughed at me and said I must have a terrible disease that made my eyebrows fall out. It was obvious I would never please them.

One evening after dinner Mama took me on her lap. "You are growing up, Vikka. You should know about your family. About your aunts especially. Aunt Zoya and Aunt Maria."

"I know about them. They live far away. But where is my Papa?"

Mama studied me a moment. "What can I tell you? You do not remember him. We were divorced when you were still a baby."

"I think I remember him," I said.

Mama laughed. "I am certain you do not. Even Nina does not. But Yuri does. And he remembers Aunt Zoya, and Aunt Maria, too."

"Will I ever see them?"

Mama sighed. "Not Aunt Maria. She has died. But maybe someday Aunt Zoya. Do you know that I had a letter from her?"

"Oh?" I said, not knowing what was expected of me, and not being particularly interested. "Can I see it?"

Mama shook her head. "No, it is not for you. She writes of things that do not concern you. But she asks about you. She remembers you from when you were a baby. And she asks that you write to her. She would like very much to hear from you."

"But I do not know her. What can I say?"

Mama smiled down at me and brushed at my hair. "Anything you wish. Whatever you write, I am sure, will please her. Ad we will send her a drawing you make just for her."

I was given paper and pencil. I stared at the blank paper wondering what to write. All that I knew about Aunt Zoya was that she was once an actress and was very beautiful. She lived alone somewhere near Moscow, and while she wanted to see us, she did not have enough money to send us so that we could visit her.

Mama said I could write anything I wanted, so I wrote:

Dear Aunt Zoya,

Mama says you remember me, but I do not remember you. I am seven years old and I am in school. Please send some apples and candy. I would like that very much.

With love,
Your niece
Victoria

That will please Aunt Zoya, I thought, and she will send the apples and candy.

ZOYA

Zoya wept all day after reading Victoria's letter. Apples and candy. Dear God, she had starved herself just to be able to receive the letter, and now her child asked her for apples and candy. "Oh, my darling one," she whispered, "ask for my life. I could give you that more easily."

She wept that the child wrote she did not remember Aunt Zoya. But how could she when she was only 11 months old when Zoya had been arrested? And now she could write and she went to school, and still she had never seen or felt the touch of her mother.

Zoya looked at the drawing Victoria had made. It was of a stick-figure girl with long spirals of curly hair that went down to the ground. To one side of the girl there was a well with a pipe sticking out the side and a bucket hanging from the pipe.

Zoya touched the paper where Victoria's hand must have rested while she drew the picture. If only she could have a photograph of the child instead of this drawing.

What did she look like? Zoya couldn't even imagine. Did she resemble her mother or her father or maybe both? But Zoya could create no picture of her daughter. It didn't surprise her. She could barely remember Jackson's face. And had she really once been a film star with a warm fur coat? Had she really once believed that no one would dare to harm her?

Zoya smiled to herself. What a fool that woman was. But if she had known what was to come, would she have behaved differently? If she had, there would have been no Victoria. There was no answer to the question.

From that day on Zoya slept with the letter and the drawing next to her. In time, she was able to read the letter without crying. One day, my darling, God willing, I will shower you with apples and candy.

It was the factory sirens all going off at once—so loudly that the women heard it in their cells—that started the rumors. Stalin was dead. At first the idea was impossible to grasp. Stalin dead? But he had been more than a human being, so how could he die? But if he *had* died? Faces that hadn't smiled in years began to show signs of softening. In all the cells of Vladimir there was new hope.

Yosh made it official when she climbed up on the table. "Attention, ladies! This is a great hour! Historical! When a creature dies whom you do not like, it is an occasion of joy!"

Zoya grabbed at her skirt. "Get down, Yosh, and lower your voice. Do you want the punishment cell?"

Yosh shook her off. "Do you hear her, ladies? That is fear, and fear is over. Soon we will all be free."

The next morning two guards came into the cell. "Gruschevskaya," one said, "you will go to the punishment cell because you have disturbed the silence of the prisoners."

The other guard ran her hand along the table. "Who is in charge of cleaning this cell today?"

Zoya stepped forward, a bitter smile on her face. They had the lists; they knew who was in charge of the cell each day. "I am."

"This place is filthy. You are going to the punishment cell, too."

Zoya handed her letter and Victoria's drawing to Leda Ruslanova to protect until she came back. She knew why she was being punished. It had nothing to do with the condition of the cell, which was no better or worse than it always was. It was because of Yosh's outburst. For some unknown reason Zoya was considered to be the leader of the cell. Since Yosh was always making speeches and Ruslanova was often demanding her rights, Zoya felt she ran a poor third as a troublemaker. But ever since her hunger strike, she was suspect when there was trouble in the cell.

When Zoya came out of the punishment cell after five days, she was allowed back into her own cell only to collect her things. The friendship between Ruslanova, Yosh, and Zoya was being broken up. Zoya embraced them both, took her letter and Victoria's drawing back from Ruslanova, and followed the guard to her new cell.

Twelve elderly women were huddled together, conducting a prayer service. They were Russian Orthodox nuns. A thirteenth woman, younger than the others, sat apart reading a book. She nodded to Zoya. When Zoya asked what she was reading, she showed Zoya that it was by Stalin. Zoya said, "It is believed that he is dead."

The woman shook her head violently. "That is not possible. It could not happen."

Zoya smiled. "Do you believe so strongly in him? If you are so loyal, why are you here?"

The woman stuck her chin up defensively. "I deserve to be punished. It was my husband. He was an enemy of the people, and he was shot. It is right that I be punished for being married to such a man."

The 12 nuns had all been together in the outside world. When they discovered that the father in charge of them was an NKVD member and was reporting everything that was done and said within their order, the women had moved away, reestablished themselves apart. The local government said this was a criminal act, and they were all arrested.

It was finally confirmed that Stalin was dead. The gossip was that he had committed suicide. The more politically aware thought his suicide unlikely, but if that was the official line, it was all to the good. Hope ran high that all the prisoners of his regime would be released.

Not long afterward Yosh was moved into Zoya's cell. They embraced and Zoya asked how Ruslanova was.

"I think she has been released," Yosh said. "At least she was ordered to get her things together, and the guard was polite when he said it. And then she was gone. I hear that her husband, the general, is back in favor again, so that is a sign."

Zoya laughed. "Darling Yosh, where do you get all your news?"

Yosh twisted her skinny little body into a seductive pose. "I have my ways. You must not ask."

"What of the rest of us?" Zoya asked.

"I am told there are officials going through the prison right now. There are some in the men's sections today. And they are making lists of names. The releases are to be in alphabetical order."

Zoya groaned. "And I am Fyodorova, the end of the alphabet."

"Cheer up!" Yosh said. "The end of the alphabet is nearer than twenty-five years!"

VICTORIA

I think only a Russian could understand the way I was as a child. Despised by everyone around me, called an enemy to my face, I was still intensely patriotic. Each day at school when we sang the song that began with "Our great-grandfather Stalin . . ." no one sang louder than I. I truly believed that he was good and wise and kind. I believed he was my great-grandfather, and I loved him.

I cried when I heard that he had died. My great-grandfather was dead. I didn't understand when Mama came home from work smiling. "Stalin is dead." She made it sound like good news.

I was outraged. "How can you smile? It means we are all going to die." To me it was as if God had died.

Mama looked at me sadly. "I will talk with you when you are a little older. You will understand then."

She gave each of us a black armband with red stripes that had been given her at her office. "They are to be worn on the left arm," Mama said. "We will only wear them in public, not at home."

I thought she was heartless, and wore my armband both at school and at home. I am not certain why I did this, why it meant so much to me. Perhaps, it was only that I liked the way the red on the armband brightened up my dark apron and dress. But more likely, the idea of Stalin as my great-grand-father was confused with the idea of a father. I did not realize then how much I hungered for a father of my own, a father like the other children at school had. I wanted anything that would make me like those favored children, and a father was the best thing one could have. A father would never let other people hurt me. He would never be too tired, the way Mama was, to love me.

The need for a father was to grow and grow in me all through my childhood and into my womanhood when it would cause me to make some terrible mistakes.

The death of Stalin, followed by the death of Beria—only a name to me, but his death pleased Mama greatly—brought about changes in the way we lived. Mama became a much happier woman, and she talked a great deal about the day when we all might be going to Moscow. For me, the big change was in the school system. Suddenly, boys and girls were to be educated together. I was in a mixed class when I entered the second grade. Otherwise, nothing changed. The new teacher hated me. She pointed me out to the other children in the class as an enemy of the people. They all stared at me as if they were looking for the horns growing out of my head.

After school I went up to the teacher. "Why did you say that? Now, no one will play with me."

She was a young, homely woman, with hard lines around her mouth. "Because it is true. And I have to protect my children."

I hated her. "You are so ugly," I said, "that you should have a broom and fly out into the sky."

She slapped me hard across the face. I cried all the way home.

But I still did not realize that if I was treated as an enemy of my country it was because the government said I was one. I believed it was only bad people around me, like that teacher, who caused my troubles. I just wanted to belong.

At the age of eight, we could become Pioneers. It was a Communist organization and joining was supposedly by choice, but our entire class was automatically enrolled and given their red scarves. Everyone but me. When I asked why I could not have a red scarf, the teacher said, "I have to have the name of your father, your patronym. It is required."

"What is that?"

When she explained, I said, "My mother and father are divorced. But her name is Alexandra Alexyevna, so my name is Alexyevna."

The teacher laughed. "What a stupid idea. Who is your *father?*"

She was looking at me in a funny way, but I didn't know what she was hinting at. Then she said, "Bring me the medical certificate of your birth. Then we will see if you can or cannot be a member."

I started to cry. She had not asked anyone else in the class to bring in their birth certificate. I did not even know if I had one. "Why are you doing this to me? Why do you hate me so?"

"You refuse to learn the truth about yourself," the teacher said. "You are an enemy. Your family is in exile here. You do not belong here. You do not belong anywhere, but because we Soviets are a generous people, we allow you to live among us. Now go home and bring me the certificate of your birth."

When I asked my mother for it, she said she would take it to the teacher herself. Of course I realize why now. "As for you, silly girl, you have the same patronym as your sister, Nina. It is Ivanova."

The next day Mama appeared after school. I didn't understand why she was furious. She told me to wait outside while she talked with my teacher. "How dare you . . ." was all I heard before the door was slammed behind me.

I got my red scarf.

ZOYA

It seemed like months since Ruslanova had left, and Zoya didn't know how long it had been since she had last seen Yosh. It was said that she, too, had been freed. But Zoya sat in the cell with the old women, waiting, listening to rumors of all kinds about the new regime and when the remaining prisoners would be released.

But another winter came, and still she waited. The prisoners were given back the clothes that had been taken away from them when they entered Vladimir. Zoya remembered with bitterness the fur coat she had given away when they brought her the threadbare coat that Olga had left in its place. When her silk stockings were returned to her, Zoya cut them and made sleeves of them, sewing them inside the leg ends of her winter underwear. She then made a head hold at the crotch and turned the whole thing into a sweater.

What made the days even longer now was that Zoya had hope of being released and of seeing her child again. Before, when Stalin lived, she had given up all hope. It made life easier. But now each day was agony, believing that at any moment the cell door might open and a guard would tell her to get her things together.

Finally it happened. She was told she was going to Lubyanka, the prison where her agony had all begun. "Will I be freed?" Zoya asked.

The guard shrugged. "I only know your orders are for Lubyanka. Be grateful for that. It is warmer there."

And indeed Lubyanka seemed like paradise after Vladimir. Zoya was put into a one-person cell that had a parquet floor, and she was allowed to go to the bathroom whenever she wanted. All she had to do was tell the guard. She was given vitamins and cod liver oil with her food. The tea was stronger than she remembered it from the first time, and there was nearly a half teaspoon of sugar with it.

The new prosecutor who saw her the day after she arrived was named Terechov. He stood up when she entered his office, and said, "Sit down, please."

It left Zoya shaken. It had been such a long, long time since anyone had spoken that way to her. "What is happening to me?" she asked.

He said, "There is a strong possibility that your sentence will be changed. We must reexamine your case."

He reached behind him and brought out the old thick dossier with the American flag still on it. Zoya groaned. He smiled. "Do not despair. I have already read the dossier. We just have to go through the main points of the charges against you, and you must explain them all to me. I will write it down, and it will all be reviewed, and then we shall see. I am sorry, but it will take time. We will begin tomorrow morning."

He stood, signaling that the first meeting was over. Zoya hesitated. "Forgive me, but if you are being kind, can you tell me what has happened to my family?"

Terechov looked in her dossier. "Your sister Alexandra has been exiled for life. She is now in Petropavlovsk, Kazakhstan, with her children, Nina and Yuri, and the child Victoria."

"For life?"

He shrugged. "It is for your crimes that she was exiled. If there is a change in your sentence, there could be a change in hers. Who can say?"

Zoya nodded. "And my sister Maria?"

He paused to light a cigarette. "I am afraid that is bad news.

Your sister Maria was sentenced to ten years in a labor camp. She was sent to the north to Vorkuta to work in a brick factory. She died in 1952."

Zoya bit her lip. Poor Maria. She was never strong. Working in a brick factory in a labor camp. Maria, who had never harmed anyone. Zoya had to dig her fingernails into her palms to keep from crying.

Day after day she met with Terechov and they went over it all again, beginning with her affair with Jackson Tate. Only this time it was all different. Terechov would ask a question, and he would listen to Zoya's answer and write it down. He never questioned the truth of what she said. Sometimes, he would nod and say, "I see, I see. So that's the way it was."

It went so slowly that Zoya despaired of its ever ending. Finally, at the end of one session, Terechov smiled at her and said, "Do not give up. I think everything will happen as you wish it to."

Zoya thought about that back in her cell. Surely that meant she would be cleared and set free.

It happened on February 23, 1954—Terechov told her the date when she came into his office.

The first thought that crossed Zoya's mind was that Victoria had turned nine while she was in Lubyanka. "Why do you tell me the date?"

"Sit down first," Terechov said. He helped Zoya into her chair. "I must tell you that this is the happiest morning in your life—you are free. All of your prison years were a terrible mistake, made under the dictator Stalin. Now under our new leader, Khrushchev, we are releasing millions. You must remember that you were not alone in your suffering."

Zoya didn't move. Her body had turned suddenly numb. Terechov looked at her. "Do you hear me, Zoya Fyodorova. It was decided this morning."

"Then I can go?" Zoya heard her own voice as if it came from far away, the words spoken by some woman who sounded half asleep.

He laughed. "Well, not until tomorrow morning. The person who is in charge of your clothes is already gone, so you will have to sleep here overnight."

"No. If I am free," Zoya said, "I will not go to the cell anymore."

"What do you mean? Where else can you sleep?"

Zoya looked around the room. "I will sleep right here. On your couch."

"Please," Terechov said, "it is not permitted. It would be bad for me if I allowed it. You can sit here for a while if you wish, but you must sleep in your cell."

She nodded. "All right, but the door is not to be locked."

"I will see," Terechov said. He turned on the radio and left the room.

It was the first music Zoya had heard in over eight years. How beautiful it was. She moved over to the sofa and sat down. It was just like sitting on a cloud, she thought.

The music changed, and a voice began to sing. It was a sad song which began, "Nobody is waiting for me anywhere." Zoya buried her face in her hands. It was true. No one was waiting for her.

Terechov returned. "I am sorry, but you must go back now."

Zoya stood up. As she neared the door, Terechov said, "Wait. There is a mirror here. Would you like to see yourself?"

He went to a closet and opened the door, revealing a full-length mirror. When Zoya hesitated, he smiled. "It is all right, I assure you. You have not become horrible. It is still Zoya Fyodorova."

Zoya walked slowly toward the mirror, staying at an angle from it so she would not see herself until she was ready. Then she braced herself. This is foolishness, she thought. Whoever is there in the mirror is me, and not looking will not change it.

She took a deep breath and stepped in front of the mirror. The woman who looked back at her was old. There was gray in her hair and puffiness around the eyes and around the cheekbones, too. The last time she had looked in a mirror she had been 33 years old. Now, she was 41. Was this the face of a 41-year-old woman or someone much older? It was not the face of a lyrical heroine, but rather her mother.

Zoya turned away.

"Do not despair so," Terechov said, laughing. "A few good meals, and you will see miracles. You are still a beautiful woman, Zoya Fyodorova."

Zoya shrugged. "Perhaps. But it is of a different kind now."

When she got back to her cell, they locked the door behind her. Zoya pounded on it until the guard unlocked it. "What do you want?"

Zoya said, "This door was not to be locked."

The guard laughed. "And who do you think you are?" She slammed the door and locked it again.

She was right, Zoya thought. Who *did* she think she was? Had she learned nothing in all her years in prison? They could do anything they wanted with her, and she could do nothing about it. They could take away eight years of her life and then say it was a mistake, and that was that. And she had to accept it.

Zoya couldn't sleep that night. Who could, on the eve of freedom?

The next day she was given a cheap coat and a beret, both smelling strongly of disinfectant.

The officer in charge asked, "Where are you going now? We have to know."

Zoya shook her head. "That is no longer your business. My sister is not in Moscow, and I don't know how my friends would feel about seeing me again. Anyway it does not concern you."

The officer said, "We have to have a better answer. Don't you have one really good friend who would take you in?"

Zoya thought a moment. "Yes, Ruslanova, the singer, but I do not know what has become of her."

The officer smiled. "She is here in Moscow. She has been free for a long time now."

"I don't know where she lives or what her telephone number is."

The guard reached for the telephone and began to dial. "We do."

The general answered the telephone. Zoya held her breath until the officer said, "You don't have to do that, sir. We will bring her to you in our car."

He walked her to the car and opened the door for her. The car began to move, and Zoya watched, stunned, as the gates of Lubyanka swung open and the car moved through.

The sight was overwhelming—trees and automobiles and

people walking on sidewalks. Zoya shrank back against the car seat. She was truly free. It was not some final horrible trick.

The driver escorted Zoya right to the general's apartment and rang the bell. Zoya heard feet running. The door was flung open and there was Ruslanova. Only it wasn't the Ruslanova Zoya remembered from Vladimir. This Ruslanova had her hair beautifully set and she was wearing something soft and warm. Tears were running down her face. "Zoyka! My Zoyka! Oh, my dear, finally I see you again."

Zoya fell into her arms and began to cry. Ruslanova held her close.

The prosecutor had told her that she could go to the head of her studio and say that she had been cleared to work, but that the necessary papers would take a few months. If there was any doubt at the studio, they could call his office for confirmation.

Zoya, wearing the smart black suit that Ruslanova had given her, went to the studio on her second day out of prison. When she told the secretary she wanted to see the studio head, the woman looked critically at her, but put through the call. "You will have to wait," she said.

Zoya waited for three hours. She smiled bitterly. She knew what this was about. Ivan the Terrible—that was what everyone at the studio always called him behind his back—was showing his power again. He had always been a man small in spirit, which made him cruel. It was his way of establishing his power, which everyone suspected masked his insecurity about himself.

Finally, Zoya was admitted. His first words were, "Are you free?"

Zoya nodded. "I have been cleared of all crimes, and I am allowed to work again."

He said, "Give me a paper to prove this."

"I don't have any papers yet," Zoya said. "They will be ready in a few months, but I have the telephone number of the prosecutor in charge of my case. He said you are to call him and he will tell you I am cleared."

He shook his head. "No papers, no work."

"I have rights," Zoya said. "It is not a case of if you don't want to, you don't have to. You must put me to work!"

He smiled. "The prosecutor's office cannot order us to do anything. When you have your papers, come in. Good-bye."

Zoya left the studio, stunned. During her two days with Ruslanova she had begun to feel as if life were starting again for her. But now it was as if she were back in prison again.

She had been totally rejected, treated as if she were dirt. Was the studio head just throwing his weight around to show his power, and could he really refuse her work until her papers came through?

Zoya walked to a little park and found an empty bench. She sat down and buried her face in her hands so that no one would see her crying. What was to become of her?

She looked into the purse that Ruslanova had given her. There weren't even five kopeks for the bus. She remembered the song she had heard on Terechov's radio. *Nobody is waiting for me anywhere.* It was true. Is this what she was released from prison for? To sit on a park bench, and to live on the kindness of Leda Ruslanova and her husband? If this is my life, why did they release me? I would be better off back in prison, or in the river. My life ended the night I was first arrested, and I have been an idiot to hang on.

Finally her tears stopped. She realized she had behaved foolishly. Self-pity accomplished nothing. It was time to do something. Anything.

She decided to walk over to the office where the actors dropped in when they were between pictures. Perhaps she would run into a friend there who would spare her a few rubles.

Luck was with her. As she was about to enter the office, a man stopped her. He had been the writer of her film *Girl-friends at the Front*. He threw his arms about her. "It is so good to see you, I cannot tell you. You must come with me. My wife will be delighted."

They gave her coffee and cake, and Zoya felt the tears coming to her eyes again. My God, she thought, there are still decent people in this world.

The writer said, "I do not wish to embarrass you, but you

must tell me something, honestly. You do not have any money, am I right?"

Zoya nodded. "And Ivan the Terrible will not give me work until my papers come through."

His wife said, "Then you must let us help you."

They gave her 2,000 rubles and told her, "Never worry about giving it back. It is from us with all our hearts."

Now she could live, and even wait, if she had to, for her work papers to come through. Soon her life would begin again. She would be working again, and her sister would come back to Moscow, and Victoria would be with her. Ah, she thought, if only I could go to Petropavlovsk and get my child. But she knew it was impossible. That was not the way to present herself to the child who did not know her.

No, she had waited this long. She would have to wait another month or two. Meanwhile, she had to build herself up for the day when she would go in front of the cameras again. And there was one thing she had to do before anything else. Victoria probably didn't even remember it, but she had written Aunt Zoya to send her apples and candy. Zoya regarded the request as a sacred obligation on her part.

VICTORIA

I think it was near the end of March, the night Mama came home from work carrying the large cardboard box. I know it was still winter because that was the day I couldn't go to school because of the wind. There were days when the wind was so strong that I could barely stand against it and it was impossible to move forward. I could only get to school if someone came along who would link arms with me and move me forward.

Anyway, the box was so large that we couldn't see Mama's face until she put it down on the table. Then we saw her grinning. "Oh yes," she said, "we are all going to Moscow very soon now."

We all gathered around the box. "What is it, Mama? Who is it from?"

"Aunt Zoya. She has left her small town and is now in Moscow, and she has sent a present to all of us."

Six pairs of wide-open eyes watched her as she took off her coat and babushka. A present! Mail had been a rarity in our lives, but a present! None of us had ever received a present through the mails. I jumped up and down. "Open it! Open it!"

Mama laughed. It thrilled me. Her laughter was such a new thing to all of us. "Patience, little one. It won't walk away."

She got a knife and slit open the box and pulled back the flaps. We all gasped. It was like looking into heaven. The box was filled with foods of all sorts, some of it food I had only seen pictures of in school, other things that I could not recognize. There was a letter on top. Mama took it and I reached into the box and pulled out what looked like a long round tube tied at both ends. I smelled it. "What is this, Mama?"

Mama shrugged. "I don't know. Let's taste it and find out."

She took the knife and sliced into the tube. Mama tasted a small piece. "It is cheese."

She cut thin slices for each of us. "Cheese," she said again so that each of us would know what we were about to taste. "If you do not like it, do not waste it."

It was like a funny-tasting candy to me. I loved it.

Then Mama emptied the whole box, and we gasped as each new treasure emerged. There were metal cans containing chicken and beef, a sausage, and a salami. Then a special box with my name on it. Mama handed it to me. "You open this one, Victoria. It has your name on it."

I ripped open the box. There were six apples and a bag of hard candies. A card said, "With all my love to you, Victoria. Aunt Zoya."

"Look! Look!" I shouted, holding up the box. "For me!"

Mama looked at me. "You will share with everyone, Vikka."

"But Aunt Zoya . . ."

"You will share."

I'll admit that I did it reluctantly, but I did give everyone an apple.

There was another box of candy at the bottom of the big box, chocolate candy. And lots of orange-colored globes. Mama took them out and put them in a bowl. "They are oranges," she said.

We stared at them at first. Then carefully, as if they might break, we reached out to touch them.

There were tears in Mama's eyes. "Tonight," she announced, "we will all eat meat! And oranges!"

Imagine, meat and oranges all in one evening. And cheese and apples—foods I had never tasted. We went crazy, even Mama. Yuri made a song of it—meat and oranges—and we joined hands in a dance around the table.

It was Mama who broke the circle and collapsed into a chair, gasping for breath. Nina and I continued to jump around like wild creatures until Mama finally stopped us. "Enough of this crazy carnival. You will make yourselves sick, and that would be a shame with such a marvelous dinner."

It took me several tastes to decide that I liked beef. It felt so strange in my mouth at first. But the oranges I liked right away. I saved the peel and put it in my pocket so that I could smell it whenever I wanted.

That was the first night I ever had enough to eat. I felt sleepy and warm. It was a lovely sensation.

Then Mama remembered the letter. As she read it, her face grew sad. "Is something wrong with Aunt Zoya?" Yuri asked.

Mama shook her head. "Aunt Zoya writes that she is lonely. She is a single woman and she has no children of her own. Doesn't that make you sad?"

"Well, maybe she will get some," I said.

Mama smiled sadly. "I was thinking that it is not right that Aunt Zoya should have no children, while I have three. It is not fair. I must give her one of mine."

She began to cry. I don't know why, but I knew that she was going to give me away to this strange aunt. I got down from my chair and backed toward the window, as far from the table as I could go.

Mama looked at me. "Wouldn't you like to live in Moscow with Aunt Zoya, Vikka? You would make her very happy, and I know she would love you very much."

I began to cry in choking sobs. "You are choosing me because I am always in trouble. You want to get rid of me! You don't love me!"

Mama came to me and wrapped me in her arms. "Oh, Vikka, you are so wrong. I love you with my heart and soul. I do not want to get rid of you. It is just that you are the youngest. Life has hardened you the least. It would be easiest for you to make a new life, to accept someone new. Aunt Zoya would be so good to you. She would love you as much as I do."

I clung to her. "No, no, please, Mama, do not send me away. I don't want a new mother."

Mama stroked my hair. "Shhh, baby, shhh. How can one have a new mother? If I am your mother now, won't I always be your mother? And it is only for a little while that we will be separated. After all, Zoya is part of our family, too. And when I come to Moscow with Nina and Yuri, we will all be together again."

She was confusing me. She seemed to be sending me away, and yet she wasn't really sending me away, because soon we would all be together again. Mama said, "Well, we don't have to decide anything right at this minute. I will think about it, and you think about it, too, Vikka."

There were letters and telegrams back and forth between Mama and Aunt Zoya, but Mama never said what was in them. And she talked more and more about when she would go to Moscow. It would be in the summer when Yuri had finished the semester in technical school. "And of course, I cannot leave my job just like that. But I do wish you were old enough to go to Moscow on your spring vacation, Vikka, and get things ready for us when we come. If you could do this, you could stay with Aunt Zoya. But you are only nine. I guess you are not really grown-up enough to do this for all of us. It would mean traveling all by yourself on the train to Moscow . . ."

"Don't you remember?" I said. "I went all by myself to Moscow to see Aunt Klava and Uncle Ivan when I was much younger."

Mama seemed surprised. "Yes, you did. I had forgotten."

"And with Aunt Zoya's help, I know I could see that everything is ready when you come."

Mama thought about that. "I don't know. It is a big responsibility."

I began to jump up and down. "I could! I could!"

Mama kissed me on the forehead. "Yes, I think maybe you could. I will think about it."

I hugged her to convince her, not realizing that I was doing exactly what she and Zoya had decided on.

One day Mama said to me, "Victoria, where is that silly hat of yours?"

It was a long brown hat that came to a point and stood almost two feet high on my head. When I wore it, I felt like Pinocchio or a wood-spirit. I loved it. "It is not silly," I said, and fished it out from under the bed.

Mama nodded. "I will write Aunt Zoya that you will be wearing such a hat when you come off the train in Moscow, so she will be certain to recognize you."

"Then I can go?"

Mama smiled. "Yes, I have thought about it, and I know that with Aunt Zoya's help you will do everything that is needed."

I threw my arms around her and kissed her.

I was so proud when we went to the railroad station. I was certain that the reason people turned to look at me was because the little bag I carried with my two dresses in it and the food Mama had packed told them that I was going to Moscow all by myself. It never occurred to me that it was the long pointed hat I wore.

"Now, don't forget," Mama said. "When you get off the train be sure to have your hat on so Aunt Zoya will recognize you. And do not move away from the car in which you sit, because I will send Aunt Zoya a telegram to tell her the number of the car. Promise me, Vikka."

"I promise." I kissed Yuri and Nina and then turned to Mama, who was wiping her eyes. "Do not worry, Mama. I will find us a nice apartment."

She bent down and kissed me, and pulled me against her breast. Muffled against her, I thought I heard her say, "It is probably the last time I will see you as my daughter," but since that made no sense, I didn't think about it.

The train came in, and Yuri helped me to get on board. I found a seat by a window and waved and waved until I couldn't see them any longer. I thought briefly about Mama's crying, but I couldn't understand why. After all, it was only for two months, and then we would all be together again.

I opened my little cardboard suitcase and took out the food Mama had packed for me. There was a sealed letter on top of my dresses with Aunt Zoya's name on it.

ZOYA

"I will die. I know it; this morning I will die. Here, feel my heart. It is going to explode."

Ruslanova laughed and continued fussing with Zoya's hair. "Nonsense, Zoyka. If Vladimir did not kill you, happiness certainly will not. Stand up and take a look at yourself."

Zoya walked to the mirror. The new suit was a deep blue and well tailored. The shoes with the heels made her ankles narrower and curved her calves. It was worth spending so much of the 3,700 rubles the government had given her—one tenth of what they had confiscated when she had been sent to prison. "What do you think?" Zoya asked.

"You look lovely. Your daughter will be very impressed."

"I don't know. I look in the mirror and I see a woman who has grown old. She will see it, too."

Ruslanova sprayed some of her perfume on Zoya. "You are being a crazy woman today. Moscow still remembers and loves you. Why shouldn't a child? You think she has seen better in Petropavlovsk?"

General Krukov stuck his head in the door. "Did you wait all these years to miss the train? It is time to go."

Zoya started trembling. "I am so afraid. What if she doesn't like me?"

Ruslanova laughed. "Why shouldn't she like you?" She went to her closet and took out her fur coat, and held it out to Zoya. "Put this on."

Zoya demurred, but Ruslanova insisted. "If she is going to have a film star for a mother, let her see a film star."

The general told the driver to go to the Kozanskyi Station. They drove in silence. Zoya kept fiddling with the clasp of her purse, and every few minutes she would open it to reread Alexandra's telegram telling her the train Victoria would come in on and the number of the car in which she would be sitting. Then she would take out a mirror and study her face and touch at nonexistent imperfections.

When they reached the station, they learned the train was four hours late. The general said, "I will leave you and come back, if that is all right with you. Or if you prefer, the driver can take you back to the apartment."

Zoya shook her head. "No. I would rather be here, just in case it comes in a little earlier."

Zoya began to pace, but never very far from the track on which Victoria's train would arrive. The time dragged by. I will go mad, Zoya thought, right here in the station if the train doesn't come soon.

She didn't realize how often she went to inquire about the train until the man who gave the information answered her once before she asked.

Her knees started to ache from the arthritis she had developed in prison. She sat down for a while but even pain could not keep her seated for long. In a few minutes she was up and pacing again. Then she was back to inquire about the train and her heart sank when the man said it was four and a half hours late.

Zoya went to the bench and sat down again. She looked at her face in the mirror. She was perspiring and there were tracks through her face powder. She patted her face with her handkerchief and applied fresh powder.

When the general came back and learned it would be another half hour, he said, "I will wait in the car. I think you would like to be alone with her?"

It was a question, but Zoya didn't know what to answer. Yes, she wanted to meet Victoria by herself, but no, she was afraid. What if she saw displeasure in the child's face?

But the general was gone. Zoya forced herself to stay seated, but her eyes were glued on the track where Victoria's train would come in. And then far away down the track, she saw it, a black spot that grew larger and larger. Zoya felt her throat close up and her hands began to tremble. Then the whole scene blurred as tears filled her eyes. She got out her handkerchief and wiped them. I will not miss this moment with tears. And I will not embarrass my child with a sobbing old lady.

Zoya stood at the head of the track as the train slid to a stop. She looked up and down the length of the train as doors opened and the first passengers stepped out. Where was the child in the funny hat?

Suddenly, the platform was filled with people pouring out onto the platform, and she could no longer see the far cars.

VICTORIA

When the lady told me we were in Moscow and I felt the train beginning to slow down, I stood up and brushed the crumbs from my dress and put on my coat. I thanked the lady who had given me the cookie.

I put on the pointed hat and tried to see myself in the train window to make sure I looked nice so that Aunt Zoya would be pleased with me. I brushed my coat to smooth it, and I bit my lips to bring out the color as I had seen older girls do.

The train stopped and everyone began to push to get off. I waited until most of them had gone and then I took my cardboard suitcase and got off, too. I straightened my hat so it stood straight up from my head. I started to walk, but then I remembered that Mama had told me to stay by the train car.

The crowd on the platform pushed past me. I looked for someone who might be my aunt, but I saw no one. And then the crowd thinned, and I saw a lady coming down the platform looking at every passing face. She was wearing a fur coat just like the beautiful lady I used to watch in Petropavlovsk. Only this lady was even more beautiful.

Suddenly, she saw me and she stopped. Then she began to

run toward me. When she reached me, I saw that she was crying. "Victoria?" she said.

I nodded. I liked the sound of her voice. "Aunt Zoya?"

The furry arms were around me, and I thought she would crush me. I felt her tears fall on me and I could feel her body trembling through her coat.

She was on her knees in front of me, looking at my face and brushing away her tears so that she could see me. "Yes," she said, "yes."

I didn't know what she meant, and I was embarrassed by her being on her knees and crying. People were looking at us, but she didn't seem to see them. She just kept staring at me. Then she pulled me to her and kissed me all over my face. Suddenly, she sagged against me. I caught her before her face hit the platform. "Aunt Zoya!" I shrieked. I thought she had died.

"I'm all right. I'm all right." Aunt Zoya dabbed at her eyes as the tears started again. She smiled at me. "Forgive me, my Vikka, but this is such a moment for me that I cannot tell you. And you don't even know what it is all about or who I am."

I thought she was treating me like a baby. "Of course I know who you are. You are my Aunt Zoya, my mother's sister."

That seemed to bring on more tears. My aunt shook her head and smiled sadly at me. "I am more than the sister of your mother. Come."

I wouldn't let her take my suitcase, but I followed her. I tried to make sense out of what she had said, but it was hopeless.

In fact, I thought it all very strange, all this crying. Mama had cried when I got on the train, and now Aunt Zoya was crying even worse.

And as far as I could see, there was nothing to cry about.

BOOK
V

VICTORIA

What Mama wrote in the letter I carried must have been very hard for Aunt Zoya to accept, but she did. Naturally, I did not see the letter for some time afterward because of what Mama had written:

> You must choose the moment very carefully when you tell her the truth of who you are. She is a very sensitive and a very nervous child, and I do not think she can take the news too quickly that she has someone else as a Mama beside me. You have to prepare her emotionally and mentally so that she can take it without shocking her for the rest of her life.

Aunt Zoya asked only that I call her "Zoya" without the "Aunt." It struck me as odd, but I agreed to her request.

But then, everything about her struck me as odd, yet I couldn't quite figure out what it was that bothered me. Mostly it was that so often she'd look at me and tears would come to her eyes. And she seemed to love me too much, more than I thought an aunt would. In the mornings, she would swoop down on me with a hug and kisses to begin my day, and the tears would come again. Or there would be more sudden hugs and kisses at odd moments during the day. And if she ever had to go out for an hour or two on some errand, she worried about leaving me alone in Ruslanova's apartment—though there was a maid to keep an eye on me. It was all just too much. It made me wonder. If she loved me this much, then why hadn't she ever come to see me in Petropavlovsk?

I suspected there was some truth about this Zoya that I did not know, but for a long time I had no idea of what it was. It was when I remembered that in the railroad station she had said to me "I am more than the sister of your mother" that confusing thoughts started to creep into my head.

At the beginning, we lived with the Krukovs, and while they were very nice to us, it was not the best arrangement. I was a wild child, and they had beautiful and delicate things in their apartment. But fine crystal and grand paintings meant nothing to me. If I wanted to play in the apartment with the ball that Zoya had brought for me, I did. And when all of the strange luxury I was living in became too much for me, I would crawl under the dining room table and refuse to come out.

After a few weeks, despite how much it must have hurt her, Zoya took me to Klava and Ivan's to live and to continue my schooling.

But she came to see me almost daily, and often with a present of a new dress or a doll. She was spoiling me and of course I loved it. And I was beginning to love Zoya very much, too. Because of the way I had lived I needed love very badly, and suddenly here was a woman who could not give me enough love.

Still I worried about Mama and Yuri and Nina. When would they come to Moscow? And where would they live if I did not find an apartment for them? But Zoya kissed me and told me not to worry. "When the time comes, it will be all right for them. The government will see to it that they are given an apartment. And I do not think they will come before the summer because of Yuri and Nina's schooling, and Alexandra's job."

I believed her, although I really didn't know much about her except that she was Mama's sister. She told me that she was an actress, that she hadn't worked in some time, but she planned to as soon as her papers came through. "It is just that there are now so many people like myself waiting for papers, that it takes time."

Usually Zoya came to see me around four o'clock in the afternoon after I returned from school. But one day, after I'd been in Moscow about two months, she didn't come. I didn't worry. I just assumed she was busy somewhere else.

Aunt Klava told me to put away my school books and to come sit beside her. I did as I was told.

"I want to talk with you. Do you ever wonder about your Aunt Zoya? Anything?"

I said a cautious "No," not certain what was expected of me. I thought that if I told Aunt Klava all of the ideas that had gone through my head about Zoya, she might be angry or think that I was insane.

Aunt Klava took my hand. "I will not tell you the whole story, because I think you are too young. But you should know, first of all, that Zoya did not live in a small town all the years you did not see her. She was in prison. It was a mistake."

I waited. I could tell there was more to come from the way Aunt Klava's hand tightened on mine. "And because she was in prison, she could not see to you as a baby, so you went with Alexandra. Alexandra is not really your mother. She is your aunt. Zoya is your mother."

I said nothing. Aunt Klava looked at me. "Are you all right? Do you understand?"

I nodded. "I am all right. I think I knew it all along."

"How?"

"I don't know, but somehow I felt it."

We were still sitting there when there was a knock at the door. Aunt Klava went to open it. It was Zoya. She looked nervously from Klava to me.

I stood up. "Mama."

She ran to me and threw her arms around me, and we both burst into tears. When we could control ourselves, she looked deep into my eyes and asked, "Is it all right?"

I said "I love you very much" and kissed her.

Later on when I asked about my father, she told me that he was a war hero, a Russian pilot who had been shot down in action. The answer satisfied me for the time being.

When Alexandra returned to Moscow with Nina and Yuri, Zoya and I went to live with them in the apartment she had been awarded. And jealousy flared up between the two sisters when I called Alexandra "Mama." Zoya couldn't stand it that I called Alexandra by the name she felt belonged only to her. "You have two children, Alexandra, and that is enough to call you Mama. But this one is mine, and only mine."

Alexandra shrugged. "What did you expect, Zoya? She grew up calling me Mama. What else could she call me now?"

I solved it as best I could by calling Alexandra "Mama" and Zoya "Mamula." But it was always difficult for Zoya to accept the fact that she did not have the title exclusively.

Finally, Mamula's papers came through, and we moved to the apartment in which I grew up, two rooms plus a tiny kitchen on Taras Shevchenko, and she went to work again in films. Lenfilm assigned her to the film *The Honeymoon*. The role was a new type for her—a middle-aged comedy role. She was done with the days of lyrical heroines.

The picture and Mamula were both a success, and her career was in full gear again.

ZOYA

It was good to be working again, but the jump from lyrical heroines to mothers, aunts, and character roles was a shock. There had been no transition period. A lyrical heroine had gone into prison and a character actress had come out. It forced Zoya's age upon her, and the fans who spoke to her in the street reinforced the change. Like the woman who had come up to her and said, "Are you Zoya Fyodorova?"

Zoya said she was. The woman said, "I thought so, but you look so much older."

Zoya looked at the woman. Was she trying to be cruel? No, Zoya didn't think so. "It has been almost ten years since I have made a film."

The woman nodded. "But there are so many wrinkles now."

"True," Zoya said, "but ten years is ten years. I assure you if you could see yourself today as you were ten years ago, you would find a completely different person."

The woman nodded her head again, as if Zoya had said a profound truth.

It wasn't the age that hurt her so much. Zoya didn't have that kind of vanity. It was the time lost, not in her career but in Victoria's childhood. When she had first regained her daughter, Victoria was already nine. And then ten and eleven and twelve. Time was racing, and before her eyes Zoya saw her child beginning to turn into a woman. Her body was lengthening, and the bones in her face were changing. There was the faintest beginning of womanly curves. Victoria was going to be a beauty, Zoya could tell that already, but she resented that the child was disappearing. It wasn't fair.

Zoya knew she was overprotective of Victoria, and she resolved over and over that she wouldn't be, but it was a difficult resolution to keep. She had had so little of her baby and now time was taking her child away, making her stretch for the independence that would one day take her away forever from her mother.

When Victoria turned 13, Zoya was troubled with another concern. What if something happens to me, she asked herself, what would become of Victoria?

Before she had gone to prison, Zoya had taken her health for granted. But since those terrible days, she had become aware of her physical condition. Her body told her things with aches and pains. Her knees always punished her when the damp weather came. And her lungs sometimes troubled her, a legacy from the punishment cells of Vladimir.

The idea that she might die before Victoria grew up preyed on Zoya. More and more, she thought of Jackson Tate, who didn't even know he had a daughter. He should know, if it were possible. Surely, the Jackson Tate Zoya had known and loved would want to know, and would want to care for, his own child. That is, if he were even alive.

Zoya tried to bring Jackson into her mind, to picture him again. But without much success. An American in a naval uniform—what was his rank?—with short hair.

There was so little to go on, and Zoya wondered how she could find him in America, so very far away. What she needed was an American she could trust, and she no longer knew any Americans.

But Zenaida Sakhnina would surely know some. She lived right in Zoya's building and they had become good friends. And Zena worked as a floor lady, a *dejournaya*, on the fifth floor of the Ukraina Hotel, where so many foreign visitors to Moscow stayed. Surely Zena could find an American to trust.

The question was, could she trust Zenaida? The NKVD was gone, but the KGB had taken its place, and it was common knowledge that all the floor ladies in Moscow were informers, reporting on everyone who stayed on their floors: who their visitors were, what time the hotel guests went in and out. To ask help from Zenaida could be a mistake.

In the summer of 1959 Zoya decided that if she were ever going to try to find Jackson Tate this was the time. The United States Trade Exhibition was in Moscow, and that meant there were many Americans involved. Surely many of them would be staying at the Ukraina. Zoya invited Zenaida to dinner on her night off.

After the meal Zoya said, "I must talk with you, Zena."

"But of course."

Zoya looked at her. "Can I trust you, Zenaida? I must know."

The woman snorted. "What a question. We are friends."

Zoya brushed that away. "You are an informer, aren't you? Tell me the truth."

"All right. Yes, I am. To you I will admit it."

Zoya ran her hand nervously through her hair. "You know that I do not like this about you, even if you are my friend. I suffered a great deal in my time and . . ."

Zenaida reached out and took her hand. "Zoyatchka, my friend, I do what I must do, but I would never betray you, I swear it. You and Vikka are like my own family to me."

Zoya took a deep breath. "All right, I trust you, too." She told Zenaida the whole story of her affair with Jackson Rogers Tate.

When she finished, Zoya said, "I know that for what I am asking you to do, you could lose your job, and even worse could happen to you."

"I know," Zenaida said, "but still I would like to do this thing for you. I am not proud that I must be an informer. All of the time, there is a guilt in me because of it. I will watch around my floor for an American I can trust, someone who will help."

Zoya kissed her. "You are a good woman."

As she was leaving, Zoya said, "Remember, Vikka must not know any of this. She still does not know who her father is."

IRINA KIRK

When word went out that Russian-speaking American citizens were being sought as guides for the United States Trade Exhibition in Moscow, Irina Kirk applied and was one of the one hundred who were accepted. For someone who had emotional roots in the Soviet Union but had never been there, it was the chance of a lifetime.

Irina Kirk's parents were among the Russians who fled at the time of the revolution. She was born in Harbin, China, and grew up speaking Russian, though along the way she also learned English, French, and some Italian.

Her mother and father—he was a journalist—divorced, and Irina and her mother went to live with her mother's father, a Russian admiral who found work in China as the caretaker in a cemetery. Irina spent her childhood years believing, as her grandfather told her, that Russia was in the hands of Bolsheviks and Communists, but one day there would be a revolution, and the czar would come back, and they would all go home to Russia. When the war began in 1941, Russia took an interest in its people in China and started sending in films and music. A Russian-language radio station was also started.

Irina remembers that in her teen years she saved her pennies so that she could go to see such films as *Girlfriends* and

The Musical Story and anything else that Zoya Fyodorova was in.

In 1946 she left China as the wife of an American marine. They settled in Hawaii and in time she gave birth to three children. But the marriage failed. She was at the University of Hawaii in 1959 when the paper came to the Russian Department giving details of how to apply for the Trade Exhibition jobs. Twenty-five of those hired were designated as private industry guides, and the remaining seventy-five were to be government guides. Irina was told she would be one of the former, assigned to Pepsi-Cola.

At the Pepsi exhibit pictures were shown of how the drink was made and while Russian girls gave out samples, Irina Kirk and her American co-workers spoke with the Russian visitors. They rarely asked about Pepsi-Cola. What they wanted to know about was the United States, and Irina Kirk answered questions from 10 A.M. until the exhibit closed at 10 P.M.

She was on duty during the so-called "kitchen debate" between then Vice-President Richard M. Nixon and Nikita Khrushchev and in fact served as the translator for the press who were there.

Irina Kirk was housed on the fifth floor of the Ukraina Hotel. Like all hotel residents she met the floor ladies who worked 24-hour shifts. They sat at desks in front of the elevators, wearing red coats with blue kerchiefs, taking in keys of those leaving and handing keys to those returning to their rooms. And they noted everything. One of them, a woman named Zenaida, seemed friendly.

It was the end of August, 1959. Irina would be going home in two more days. To her amazement, when she stopped to pick up her key, Zenaida took her aside and invited her to her home for dinner. Irina accepted eagerly. An invitation to visit a Russian home was extremely rare.

Irina asked if she could bring her roommate along, and Zenaida said, "No, no. Just you." Irina had the impression that she was frightened.

Zenaida leaned close so that she could speak softly. "Only you, and don't tell anyone that I invited you. Not even your friend."

"All right."

"You will be in front of the hotel at seven o'clock. I will be across the street. Do not even look like you know me. Just follow me on your side of the street."

Irina agreed.

She was in front of the hotel at five minutes to seven. At seven sharp, she saw Zenaida across the street, walking without stopping or even glancing at her.

Irina followed along on her side of the street, keeping track of Zenaida's direction out of the corner of her eye. At the time, it all seemed to her like something out of a bad movie. She had been in Moscow long enough to know that Zenaida was taking a risk inviting an American citizen to her home, but that the purpose was anything more than dinner didn't occur to her.

Zenaida left the busy thoroughfare and turned down a narrow street. Irina followed on the opposite side. Finally, the floor lady entered a dark building passageway. Irina walked on, casually glancing about her to make certain the street was empty. Then she turned back and went into the building. Zenaida was waiting for her halfway up the stairs and led her into a one-room apartment. The first thing Irina saw was an attractive blond woman and a young girl somewhere in her early teens, who was pretty but had a certain tenseness to her face. The blond woman stood. There was something familiar about her.

Zenaida made the introductions. "This is Zoya Fyodorova and her daughter, Victoria."

The face came back to Irina from her childhood. "*The* Zoya Fyodorova? The actress?"

"You know me?" Zoya said. She seemed both nervous and pleased.

Irina explained how she knew Zoya. The actress seemed to relax. She pushed her daughter forward to shake hands with the visitor. Irina looked into the enormous green eyes and found something disturbing there in so young a person. It was pain or perhaps a fierce aloneness. She couldn't decide which. But she did note how little the child resembled her mother.

The dinner was pleasant and friendly. The only odd note to

Irina was how often the child looked to her mother, as if seeking approval. Zoya would always pat her on the head and smile at her, and then Victoria would return to her food. She didn't speak throughout the meal.

After dinner Zoya told her daughter to go home and do her homework and she would follow shortly. Victoria left after thanking Zenaida very formally and giving Irina a stiff little bow.

Zoya helped Zenaida clear the table. After tea was served, Zenaida began. "You understand that much as I would like to have you here for dinner, it is no easy matter in Russia today. I mean, you are an American, and . . ."

Zoya leaned forward. "Zena is my best friend. She has done this service for me. I need very much to speak with an American, one that can be trusted."

She then told Irina the whole story of herself and Jackson Tate, and of the prison years that followed. "But now I worry. If something should happen to me, my Vikka would be alone. I would like you to find Jackson and tell him he has a daughter. Give him this."

She handed Irina Victoria's photograph. Irina asked, "Does the child know any of this?"

Zoya shook her head. "No. She believes her father was a Russian pilot who was killed during the war. I will tell her the truth when you find her father. Then it will be time enough."

Irina said, "You must tell me everything you can about this Jackson Tate. It could be difficult to find him after so many years."

Zoya shrugged. "I know so little. He was in the American Navy. An officer with gold on his sleeves. He was in some way connected with your embassy here in Moscow during the war."

"Can you tell me his rank at the time? Did he ever say what state he lived in?"

"No." Zoya shook her head. "If he did, I do not remember. But he had gold stripes on his sleeves. More than one, I am certain."

"All right," Irina said. "As soon as I get home, I will write to the Department of the Navy. They should know. But how do I let you know?"

"Don't write to me," Zoya said quickly. "Write instead to Zena at the hotel."

She looked at Zenaida for approval. The woman said, "It will be all right because you lived on my floor for so long. But a postcard only. A letter would look strange. And write only if you find him. Say that you visited Paris on the way home and that while you liked Paris a lot, you liked Moscow better. I think the authorities would approve of such a message. And we will know that you have found him."

Irina agreed. When it came time to leave, Zoya said that she would walk partway with her. Zena advised her not to. Americans were too easily spotted because of their clothes. But Zoya insisted. She would be careful.

When they were outside, Zoya looked around, then put a piece of paper in Irina's hand. "What is it?" Irina asked.

"My address and telephone number. If you should come back to Moscow, get in touch with me, please."

Irina was confused. "But I thought you didn't want me to."

"Not to write," Zoya said, "but come see me if you come back. Because if I am not there, it will mean that she has betrayed me."

"Zenaida? Your best friend?"

"No one knows about this but her." Zoya made a sad gesture of helplessness. "I don't trust her completely."

As they approached the lights of the main thoroughfare, Zoya said goodnight and left Irina.

A few days later, Irina Kirk returned to Hawaii.

She wrote to the Department of the Navy in Washington, D.C.:

Dear Sirs:

I would greatly appreciate it if you could provide me with the address of Jackson Tate. He was a naval officer in 1945 attached to the American Embassy in Moscow. His former or present rank is unknown to me.

Yours truly,
Irina Kirk

She received no reply. After waiting a month, she wrote again, not knowing where else to turn. Again there was no answer. She wrote the Department of the Navy several more times, sometimes waiting for as long as two months between letters. None of her letters were ever answered.

In time, her work at the University of Hawaii and the problems of raising three children pushed the evening at Zenaida's apartment to the back of her mind.

JACKSON TATE

By 1959 Jack Tate had been retired from the Navy for nine years. He made the decision to retire shortly after he went up from Terminal Island to take over the air station at Alameda, California.

On March 10, 1949, he became Rear Admiral Jackson Rogers Tate. He was pleased, of course, but he wasn't thrilled. Jack Tate was always a logical man, as well as a man whose emotions were kept private. Making rear admiral wasn't so much an honor as an accomplishment to him, one he had worked years for. It wasn't every man who went into the Navy as a second-class seaman and made it to rear admiral.

And Jack had no illusions about the appointment. Not everybody in the Navy would be pleased by it. Jack was a "mustang," not one of the insiders of the Navy elite. Men who had come up through the ranks without being part of the Annapolis establishment never were.

But that was all right by Jack. He had served the Navy well, and it had recognized that service and rewarded him for it. That was right and fair. Cut and dried. He had given the Navy over 30 years of his life, and it had given him the life he had wanted. There were no emotional ties either way.

Rear Admiral Tate figured it out. Alameda was a big responsibility, with new headaches every day, not the least of which were the many Civil Service personnel on the base, all of whom had to be handled with tact and caution. When he considered that he could earn 75 percent of his salary as retirement pay, a man would have to be crazy to work his tail off for only 25 percent more.

In 1950 Jack Tate retired. As soon as he had his civilian wardrobe, he gathered together his navy uniforms and burned them. He had no intention of being one of those old men who trotted out their uniforms on holidays and squeezed their sagging bodies into them. He could be sentimental about his navy days when he was alone or with a few close friends. The rest was needless show, and pointless. Jack still had a chunk of life ahead of him, and it was time to get on with it.

Jack took off for Baja, California, as the guest of Erle Stanley Gardner, a friend he had made during his naval wanderings. He had no idea how long he would stay, but then he didn't have to know. He was a free man with no one waiting for him anywhere.

As it turned out, he liked Baja, California, enormously, and he spent a year and a half exploring the area in a specially built jeep. Then there were various jobs that kept him moving around the United States. For a while he was with an organization called Exhibition Ships and then a company in San Francisco that built airborne radars and dunking sonars. After that it was Westinghouse in Baltimore, Maryland.

When Irina Kirk's first letter reached him from the Department of the Navy he read it and threw it away. The letter told him nothing and he couldn't remember ever meeting a woman named Irina Kirk.

Through the years there had been other letters forwarded to him from people whom he either couldn't remember, or who had crossed his path so briefly that he saw no reason to respond. Happily, the Navy never gave out a man's address. They would just forward the mail, and the man could take it from there if he so desired.

Other letters reached him from the unknown Irina Kirk, and he threw them all away. Whoever she was, he thought, she sure didn't know her way around the Navy. All she had to do was write a letter to him and state her business, and he'd get it. That way, at least he'd know what she wanted.

And she wanted something. That much was certain. Might even be some navy widow who knew he was a widower and was looking for a new husband. He had had a few letters like that in the past.

No, whoever this Irina Kirk was, he wasn't interested. And he wasn't curious.

His last job, which kept him traveling back and forth between Florida and Washington, D.C., was with a company concerned with heavy sands. But in time, Jack got fed up with the operation and moved to Virginia Beach, Virginia, where his son, Hugh John Tate,* was living in retirement as a naval captain.

While he was living in Virginia Beach, Jack got a letter from a friend named Travis Fletcher, who had been in India for the Lowell Thomas Foundation. Fletcher thought Jack would be a good man to take his place relocating the refugees streaming out of Tibet. He wrote:

> You won't make much money at this, but you'll be doing a service which I think is necessary. You will have an air-conditioned suite in a hotel in New Delhi. You will have an office in Hong Kong, and another one in Afghanistan. However, you will spend most of your time up in the hills.

The hills, when Jack looked them up on a map, turned out to be the Himalayas. He thought about it, and then decided, why not? He was bored with his life, and this would shake it up. He wrote Travis Fletcher indicating his interest.

Before he had committed himself, however, Jack met Hazel Culley, a widow who worked as a real estate developer on her own land holdings. She was a tiny thing, only five feet tall with flaming red hair, and was affectionately called Hazy.

Jack and Hazy began seeing a great deal of each other, and

---

* Hugh John Tate had been christened Hugh John Spann, the son of Helen Spann, who was Jackson Tate's second wife. It was admiration for his stepfather and his stepfather's career that caused Hugh to take Jack's last name. In time Jack adopted him.

Jack reconsidered the whole idea of the job he had been offered. He had been interested because his life was empty. But it wasn't empty anymore, so maybe India wasn't such a good idea.

VICTORIA

Life with Mamula was exciting. In my thirteenth summer I went to the Ukraine with her, where she was filming a picture. I cannot say that I thought about becoming an actress then, but I enjoyed being on the set with her, although after a while, I found it too confining to have to sit still and be quiet.

I much preferred to go out in the streets and to play with boys. I don't know why, but girls and their games didn't interest me as much as the rough times spent with boys.

It was that summer that I became a woman. Luckily, I was in our apartment when it happened. I was confused more than frightened, but when I told Mamula, she just laughed and hugged me, and told me it was perfectly normal.

Though she really hadn't prepared me for it, she did handle the situation well. She even told me a little about sex, perhaps not everything, but enough. In any case, I wasn't particularly interested then, maybe because I was such a private person, such a loner.

I don't know what Mamula made of that because she was and is a very outgoing person. When I think of her, I always see her surrounded by people. Any apartment we lived in had a constant flow of visitors. The conversations went on long after I went to bed. I often fell asleep listening to laughter and to talk that I couldn't really understand.

But I would catch bits and pieces, and some of it puzzled me. And when I would hear my name mentioned and Mamula shushing and whispering, I would strain to hear what was being said.

I remember a woman coming to visit and saying to Mamula, "Victoria? It is not a name you hear too often in Russia."

And another lady, who patted me on my cheek and said to Mamula, "She is going to be very pretty, but she certainly doesn't look like a Russian child." They both laughed.

Finally, when I was 14 or 15, I confronted her. "Mamula, is it true that my father was a Russian pilot who was killed in the war?"

She looked at me curiously. "Why do you ask?"

"Because I don't understand. I was born in January of 1946, and the war ended in May of 1945. If you have to be pregnant for nine months to have a baby, then my papa would have been killed at the very end of the war. The last day maybe. Did that happen?"

Mamula smiled. "You are growing up, Vikka, I can see that. I think it is time for a grown-up talk between us."

We sat down at the table. Mamula took my hand. "Have you been hearing gossip?"

I shook my head. "No, but I hear you and your friends talk, and sometimes funny things are said. They make me wonder."

Mamula nodded her head. "I did not tell you before because I didn't think you could understand. But I think you are ready for the truth now."

She told me the whole story from the beginning of their love for each other, of how he had been sent out of the country, and of her years in prison because of her love for him. She made their love seem beautiful to me. "And so we never married, your father and I, because we were not allowed to be together. But our love was strong, and we wanted you."

I didn't say anything right away, not because I was shocked, but because I was caught up in the story. Mamula looked at me, and there was worry in her eyes. "You understand, Vikka? It is all right?"

I kissed her. "Of course."

Then I began to barrage her with questions about my father. What did he look like? How tall was he? What color were his eyes? Finally, Mamula stopped me. "If you want to see your papa, go stand in front of a mirror and look carefully at your own face. You will see his."

I ran to the mirror. At first, all I could see was a girl who was too tall and skinny, with arms and legs like string beans. But then I began to compare my face to Mamula's and what wasn't in her face had to be my father's. The green eyes and the dark hair and the defined cheekbones. And my height—my father must be tall, too.

I ran back to Mamula. "Let me see his picture."

"Everything is gone," she said. "When I was arrested, they confiscated everything."

"But you must have something of my papa. Something!"

"No, nothing." Then she put a hand to her mouth. "Wait, there is one thing."

She went to the bureau and started rummaging through the drawers. "Here," she said, "this was his."

She handed me a flashlight with a black and red top. "See where it says 'Made in U.S.A.'? It was his. He left it here. That is all I have."

I took it and held it against my body as if it contained some feel of him. Of course the flashlight didn't work. The batteries had been long gone, and new batteries for an American flashlight didn't exist in Russia. But it was his. That was what mattered. Something of my father was now mine.

The flashlight became my talisman. I would look at it by the hour and picture my father's hand holding it. And then my fantasy would extend and I would imagine my father standing in front of me, handsome and tall, holding the flashlight.

I said to my mother, "One day, I will meet my father."

She snorted. "Don't be silly, Vikka. We don't know where he is, or even if he is still alive."

"I will find him. You will see."

Mamula placed her hands on my shoulders. "Listen to me, Vikka. This is serious. I understand that you should want to see your papa. That is natural, but there is no way. It is very dangerous what you are saying. It could get you into a great deal of trouble."

"I don't care."

"Vikka, he was older than I. He could be dead. I know nothing about him all these years, just his name. And I think that was not enough."

I asked her what she meant by that. "Remember the night when we had dinner at Zenaida's house, and there was an American lady there named Irina Kirk?"

I dimly remembered it. "I asked her to find your papa. She said she would, and if she did she would send word. There has never been anything from her."

That upset me. If an American could not find him, how could I hope to from inside Russia? Well, I would. Somehow I would. And he would be alive. Enough had been done to me in my short life. God would not let me know about my papa if he were dead.

IRINA KIRK

In the summer of 1962 Irini Kirk, who now lived in Blooming-
ton, Indiana, and taught at Indiana University, found herself
nearly broke in Mallorca, Spain, where she had gone with her
children to work on her first novel. She wrote to the chairman
of her department at the university asking for advice. He wired
back that if she could leave the children at some Danish camp,
and then catch the Indiana University tour flight from Copenhagen to Moscow, she could serve as a tour leader, which would
provide her and her children with passage home.

Moscow was the last stop on the six-week, eight-city tour.
When she arrived, Irina realized that she had left Zoya's
address and telephone number back home. Since telephone
directories were unknown in Moscow, there was no way of
locating Zoya. But there was still Zenaida.

Irina went to the fifth floor of the Ukraina Hotel at the time
when shifts changed. There were two floor ladies there whom
Irina recognized, but neither was Zenaida. But the women
recognized Irina and seemed pleased to see her, which made it
easier to ask for Zenaida.

The women looked at each other and then intently at Irina.
It was a Russian look that Irina recognized the significance of
immediately. It meant, "We will tell you something, but we

are saying something more than we can put in words." One of the floor ladies took her off to a side. "Zena is not here."

"I can see that," Irina said. "Where is she? I would like to see her."

"We do not know. She was fired the day after you left."

Irina felt a chill. Though she could have sworn that no one had seen her entering or leaving Zenaida's apartment the night she had gone for dinner, someone obviously had. It sounded like the KGB. Had Zena been arrested or merely discharged? The chances are that she would never know.

Irina thanked the women and left the hotel. She decided not to try to locate Zoya on her own. If the KGB knew about the dinner meeting at Zenaida's, to look for Zoya might cause her harm. And why do that, when she had absolutely no news of Jack Tate? Irina Kirk returned to Indiana with her student tour.

In the summer of 1963 she went to Peru to visit a friend she hadn't seen since her childhood in China. On the day before she was to leave Peru, she called several friends and acquaintances to say good-bye. One woman she spoke with mentioned having been at a party the previous night. "A good party?" Irina asked, making polite conversation.

"No, a very boring party."

Irina laughed. "Oh, surely there must have been someone interesting there."

"Well, yes, there was one person, but only because he had been in Russia at the American Embassy in 1945."

Irina felt as if she had been struck in the chest. She screamed into the phone, "What was his name?"

The woman gasped. "Irina, what's the matter with you? I don't remember his name."

"Then give me the hostess's name and telephone number."

Irina called her immediately and described the man. "Oh, yes," the woman said and gave a name that meant nothing to Irina. For a second, she felt let down. She was hoping that it was Jackson Tate.

She got the man's telephone number and rang him up. "Yes," he said, "I remember Jack Tate."

"Please," Irina said, "I am trying to find him. Can you tell me where he is?"

"Sorry, but I haven't seen him in years. I can't help you."

He sounded ready to hang up. "Please, I have been trying to locate him for years. Don't you know any way?"

The man hesitated and then said, "Well, I do know one person in South Carolina who I believe still keeps in touch with Jack." He gave her the name and address.*

As soon as she returned home, Irina wrote to the man in South Carolina asking for Jack Tate's address. After waiting three months for a reply, Irina decided the search for Jack Tate was a lost cause.

Then several weeks later she received a letter postmarked South Carolina. The man apologized for the delay in answering, saying he simply had misplaced her letter. And he gave her Jackson Tate's current naval status and his address in Virginia Beach, Virginia. Irina stared at the paper. She could hardly believe she had in her hands what she had so long sought.

When the children had gone to bed, Irina sat down at her desk and pondered what to say in her letter to Admiral Tate. If only she knew something about him, it would be so much easier. Was he married or single? Did he have children? Did he have a wife who opened his mail? How would he respond to having his past catch up to him?

Finally, she wrote:

> Dear Admiral Tate:
>   I have news of an intimate nature for you. If you care, please phone me at this number.
>
>   Sincerely yours,
>   Irina Kirk

It was an abrupt note, she realized that, but what else could she say without risking someone destroying the letter before he saw it? And she couldn't tell him about his daughter just like that. She might then never hear from him at all. No, he had to

---

*Neither Irina Kirk nor Jackson Tate can remember the name of either the embassy man or the man in South Carolina.

call her so that she could hear his voice when she told him. That way she would know if the man cared at all for Zoya and their child.

She was at the dinner table with the children when the call came.

The voice was deep with a slight Southern slur to it, and it had a no-nonsense, commanding tone. "This is Admiral Tate. You wrote me."

It caught Irina off guard for a moment. "That is true."

"Well?"

"Forgive me, Admiral, but are you married?"

The voice sounded suspicious and a little angry. "Why do you want to know? Who are you?"

Irina had regained her composure. "I'm sorry, but first you must answer my question."

There was a pause. "No, I am not."

Irina said, "What does the name Zoya mean to you?"

She could hear the sharp intake of breath through the telephone. When he spoke again, his voice was gentler. "It means everything."

"I have seen Zoya. She wants you to know you have a daughter in Russia."

There was a grunt. Then he spoke again, and there was suspicion in his voice. "Tell me her name."

"Victoria."

He said nothing. After a few moments, Irina thought the line had gone dead. "Admiral Tate, are you there?"

He was crying. "Forgive me, Mrs. Kirk. I didn't trust you at first. Please tell me everything you know."

So the man wasn't made of iron altogether. But was it shock or sentiment that caused the tears, Irina wondered? Well, what did it matter at this point? "Look, Admiral, this is long-distance, and it is difficult for me to talk. My children are here, and it is noisy. I promise to write you a long letter with every detail I can recall. And I have a picture of Victoria which I will send to you."

That evening she sat down and wrote Jack Tate, enclosing the picture of Victoria. She sent it off the next morning by special delivery.

Two days later at two in the morning Irina Kirk's telephone rang. It was Jack Tate and he sounded drunk to her. "Irene?" He was always to call her Irene.

"Yes."

"This is Jack Tate. I'm sorry to be calling you at this hour, but you are the only one who knows the story."

"Yes?" She thought of her own children and felt a little sorry for Jack Tate. What was it like to be 65 and look at a child's picture, and to know that the child is yours and you will probably never see her?

"I've been drinking. I guess you can tell. And I've been looking at Victoria's picture, and she looks so much like my mother."

Then he told her the story she already knew of his romance with Zoya, but from his viewpoint. It added a few facts that Zoya couldn't have known. He concluded the long story with "Irene, what should I do?"

"What does your heart tell you to do?" Irina said. "I don't know how you feel about this whole thing."

"Well, I think I should get in touch with the State Department."

"No," Irina said. "It is the last thing you want to do. You don't get in touch with any officials. If you want to see Zoya and Victoria, you should go to Russia as a tourist. You call Zoya from a telephone booth, not from your hotel."

"Well, I'm thinking of what I should do. At the moment, there's a possibility that I'll be going to India on a job."

The conversation went on for another half hour, and the more he talked, the more the conviction grew in Irina Kirk that Jack Tate wasn't going to do anything. It wasn't that he didn't care, she decided, but rather that he was an old man floundering around in a dream that had blown up in his face. The affair with Zoya had been a beautiful thing in his life and he wanted to keep it that way, a dream he could always return to. But if he went and saw her, the dream would explode in the reality of an old man facing his lost love without the magic they had once shared.

When he finally hung up, Irina felt sad. It was all over, and she had accomplished her mission, and she didn't believe any-

thing would come of it. Worse yet, because of the disappearance of Zenaida, there was no way to notify Zoya that she had
found her Jackson, and Victoria wouldn't know that her father
was alive.

Well, whatever was to happen now would be up to Jack Tate.

In September of 1963, Irina Kirk went to Europe for a year
and a half to work on her Ph.D. She did not go to Russia during this time.

As things were to turn out, it was not the last time she would
be in contact with Jackson Tate. They never met face to face
but their relationship was a long one via mail and telephone.
Though they were to work together to help Victoria and Zoya,
the relationship was never a good one. They were two people
who could never understand each other.

Jack was a man who believed in doing everything directly.
Though he had been in Moscow, he still was not wise to the
Russian way of thinking. His blunt approach seemed like na-
iveté to Irina Kirk, who was Russian to the bone though she had
never lived in that country. She understood the need for de-
viousness and subtlety when dealing with Russians. Jack's
American directness and bluntness maddened her. He was a
perpetual bull in a Russian china shop, always on the verge of
wrecking everything. Jack, for his part, found Irina frustrating
and confusing. She was forever doing things off-center in an in-
direct way that he couldn't understand. To a man used to command, she always seemed to be sneaking up on things to
bypass them, while he favored a straight plunge through center.

Later on, when Irina published her book, *Profiles in Russian
Resistance,* he came to fear her. She was involved with all sorts
of dissidents, and he felt association with her could bring harm
to Victoria and Zoya.

Though they needed each other through the years ahead
working on behalf of Victoria, it was a relationship that deterio-
rated from its very beginning. Throughout its entirety, Jack felt
Irina misunderstood what he did, and Irina felt he misunderstood what she did. And on that point, each was correct.

VICTORIA

In 1962, at the age of 16, I graduated from school and entered the Dramatic Art Studio to become an actress. My interest in a film career came about, I think, from the time I spent with my mother when she was making films. I know the choice pleased her. She had said to me the year before, when I began to show some interest: "Yes, I wish you would become an actress, but it must be your decision. I do not think it right that I should help you. There is nothing worse than an actress without talent or skill. You must prove yourself, and if you can show that you have the talent, then I will welcome you with all my heart. My second life is in you, Vikka."

There was a theater attached to the studio where I appeared in plays along with the other students. One day a lady from Mosfilm came to our school and to the room where I was with about 20 other students. She had us line up and she walked in front of us, studying us. Then she said, "Well, this one" and then, "That one." And I was one of the "ones" she chose.

"Those of you I have selected," she said, "please come to the studio tomorrow morning and we will see what can be done with you. It is a new film, and there are some parts. . . ."

She turned to leave, but those of us she had picked rushed

after her to find out what the film was. It was to be called
Good-bye, Boys, a drama about life in Russia in 1938–39, based
on a very popular current novel.

As soon as I could leave school for the day I bought a copy of
the book and read it through that evening. In my mind I saw
myself as the heroine, of course. I didn't sleep that night.

The next morning when I arrived at the studio, I discovered
that our school wasn't the only one the lady had visited. There
were about 50 young people in the room. I knew I didn't look
typically Russian but I convinced myself that that was an asset.
I would be so strikingly different they would have to choose
me for the film.

But then the director came into the room, and my heart
sank. He was a short man, at least a head shorter than I was. I
knew he would never choose me. And he didn't. He barely
glanced at me as he passed by to stop and talk with others.

As he started to leave the room, without thinking, I shouted,
"What about me?"

He turned and looked at me. "What about you?"

"Well, you brought me here, and I am an actress and I want
to work in this film."

He seemed amused by my nerve. "With that body and that
face?"

I felt myself blushing. While I thought myself too tall and
too thin, I knew that I was attractive—enough of Mamula's
friends had told me so. But I wasn't vain about it. It was how I
looked, that was all, and it could be of use to me as an actress.
"What's wrong with my face and body?"

I was amazed at my nerve. I thought that at any second the
director would have me thrown out of the studio. Instead, he
came over to me. "If you have read the book, you know that
the heroine is a tiny girl who lives near the sea. I see her as a
very romantic, lyrical type. You are much too tall."

"But I can play the part."

He patted my face. "Forget it, my darling." He studied me
for a moment. "But I think there is another part that you would
be exactly right for just as you are."

I made my screen debut as one of the heroine's two girl
friends. It was a fairly good part with quite a few lines, at least

in the script, but by the time the film was edited, it was reduced to a small part. But it was a beginning.

As soon as I finished *Good-bye, Boys*, I went into my second picture, *Lost Music*, which was filmed in Leningrad. This time I had one of the leading roles, but it wasn't much of a picture and it made few demands on me as an actress. It was a mild love story in which I played an 18-year-old girl. This film, like so many of my others, made use of the fact that I was becoming pretty and very little use of what I like to think of as my talent, but at the beginning I was grateful to be working. And Mamula was proud.

My third movie was a good one, one of the best I was ever in. It was called *Dvoe*, which means two, and it won a gold medal at the Moscow International Festival. I played a deaf-mute, and at 18 I found myself a recognized actress. Mamula saw the movie several times, and each time she cried.

The film played all over the world under the title *Ballad of Love*. I was told that it would even play in the United States, and I prayed that my father would see it and recognize me, and come to Moscow to see me.

For as exciting as my career was becoming, I never forgot my father and my dreams about seeing him. I wanted that more than anything else in the world. Yet I rarely spoke about him outside of our home. Mamula had warned me, shortly after she told me the truth, that I must not repeat it to the children at school. "You could be hurt. It is enough that you know it. For others, if they ask, your father was a Russian pilot who died during the war. Promise me, Vikka."

As time went by and we did not hear from Irina Kirk, it even became difficult for me to discuss my father with Mamula. I would see her mouth tense up with bitterness when I started to ask questions about him. "Vikka, let it be. You know about him, and that must be enough. Either Irina Kirk did not find him, or she found him dead."

"But, Mamula, I cannot leave it like that. He is my papa."

Her smile was a sour one. "And he was something more to me, and I never heard one word from him. And I have lived with that. You must, too."

I cried in bed that night, hugging his flashlight. It couldn't end this way, in nothingness.

He started appearing in my dreams. There was one in particular that was so strong and vivid that it carried over into my waking life. It became a part of my daylight fantasy-world, which was strongly built around him.

I saw him in Moscow, telephoning me from the hotel in which he was staying. He spoke in Russian but with what my dream self said was a strong American accent. "Victoria, can you guess who is calling?"

"I said, "No."

"Don't you remember what you asked Irina Kirk to do?"

I felt as if there were electric wires running through my body. "I cannot believe it!"

"Yes, it is your father, and I am here at the hotel, right across the street from your apartment building."

"When can I see you?"

He laughed. "Right now, but don't tell your mother that I am here."

"How will I recognize you?"

Another laugh. There was such wonderful warmth in his laugh. "Don't worry, I will know you. Remember, your mother sent me a picture."

I ran like a wild thing from our apartment and across the street to the hotel, which had a very long flight of stairs leading up to the door. I ran up all of them. There were people all over the top step, but none of them was my father. I started to panic, but then I saw him coming through the crowd, which parted in front of him like wheat in the wind.

He was a tall man with a good, strong body, about 50 years old. He was wearing a gray suit and he had some newspapers under his arm. He smiled at me, and we ran to each other and cried in each other's arms.

Then he kissed me and said, "I am very glad to see you. Don't tell your mother anything, because I don't want to disappoint her. I have this chance to be here for only two or three hours and that is all. Then I am leaving."

I threw my arms around him again. "Can't you stay here for just this one day, Papa?"

He smiled down at me. "No, it is against the laws of the Soviet Union. I came only to see you, and now I must go."

He kissed my forehead and then turned into the crowd on the steps and disappeared.

I wanted to stop him, but I couldn't seem to move.

When I awoke, there were tears on my face, but I felt happy. And the dream stayed with me and became a part of the truth of my life. I began to believe I had really seen my father. I wove the dream into my life and even embroidered on it.

I told several of Mamula's friends that I had seen my father. They were surprised, but I convinced them that I was telling the truth. I even described him for them. And I told them my mother didn't know, because he didn't want her to. He had sneaked into the Soviet Union, which was very dangerous, just to see me.

Many of her friends accepted the story as truth, though they all found it difficult to believe that Mamula didn't know. "Oh," I said, "that is because he is married in America and cannot be with her. He came only for me, because he loves me."

In time Mamula found out what I was telling her friends. She sat down with me one night. There was concern in her face. "Why are you telling this story, Vikka? Don't you know the difference between a dream and reality?"

"I saw him, Mamula, as real as life itself."

She smiled. "You saw him because you wanted to see him, that is all. But we both know it was a dream. Put him back in your dreams, Vikka. That is where he belongs."

I leaned against her and she wrapped her arms around me. "It is not enough. I need him so badly."

"I know, Vikka, I know. But no one ever gets everything he wants. And very often we do not get what we want most. That's the way life is. You have him, Vikka, as much as you ever will. Let it be enough."

I said nothing. I didn't want to hurt Mamula. But I couldn't put my father away. How could I forget what I had never had?

I made a silent promise to myself that I would try not to speak about him in front of my mother.

* * *

Appearing in a successful film at the age of 18, having people recognize me in the streets of Moscow, were both wonderful and frightening. But it happened too quickly, and I knew that I really didn't have much technique behind me as an actress. How long could I get by on raw talent? And without a diploma as an actress, I would have a hard time getting work in films. For every part available to a "free artist," 350 people showed up.

I talked it over with Mamula and with other actors whom I respected. A diploma was the answer. I would improve both my technique and my salary.

I applied for admittance to the Soviet Institute of Cinematography, the only school of its kind in all of the Soviet Union. The competition each year was very strong, with hundreds of people auditioning for each opening. The year that I auditioned there were 360 applicants for each of the 19 places that were open.

I studied as I had never studied before and passed both the examinations in my academic subjects and the four auditions required of aspiring acting students.

I entered the four-year course of study at the Institute.

For a while, only my work at the Institute—and my fantasies about my father—filled my mind.

JACKSON TATE / IRINA KIRK

While Irina Kirk was in Europe working on her Ph.D., Jackson Tate and Hazel Culley were married. Soon afterward, they moved to Orange Park, Florida.

In the summer of 1966 Irina Kirk again had the opportunity to go into Russia as a student-tour leader. Since she was determined that on this trip she would locate Zoya and Victoria, she sent a letter to Jack asking if he had any message for her to take. Her letter was returned to her marked "Return to Sender. Addressee Unknown." Irina then telephoned the Virginia Beach number and was told by an operator that the telephone number was no longer operative. She was stunned. Jackson Tate had disappeared again.

When Irina Kirk hung up the telephone, it marked the beginning of an approximately five-year break in communication between them. It also marks a strange, unexplained portion of the story.

Jack and Hazel Tate say they were easy to reach. They had left a forwarding address with the post office, and to their knowledge all mail sent to them in Virginia Beach was forwarded. Furthermore, Jack distinctly remembered that in one of his telephone conversations with Irina, he had told her she could always reach him through the Department of the Navy. All she had to do was address the letter to him in care of the Navy and it would be forwarded. But she never did that. Jack could never figure out why.

Irina, on the other hand, could never understand why Jack Tate did nothing after she told him about the existence of his daughter. The answer lies somewhere in the personality of Jackson Rogers Tate. It was not that he didn't care about the daughter he had never seen, and it was not that he wasn't certain that a daughter of Zoya's existed fathered by him. He had known that to be a fact since the moment Irina told him the name. But he was a man in his late 60s, tired by life and failing in health. He cared that a daughter of his existed, but there was a remoteness to his caring because he had never seen her.

Furthermore, he didn't know what it was that he could do. He didn't believe Victoria could come out of Russia, and he was certain that he couldn't get in. They had expelled him once, and his impression of the Soviet government was that they didn't forget anything.

Probably the most important reason for his lack of activity was his distrust of Irina Kirk. It began almost from the very beginning when she was writing the Department of the Navy trying to locate him without saying why, instead of addressing a letter to him in care of the Navy. And her questions—"Are you married?" "Does the name Zoya mean anything to you?"—what were they all about? No matter how he had answered her questions, the fact that he had a daughter was still the same. Why was she always so mysterious instead of direct?

No, Jack did not trust Irina Kirk. When speaking about her, he said, "I was keeping my fingers strictly on my number. I learned that in the Navy. That's the way you keep out of trouble in this world."

In the few days that the tour allowed Irina to be in Moscow, she did not succeed in seeing Zoya. Making discreet inquiries through friends, she learned that Zoya and Victoria were out of the city at Zoya's dacha. She did learn, however, that Victoria had begun a successful film career and that Zoya was as popular as ever.

Beyond that, Irina felt a sense of total frustration. At home she had not been able to find the slip of paper with Zoya's address and telephone number on it that the actress had pressed into her hand the night they had met. And in Moscow she found no one who could give her the information, and she didn't dare inquire at Zoya's studio, not after the disappearance of Zenaida. To ask, and therefore to identify herself, might bring harm to the mother and daughter.

It had been seven years since Zoya had told her story to Irina, and now Irina had to face the fact that she had lost everyone involved.

VICTORIA

I look back on the men in my life, and I don't know exactly what to make of myself. In America, where there is so much talk of psychology, and every action can be explained in terms of subconscious drives, someone would probably come up with an answer. But I was 19 when Erakli came into my life, and the place was Moscow. Freud and psychiatry are known there, but the people do not walk around psychoanalyzing themselves. One is what one is, and one tries to do better, that is all. We do not search for our motivations.

I have been told that probably I have always been looking for a father, that I find him in every man I get involved with, and that in time the relationship fails, because for me it must fail so that my father can go out of my life the way he went out of my mother's. I have been told, too, that I want to be a victim, that I am most comfortable in that role, because my childhood was spent among people who considered me an enemy and rejected me, enforcing in me the idea that I should be rejected. What can I say to all of that? Perhaps it is the truth. Certainly it is an explanation, which is all I can say for any of it. I don't know.

* * *

Erakli was at the Institute when I was there. He was studying to be a film director like his father, who was rather famous. Erakli was tall and slim, with brown hair and dark eyes, quite handsome. And he was half-Georgian, which meant Mamula didn't like him before she met him. She never forgot that Stalin and Beria were Georgians. "They are all tyrants," she said. "They are wild people, and terribly jealous."

Her opinion of Georgians, and Erakli in particular, didn't bother me, because I wasn't that interested in him at first. He was just one of many men at the Institute that I went out with. I paid no particular attention to him, though I knew he was very interested in me. I often found him waiting in front of our apartment house for me to come out, or he'd be in front of the room in which I had a class at the Institute.

And then one of the deans at the Institute called me in and asked me to pay some attention to Erakli. "He has stopped studying, did you know that? He forgets his classes to go and stand in front of a room that you are in."

"But what can I do?" I said. "I don't think of him seriously because he is still so young." Actually, he was the same age as I, but what did that matter? I didn't want to be in love or get married to anyone at that point.

"His father is very upset," the dean said. "Be kind to Erakli."

Romance began when Erakli was home in Georgia, and I was sent to a film festival in that part of the country, though in a different city. Erakli called me every day inviting me to come visit him at his home. I had one free day, and I thought, why not?

I went to his family's home for dinner, and after the meal, his parents began to plead Erakli's case for him. His mother said, "I can see that he is truly in love with you."

The father chimed in. "He has lost his head, no doubt of it."

I stared at my tea, too embarrassed to look up. I wondered what Erakli was doing across the table.

"You must really decide, my dear," his mother said. "It is not fair to our son."

I probably should have ended it right then, but I said nothing. Besides, I liked Erakli. I was not in love with him, but I was not in love with anybody else, so there was no need to end it.

When we both returned to the Institute, I began to see more of him. We studied together a great deal, and I always found him warm and kind to me. Even Mamula seemed to like him, despite his being a Georgian.

We went together for a year and a half, and during the third year at the Institute we were married. I know now I didn't love him, but I thought I did.

Because we were married in January, near the time of exams at the Institute, we didn't have a honeymoon. We went directly from the wedding to Mamula's apartment to begin our marriage. A husband and wife and the mother of one of them, all in a two-room apartment, is never a good idea, but we had no choice. This was the apartment I was registered to live in, so there was nothing we could do, any of us, but make the best of it.

It affected our sex life from the very beginning. We never knew when Mamula might come bursting into our room. It put a nervous edge to the act so that unless we were burning with passion, it was easier to put the desire aside for another day. Our other solution, to meet in the apartment when Mamula was out, was far from satisfactory. It made the act of love somehow sneaky and therefore cheap, as if we were doing something that we shouldn't. Sex left our marriage early.

In a very short time, I realized that we were both too young for marriage. We were students with careers ahead of us. Marriage was a settling down, and we were far from ready to do that. I don't know if Erakli sensed it, but I did.

And I soon realized that I wasn't getting the interest, the attention, the emotional support, I needed from a husband. When I came to him with my troubles, I could see confusion in his eyes, and sometimes annoyance that I was interrupting whatever he was doing. He would hold me for a moment, then pat me on the back as if I were some pet animal he was dismissing.

Erakli was a quiet man of intelligence, but there was also a wild Georgian streak in him. I first became aware of it one night when we went to a friend's apartment for an evening of cards. Wine was served while we played, but I do not think Erakli drank enough to make him drunk. Something upset him, I don't remember what, and suddenly he grabbed an empty wine bottle by the neck and broke it over the top of his head. He looked at me as he did it, and I guess he saw what he wanted. I was both shocked and embarrassed. He took another empty bottle and repeated the ridiculous performance. The evening ended shortly after.

I was furious on the way home. "What do you think you were doing back there?"

His head went up and he didn't answer me. But it was the beginning of many exhibitions of this strange behavior. I could feel myself literally drawing away from this man I called my husband, thinking of him as some strange child I couldn't understand.

I also came to realize that the episodes of wildness often occurred when I had been talking too long with some male friend of ours. When I asked Erakli if it was jealousy that caused him to make a fool of himself in public, I got no answer.

Of course I didn't tell Mamula about any of this. I didn't need another one of her speeches on what she thought of Georgians.

I think we had been married about six months when the next major incident occurred. It was at our apartment, an evening when we had friends from the Institute in. Mamula was somewhere outside of Moscow making a film. We had wine and vodka for our guests, and it was a happy evening. Except for Erakli's behavior. He grew more and more silent. Finally, I went over to him and I said in a low voice, so that our friends couldn't hear, "What is the matter with you? We have company. Why aren't you joining in?"

He looked at me with hurt eyes. "I don't think you need me. You seem to laugh more with our friends than you do with me."

I was fed up with that hurt-little-boy attitude of his. I said, "If you think that is the case, then why don't you go out somewhere where you *will* feel needed?"

He nodded curtly, with that I'll-show-you mannerism I had gotten so used to, and walked into the next room, Mamula's bedroom. I turned back to our guests, determined for once not to let Erakli and his childish sulks upset another evening for me.

About fifteen minutes later one of our guests went into the other room. He shouted for me. "Vikka!"

I ran in. Erakli was sitting on the side of Mamula's bed. His straight-edge razor was on the floor. Blood was trickling from both of his wrists into a shoebox he had placed at his feet. When I called to him, he looked up but his eyes seemed glazed.

I took him to the hospital where they stitched his wrists. He hadn't cut very deeply. When I asked Erakli why he had done such a terrible thing, he said, "You know," and that was all I ever learned.

When Mamula heard about it, she pronounced him crazy.

Three months later, he did it again, this time along the back of the wrists. Again, he did it in our apartment so that I would find him in time. I waited until they had stitched his hands, and then we walked home together. "They told me that you didn't cut very deeply, Erakli. Tell me why. Is it that you don't really want to kill yourself? That you do this so that I will see you bleeding and be punished?"

I got no answer. "This is no marriage, Erakli," I said. "We both know that. If I make you so unhappy that you take a razor to yourself, why do we stay together?"

He looked at me. "I love you very much, Vikka."

"What kind of love is it that comes with razors?"

He promised he would never do it again, and he never did. But the marriage was over. I knew it, and I am certain he knew it, too. Still, we went on for a little over a year.

Every evening was the same. After we came home from our classes, Mamula would go into her room, and we would go into ours, never speaking. The silence finally got to me. One night I could stand it no longer. "How long are we going to go on in this crazy way, Erakli?"

"We are married," he said.

"No!" I shouted. "We have a piece of paper between us, that is all we share."

"Are you blaming me?"

"It is not a question of blame. It is a question of what is between us, and there is nothing. We are just taking up each other's lives. We do not belong together."

He stood up and put on his overcoat. "If we do not belong together, then I am going out."

I stepped in front of him. "Why don't you stay and talk instead? You are running away! You go out, you cut your wrists, you smash bottles—everything is a running away for you!"

He started for the door when Mamula came into our room. "Enough, please! Do you want the whole building to hear?"

"Hear?" I shouted. "What will they hear? They will only hear my husband going out, that's all." I looked at Erakli. "Well, if you are going, go!"

Before Mamula or I realized what was happening Erakli ran across the room and crashed against the window. I screamed. We were eight floors above the sidewalk. But his shoulders were too wide for the narrow window, so that only his head went through the glass, and he was stuck, his shoulders wedged against the frame.

Mamula and I eased him out. Blood was pouring down his face, but by some miracle he wasn't too badly hurt. There was only one deep cut—the rest were all minor.

We cleaned him up, and later, when we were all calmer, I said, "Erakli, what is the sense of us anymore?"

He said, "I know, Vikka, you are right."

We separated, and in 1969 I went back to the same office in which we had been married and filled out the divorce papers.

I met my second husband, Sergei, while I was still married to Erakli, though of course I didn't know he would be my second husband. What is more, he came into my life out of my mother's past.

Mamula and Nadja, Sergei's mother, had been classmates at the Institute. But Nadja didn't become an actress. She felt her talent wasn't strong enough, so she studied law and became a lawyer. She and Sergei's father were separated shortly after the boy's birth.

Years later Nadja admired me in one of my films, and when she saw my name on the screen, she thought of her friend Zoya and guessed that I might be her daughter. She telephoned Mamula, they were reunited, and I met Sergei.

Nadja knew of my fights with Erakli. I think she was even at the apartment when one occurred. In any case, she knew when the marriage ended, and I think she had me picked out for her son. Why, I do not know, since she turned out to be a very possessive mother who didn't really want to part with her only child.

Sergei was 29, with blond hair, blue eyes, and the build of an American football player. He was an architect, from a different world than mine. His world had a calm, factual approach to things, as opposed to the emotional world of actors. I think that, in part, is what drew me to him, the contrast between him and Erakli.

I was impressed with Sergei's intelligence. He spoke German and English, as well as Russian. He was well read, with opinions on everything, and he was kind to me. He introduced me to his friends, and I brought him to gatherings of mine. And that seemed exciting because the two groups were so different. What I didn't realize was that we never mixed our worlds. We didn't even try.

You would think that after one bad marriage I would have learned something. And yet when Sergei gave me a ring with a diamond in it, I accepted it, knowing that I was not in love with him. He did not excite me sexually. But I respected him greatly, and I felt comfortable and safe with him, and I guess I confused that with love.

Yet I had learned one thing and that was a fear of marriage. I didn't want to fail again. Although I moved in with Sergei, into a six-room apartment he shared with his mother, I made it clear I did not want to marry him. Not yet. I needed time. We had our own rooms in the apartment and his mother never came barging in on us as Mamula had done to Erakli and me. But life with Nadja wasn't easy. It struck me as funny at first. The man I was living with trusted me, but his mother didn't. She had chosen me for her son, and she was going to make certain that nothing took me away from him. I soon became aware that whenever I got a telephone call, she would pick up the extension and listen in. And several times I discovered that she followed me when I went out of the apartment to see where I went and to whom I spoke. It wasn't that she cared so much about me and my reputation. She only cared about her son's reputation. His woman had to be perfect and, if Nadja could arrange it, have no life outside of him.

Sergei accepted our arrangement. I had said to him, "I really don't want to get married. Let it be enough that I am living with you. I belong to you, and I share your happiness."

Sergei agreed to these terms, and we truly enjoyed each other's company. I think Mamula accepted the arrangement, too. Or if she didn't, I cannot remember her saying anything against it. After all, she, too, remembered Erakli.

The most Sergei ever said about marriage was that he hoped one day soon I would reconsider. It wasn't only that he loved me, but it would be better for his career if he were married. Our arrangement had earned him a little black mark in his dossier.

But Nadja couldn't accept the arrangement. Why should her perfect son have a mark in his dossier? Wasn't marriage to her Sergei the best possible life for a woman? What was the matter with me?

I have never been able to take pressure. After five months of living with Sergei and having Nadja work on me, I gave in. Perhaps Nadja was right. What was the matter with me? I was happy enough with Sergei, and life with him was good. So we went down to the registry office and got the official stamp. We were married in 1971.

I wish I could say the situation with Nadja changed once we were married, but it didn't. The only thing that helped was the arrival of Uncle Anatoly, Nadja's brother. He was a delightful man who understood Sergei and me, and saw what his sister was doing. Of course, she didn't listen to him either. She shouted at him, "You cannot understand what it is to be a parent. How could you when you have never even married?"

He only laughed at her. "Does marriage give you special brains, Nadja?"

In 1971 I was lucky to work again with Misha Bogin, the director who had chosen me for *Dvoe.* The new film was called *About Love,* and I played a sculptor who couldn't compromise her artistic ideals to conform to the standard love-and-marriage role of the average woman.

You would think that Nadja would have been pleased that her daughter-in-law was a film actress, and one for whom people predicted a bright future. But I think she saw my film work as taking precedence over my duties as Sergei's wife. Though she could not follow me into the studio, she was again following me in the streets and listening in on my telephone calls.

When I wasn't working on a film, Nadja and Sergei made my life so comfortable that it was almost as if they were destroying me with luxury. The maid would bring me breakfast in bed, no matter how many times I told Nadja that I preferred to get up and come to the table. In between times Nadja anticipated almost everything I might want to leave the house to get. I began to feel as if I were a pet bird living in a cage. I gained weight and I grew lazy, taking naps in the middle of the day to rest up from mornings in which I did nothing.

But even without Nadja, my life with Sergei was not going well. He was working on an advanced degree so he wasn't too eager to go out evenings. And when we did, he preferred we see his friends. Although I could understand this and they were all polite and friendly to me, we really had nothing to say to each other. I knew nothing of the scientific world that interested them, so I spent my time smiling and saying nothing.

When we visited with my friends, Sergei was quiet. He didn't feel comfortable in the theatrical and film world. And his silence made my friends uncomfortable.

But more than anything else, Nadja's continual butting in was the major problem. After one particularly unpleasant scene over her following me in the streets, she took a new tactic. Now it was a baby. Each night at dinner, she turned the conversation to our having a child. Why didn't we? Sergei should be a father while he was still young. What was the future for us, what were we working for if not for a child? Though I told her in no uncertain terms that I didn't feel ready to become a mother, and Sergei backed me up in this, Nadja went right on campaigning for the grandchild she wanted.

Finally, I told Sergei and his mother I had taken all I was going to take. Mamula had moved to a new and larger apartment on Kutuzovsky Prospekt, and I was going to move in with her.

"I am leaving with you," Sergei said.

What could I say? I was pleased that Sergei saw things my way, but in truth I would not have been terribly unhappy if he had stayed with his mother. I knew that no matter where we lived, so long as I was with Sergei, Nadja would always be a problem in our lives.

We were only at Mamula's a little over a month when I got a call to go to Leningrad to appear in a film. When I realized that I wanted to go far more than I wanted to be with Sergei, I knew our marriage was over. I told Mamula, "I don't care about his great future, or the prestige of his job, or any of it. I must be free."

Mamula shook her head. "I don't understand you. Vikka, what is it you want? You will never find a better man than Sergei. He is perfect for you. Are you throwing him away because of his mother?"

"No. Even without her it would be over. I just don't love him."

"All right," she said. She came to me and took my face in her hands. "What happened to you, Vikka, in the years when I was not with you? Can you love any man?"

"Of course," I said, but her question frightened me. I felt as if there were an icicle moving down inside my body. It was a question I had asked myself. I was 25 years old, and already I had two bad marriages. I shoved the question out of my mind. It was like a disease I didn't want to think about.

When I told Sergei that I was going to Leningrad and I wasn't coming back to him, he said, "I will wait for you."

He moved back to Nadja's apartment while I was away. Two or three months after my return he called me. I had had plenty of time to think of my life with Sergei, and there were things I missed. He was a good man, and perhaps if I tried harder I could make it work. So when he asked if I would come back to him and give it another chance, I said yes.

Uncle Anatoly burst into tears when I came into the apartment. He threw his arms around me. Nadja kissed me and even apologized for the past, but I watched her face as she spoke. There was no expression, no true warmth in her eyes, and she sounded as if she were reciting a piece she had learned by heart.

The minute I entered the room Sergei and I shared when we first married, I felt my throat close up and my arms grow rigid. It was as if every stick of furniture was reaching out to smother me. Sergei closed the door and came to me. He put his arms around me, and suddenly I wanted to scream. I wriggled free. "Please don't, Sergei. Maybe tomorrow, but not now. Right now, I can't sleep with you. I've got to sort it all out."

We slept that night side by side as if we were two soldiers sharing a small tent. Well, Sergei slept. I lay most of the night staring up at the ceiling.

The next day I realized that our marriage couldn't be saved, at least not as far as I was concerned. The room, the apartment, held too many unhappy memories for me. I told Sergei that it was not his fault. It was just over, and I should have realized it and not come back to him at all.

I had to face what I had felt way back at the beginning of it all. I did not love Sergei. And being told that he was a wonderful man and a desirable husband was meaningless.

We were divorced in 1972. I pushed that nagging question— could I love anyone?—far, far back in my mind, and told myself instead that I had had enough of marriage. I had a good career, many friends, and many men interested in me. Sometime, someday, I would love, but not now. Now, I had too much else to do.

I was happy for a while with my freedom. Only when I thought of my father did I become sad. Where was he? Why didn't he come to see me? Why didn't he write? And most frightening of all, why didn't he want me?

Then Kolia took over my life completely. All of the worst moments of my life before Kolia were paradise by comparison to the years with him. He came closer to destroying me than all of Kazakhstan ever had.

IRINA KIRK

The year 1973 was an important one for Dr. Irina Kirk, now a professor of Russian Literature at the University of Connecticut. It was the year she was to establish contact again with all the parties involved in the Fyodorova-Tate story.

She had begun work on her book *Profiles in Russian Resistance*, a collection of interviews she conducted with Soviet dissidents, which would be published in 1975. She was interviewing a man whose field was international law, a man she had no reason to believe would know anyone connected with the Russian theater. Directly after the interview she was taking off for Russia. Whether it was simply making conversation or something intuitive, Irina Kirk does not know, but she turned in the doorway and said, "Do you happen to know either Zoya Fyodorova or her daughter, Victoria Fyodorova?"

He said, "Yes, I do. Victoria was married to a friend of mine when I was in Russia and I used to call often at their apartment."

He was able to supply Irina with the telephone number from memory, but then asked, "Why do you want to see her?"

Irina shook her head. "It is for private reasons."

"Frankly I wouldn't advise it," the man said. "Victoria has a drinking problem. While I do not believe that she would betray you or do anything to bring harm to you, who knows what she might say if she has enough to drink? And would she be able to know then if there were KGB people in the room? I really would avoid her if I were you."

Irina thanked him and immediately decided to ignore his advice though his news startled her. The last time she had seen Victoria she had been a girl, 13 or 14 years old, being sent home to do her schoolwork. It had been enough of a shock when Irina had seen the film *Ballad of Love* and realized that the child had become a woman. But now to learn that she was a divorcée with a drinking problem!

As soon as Irina arrived in Moscow, she went to a telephone outside of her hotel and dialed Zoya's number. A woman's voice answered, sharp and impatient. "Yes?"

"Zoya?"

"Not home," the woman snapped.

"When will she be home?"

"She is away for the summer. Who is this?"

"Is Victoria there?"

"Also away. Who *is* this?"

"You don't know me," Irina said, beginning to feel annoyance with the rudeness from the other end of the line. "Will you at least take a message for Zoya?"

"Very well. What is it?"

Not knowing to whom she was speaking, Irina chose her words carefully. "Please tell Zoya that a friend of hers called, a friend she has not seen since 1959, someone who is not from here."

The voice softened. "You are not Irina, are you?"

"Yes."

"Forgive me, I know all about you. I am Zoya's sister, Alexandra, just visiting. I thought you were one of those silly girls—fans—who call here at all hours. I always tell them they are away indefinitely. Please, please call back in half an hour. Zoya just went to the store."

When Irina called back, Zoya picked up in the middle of the first ring. She had to have been sitting beside the telephone. "Iritchka?"

"Zoyka?" The bond between them made them leap to the familiar forms right away, not a common occurrence among Russians.

"When can I see you?" Zoya asked.

"Right away."

"Good. Tell me your hotel."

Irina told her, and Zoya said she would meet her outside the hotel in ten minutes.

As she stood in the street looking for a familiar face among the hundreds passing by, Irina wondered if she would recognize Zoya. But then she saw heads turning as a woman walked by, and two young girls running up to her, grabbing her hands. It was Zoya.

The two women embraced. Irina expected the first question to be about Jack Tate. Instead, Zoya said, "Let's go to see Victoria."

"Where is she?"

"She is at our dacha," and she named a town in an area the Russians refer to as Little Switzerland, perhaps because it contains a few low hills. Irina knew that as a tourist she was restricted to a 25-mile radius, and the dacha was 50 miles or more away. Since she was working on her book while in the Soviet Union, she was not anxious to do anything that could get her expelled. "Couldn't we telephone Victoria and ask her to come to Moscow?"

Zoya shook her head. "There is no telephone there, and I begin a new film early tomorrow morning, so there is only today."

She looked so disappointed that Irina decided to take the chance.

Throughout the entire train ride and the bus ride that followed, Zoya never once asked about Jack Tate. That surprised Irina, but she decided that Zoya was being cautious because of the other people in the compartment.

Zoya talked about Victoria and how well she was doing in motion pictures.

Irina told her that she had seen Victoria in *Ballad of Love* and thought she was very beautiful and a good actress.

Zoya beamed, like the proud mother she was. But then a

shadow seemed to pass over her face. "When we get there, you will probably meet Kolia. I am certain he is still there."

"Oh? Who is he?"

"He is a very well-known screenwriter," Zoya said. "He has even taught at the Institute."

"Why should he be at the dacha?"

"Because Victoria is living with him—why, I do not really know. He is so much older than she."

It was the bitter edge to Zoya's voice that told Irina Zoya did not like Kolia. "Perhaps he is a father figure to Victoria."

"Father figure? What does that mean, Iritchka?"

When Irina explained what she meant, she observed from Zoya's reaction that she had struck home. Zoya was a bright woman, and Irina could almost see her digesting this new bit of information and tucking it away inside of herself.

The dacha was on the shore of the Moscow River. There was a man sitting on the porch and Irina knew immediately that this had to be Kolia, but she was shocked. When Zoya said he was older, she had pictured someone perhaps in his late 30s or early 40s, but this man looked well into his 50s.

VICTORIA

I was 26 or 27 when Kolia came into my life. I had met him long before that, first, I think, when I was 18. Someone introduced us at a party. Naturally, I had heard of him. Kolia was, and is, a very well-known film writer in Russia with a marvelous sense of comedy. Later on, I encountered him several times at the Institute, where he taught a course in screen writing. But except for his fame as a screenwriter, he meant nothing to me in those days. For one thing, he was 25 years older than I. For another thing, he was a member of the Communist Party, which meant that he had political interests. I did not. I have never been a political person. Also, I heard that he had a drinking problem. Not that I ever saw him drunk at the Institute, but the idea of it didn't make him any more appealing to me.

After my divorce from Sergei, I was very unsure of myself. I had been through two divorces, and that frightened me. Had I chosen the wrong men, or was it me? I couldn't escape from the question, but I did my best to run away from it. I buried myself in my film work, and I went to every party to which I was invited. But if I met a man who attracted me and I could tell he was interested, the question popped up. Did I dare to get involved again?

It was at a party given by an actress friend. Kolia was suddenly standing in front of me. I could tell that he was a little drunk, but it meant nothing to me. After all, it was a party. He had two glasses in his hand. He shoved one at me. "What is it?" I asked.

He laughed. "What else is that color? Vodka, of course."

I tried to hand it back to him. "It is too much for me."

"You drink, don't you?" I nodded my head. "Then drink this. It can only make you feel better. And if you get drunk, so what? What can happen to you in the middle of all these people? To your health!"

He drank his in one long swallow. I took a sip of mine. Before I knew what was happening, he had his hand under my elbow and was steering me to a corner of the room. "Come, we will talk."

From that moment I was Kolia's property. It was his way. He just took me over completely. Come here, go there, drink this.

Kolia was not a handsome older man, not at all. There was a perpetually messy look about him, but I began to find him attractive. I think it was his great sense of authority and the confidence he had about himself. It was such a change from the warmth and patience of Sergei and the hungry-puppy-dog attitude of Erakli. If ever there was a man who was like a fantasy father it was Kolia. He just took over and I didn't have to think at all.

"Sit here," he said and motioned to two women to get off the sofa. "Now, we will talk. I saw your last film."

"Did you like it?"

"It was trash. And you were dreadful in it."

How dare he? I started to get up.

"Sit," he said, and pushed me back down. "Did you think the picture was any good?"

"Well, no."

"Then how could you be any good in it?"

I had to smile. The man was outrageous.

He called to someone, and two new glasses of vodka were

brought to us. "Finish that one," he said to me, "and drink this. And I will tell you about greatness in film."

I was fascinated by him. It was like being hypnotized. He just overwhelmed me with his sheer power. Also the vodka was beginning to affect me. I forgot that we were in a room filled with people. There was only Kolia. How impressed I was that he had chosen me. Everyone in the Russian film world knew his work. He was supposed to be a genius, and I didn't doubt it for a moment. Not then, at least.

I did try to refuse the second drink. "Please, I am dizzy already."

"Vodka makes the world a more beautiful place. And you are with me. I will see that you get home."

I obeyed him and all I can remember after that is that we talked late into the night—or Kolia talked.

I remember that he tried to force his way into Mamula's apartment, but I kept him out. I remember also that he kissed me several times and ran his hands over my body before I finally got free of him and closed the door in his face.

The next morning I was barely through my first coffee when the telephone rang. It was Kolia. He wanted to see me that evening. I told him that I was going to dinner with some friends. He told me to cancel it, and like a fool, I allowed him to talk me into doing it.

In a very short time I belonged to him, and he turned my life into a hell. His solution to all my problems was vodka or cognac. I became an alcoholic. I also became his victim.

What had first attracted me to him, his great sense of confidence that seemed to make the world safe for me, soon changed to a dominance that crushed me. I have no doubt that Kolia loved me—he told me often enough—but his love turned me into his property, something he owned. In giving myself to him, I soon discovered that I had given up myself. He told me what to think and how to think. And if I dared to think for myself, or to question something he said, he could be viciously cruel, even in public.

At first I drank because he insisted on it, and later because it was an escape from him, the only way I knew to escape. Kolia could destroy me with words but there was no destroying him. He was absolutely insensitive.

When Mamula was away on a film, he moved into the apartment. When she returned, there he was, and there seemed to be nothing she could do about it.

Kolia was still asleep the morning Mamula caught me having a drink to stop my hands from trembling. "Vikka, what are you doing?"

I turned away from her and downed the drink. "Please, Mamula, don't say anything. It helps me."

"It will kill you. That man will kill you."

I shook my head. "He says he loves me."

"And do you love him?"

"I don't know anymore."

Mamula put her hands on my shoulders. "And your work? Is that over, too?"

"Of course not. When I go to work again, I will not drink."

"I hope so," Mamula said.

Mamula, of course, hated Kolia for what he was doing to me. She never looked at him without glowering. If he tried to be charming or just friendly, she turned away from him. Naturally, that did not bother him. Nothing bothered Kolia. What other people thought of him didn't interest him in the least.

But the way she treated him bothered me. "You don't give him a chance," I told her.

She looked at me with cold eyes. "A chance for what? To make a drunkard of me, too?"

"I am not a drunkard," I said.

"No? You should look at yourself in the mirror. This is not my Vikka I am seeing."

Her words hurt me, probably because I knew they were true, but I wasn't ready to face them yet. So I put them aside. "He is a genius, Mamula. You have seen the films he has written. Talk with him, listen to him, and you will see."

Mamula shook her head. "You are my life, Vikka. You are the one I care about. Not your Kolia. I will happily go to see his motion pictures, and I will laugh my head off. But let him go somewhere else to write them. Let him destroy some other woman."

Her attitude made our life in the apartment very difficult, which made me drink all the more to escape the tension.

When I got a call for a new film, however, I made up my

mind I wouldn't have anything to drink for the entire week before I was to report. I worked out a daily routine of long, hot baths and long walks, determined to get my body back into shape.

The first two days were very difficult. I craved a drink, and Kolia didn't make it easy for me. "If you want to drink, then drink. Life is too short, and there are too few pleasures in it. If you know of a pleasure, take it." But I refused.

When I began to feel better physically, I told Mamula proudly, "See? I told you I could stop drinking. You cannot call me a drunkard."

She took me in her arms and kissed me. "I hope I will never call you that again."

The trouble with being sober was that it made me see Kolia the way he was. A man who said he loved me should have been pleased to see me clear-eyed and in command of myself again. But as an alcoholic, Kolia hated my escaping from what he could not and would not even try to escape from. I think it frightened him. It was a sign that I was breaking free of him. And it made him more possessive than ever. "Where are you going?" he asked one morning as I put on my coat.

"For a walk. You know that."

"I don't want you to go," he said, and stepped in front of the door.

"Kolia, don't be silly. I have to be in shape to work next week."

He laughed. "Unless you are doing a hiking story, you do not need to have strong legs."

I tried to pull him away from the door. "Get out of my way, Kolia."

He shoved me backward so that I fell against a table. "Is it walking, really, Vikka? Or is there some man waiting out there for you?"

"You disgust me with your filthy mind!"

He shrugged his shoulders. "Nevertheless, you are not going out. I do not want it."

We stood facing each other, neither making a move. I looked at the glass he held in his hand. I knew when it was empty, he would have to refill it.

I took off my coat and put it casually over a chair not far from the door. Then I sat down and pretended to read a magazine, ignoring him.

It took something like 20 minutes before his need for alcohol got the better of him. "Here, Vikka. Get me another drink."

I looked over at him. "I am not a servant, Kolia. If you want a drink, get it. But don't bother me."

He grunted to himself. I waited. And finally he moved away from the door. When he was across the room, I grabbed my coat and ran from the apartment. I felt proud of myself for having outsmarted Kolia, which shows you how foolish I was. I didn't even consider what would happen when I went back.

The minute I came in he grabbed me by the arms, so tightly that pain shot through me. "You're hurting me, Kolia."

He smiled. "Good. Then you will learn to do as I say."

Later on, I tried to talk to him. "Why do you do these things to me, Kolia? You say you love me, and yet you are terrible to me. You know I am going to make a film starting on Monday. That is hard work—you know that. I must look my best and feel good. You should want me to."

He put his hand under my chin and tilted my face to look up at his. "Your place is with me wherever I am. That is all."

"I am an actress, Kolia."

He threw back his head and laughed. " 'I am an actress, Kolia!' You say that as if it meant something. What is an actress? A face and a body that moves to other people's directions and says words that other people have thought of and written down. An actress is a windup toy that performs, that is all."

"Perhaps you are right," I said, knowing that Kolia was off on one of his interminable speeches. It was easier to agree with him.

I made the film, and I did not drink throughout the weeks of filming. But it was not my best work. Too often, as I was going into a scene, I would be distracted by seeing Kolia somewhere on the set watching me, with that sneering, possessive look of his.

When the picture was finished, and there was nothing to take me away from the apartment and Kolia, I began drinking again.

For months I floated in my alcoholic world. At odd moments I realized that my life was getting away from me, but I only made an effort to take control of myself at those times when I had a film to make. And as long as I could fight my way back, I was certain that I was all right. While I drank, Kolia was somewhere far outside of me, like a whirlwind, and I lived safely in my own quiet place in the middle of the storm. I could hear him, but he couldn't hurt me. And although I could see Mamula's concern, I didn't have to think about why she should be concerned.

IRINA KIRK

As Irina and Zoya started up the steps of the dacha, the man looked up. There was suspicion on his face. "Who is this?" he asked.

Zoya's back stiffened. There was contempt in her voice. "This is *our* friend, Irina Kirk." She turned to Irina. "And that is Kolia, whom I told you about."

He roared with laughter and saluted Irina with his glass. "I am sure she told you about me. I can imagine."

Irina disliked him immediately. His coarseness offended her.

Kolia took another swallow of his drink and went back to reading the script in his lap.

Zoya said, "Where is Vikka?"

He motioned to the house. "Upstairs." Then glancing at Irina, "Is this one staying?"

Zoya turned on him. "*This one* is a professor. You could show a little respect."

Kolia pulled himself to his feet, grinning. "Well, a professor! At last an intelligent woman around this place."

"It is true," Zoya said. "Victoria is not intelligent. I can see that. If she were, she would have thrown you out long ago. Come, Iritchka."

They went into the house and Irina followed Zoya up the narrow wooden stairs. Zoya opened the first door on the right. Victoria was asleep on top of the rumpled bed. Zoya went to her and shook her shoulder. "Vikka, wake up. Look who is here."

Victoria's eyes opened for an instant. Irina noted what a beautiful woman she had become. Then she closed her eyes again and turned her head away. Zoya shook her another time. "Vikka, you must wake up. You must see who is here."

Zoya sat her up and put her legs over the side of the bed. Victoria looked blankly at Irina, then shook her head. "I don't know who it is."

Zoya looked stricken, and Irina said, "Zoyka, how could she remember me? She was only a child. Victoria, I am Irina Kirk, and . . ."

The sleep vanished from Victoria's eyes. They grew wide with fear. She clamped her hands to her ears and began screaming. "I don't want to hear! I won't listen. I won't!"

Irina was startled. "What are you talking about?"

Victoria began shaking her head wildly. "I know! I know! Zenaida told Mamula! I don't want to hear anymore."

Zenaida's name came as more of a shock to Irina than Victoria's strange behavior. Irina had thought Zenaida had gone out of all of their lives. That was what the floor ladies had said when she had tried to find her at the hotel in 1962. They told her Zenaida had disappeared.

The door burst open, and Kolia came in. He looked at the hysterical woman on the bed. "Are you pleased now?" he shouted at her. "You wanted to live in a dream of the Papatchka, didn't you? Such a pretty little dream and now it has exploded in your face!"

"Shut up!" Irina shouted at him, furious at the way he was treating Victoria.

Kolia's eyes widened. Obviously he was not used to women talking that way to him. He started to speak.

"I said shut up!" Irina repeated, and she turned and left the room, shaken by her own rage.

Zoya followed her downstairs. When Irina had pulled herself together, she asked Zoya, "What was Victoria talking about?"

"She knows everything. She knows what you told Zena in 1962 at the hotel."

"But I didn't see Zena. I was at the hotel in 1962, but the women there told me she had been fired."

Now Zoya looked confused. "But Zena never lost her job. She told me she had seen you at the hotel in 1962. She telephoned me and asked me to come to her apartment, that she had news for me. I knew what she meant. She told me that you had said you had found Jackson Tate. He had come to your house in a big black car, and you had given him Vikka's picture. And he took a look at it and then he tore it into pieces and threw it on the ground. You said he told you, 'This is no proof, and until someone proves it to me, I'm not going to accept this.' And he got back into his limousine and drove away."

"It is a lie," Irina said. "All of it. I have spoken with Jackson Tate by telephone, I have written to him, but he has never been to my house. We have never met face to face. Let's get Victoria and go back to Moscow right now and see Zenaida. I want to confront her!"

Zoya shook her head. "Zena died a year ago. Vikka and I were with her at the hospital when she died."

"Well, I tell you it is a lie. I think the KGB got to her and made her say that. It sounds like it to me. The big black limousine. In their minds all Americans whom they want to slander are always in big black limousines."

Zoya took her hand. "Please, I have no bitterness toward Zena. Perhaps she had to tell this lie. You go upstairs, Iritchka, and tell Vikka. Please."

Irina went back upstairs. Victoria was still lying on the bed, her body turned to the wall. Irina sat down on the bed beside her. "It is Irina Kirk, Vikka. Won't you listen to me?"

She shook her head. "No. I don't have any father. I don't want to hear about him."

"Zenaida told a lie. Won't you trust me, Vikka?"

"No. I don't trust anybody."

Irina patted Victoria's shoulder. "How can I make you trust me? You know that I am a writer, and in 1959 when your mother told me the story of herself and Jackson Tate, I was also a woman alone trying to raise three young children. I could have written your mother's story and sold it for a great deal of money, but I never did. Because I made a promise to myself that I never would until you and your father were together."

Victoria turned over. Her face was wet. "Tell me about him."

When Irina finished, Victoria bent forward and kissed her on the cheek. "Thank you, Iritchka, and forgive me. I do trust you." She hesitated for a moment and then said, "Then he never tore up my picture? He never said he didn't believe I was his daughter?"

"No," Irina said. "The minute he heard your name, he knew you were his."

Victoria smiled for the first time, but her face clouded again. "Then why has he never come to see me? Why did he never write to me?"

They were the same questions that had gone through Irina's mind, and she didn't know the answers. But she knew she had to give answers to Victoria. "There could be so many reasons, Victoria. He is an old man now, you know that. He could be ill, or he might even have died."

Victoria shook her head violently, and her tears started again. "No. You mustn't say that. He has to be alive!"

Irina took her hand to calm her. "There could even be other reasons. You know that he was once put out of the Soviet Union. Such things are not forgotten. He probably could not get a visa to come to you. . . ."

But Victoria wasn't listening. "I know he is not dead. I feel it. I have to see him, even if it is only for one minute. You don't understand. No one does."

"I do, Victoria."

"No, no one can know what it is to be illegitimate all your life. To be reminded of it wherever I go. Whenever I fill out an application, I always have to draw a line where it says father. And I cannot write in 'none' or 'unknown.' That would be like saying I do not know him, that he doesn't exist." She grabbed Irina's hand in her own hands. "You must find him for me, Irina. I need him so much."

"I will try again. But you must be prepared that he could be dead."

"Then you must find his grave and send me a picture of it. I must have something.

"All right, I will try."

Victoria kissed her again. Irina stood up and looked down at her. "It could take time."

"I know."

"And when I do find him, will you be here, Victoria?" Irina said the words slowly so that the woman on the bed would understand her meaning.

Victoria flushed. "Say what you mean, Iritchka."

"Very well. If you and your father could meet, would you want him to see you as you are now? If he is alive when I find him, will you be?"

Victoria smiled. "I will be alive. I have stopped drinking as of this minute."

Irina looked at her, wondering if she were hearing the truth, or simply an actress caught up in an emotional moment.

Victoria nodded. "You will see, Iritchka. I have something to live for now."

VICTORIA

I had stopped drinking completely by the time we returned to Moscow, and I saw Kolia as I had never seen him before. He was a monster who loved only himself. His talent was the only talent he recognized. The love he claimed to have for me was no different than what he felt for his toothbrush or his jacket. They were his, he owned them. That was how he felt about me.

He hated me for doing what he could not do, so he tortured me with words. "Do you think God is saying how wonderful you are because you are not drinking? Do you think God is saying, 'Well, I have to reward her for not drinking, so I will make her papa be alive and let that professor woman find him for my wonderful Victoria?"

I realized at last what I had chosen to give myself to. "You are horrible, Kolia. I am not doing this for anyone but myself."

"Hah! What a pretty speech! Is it from one of your films? You are a child, Vikka, a grown-up child who gets movie stories all mixed up with life. Wake up, Vikka. This is not the cinema. Your father is probably dead, and whether or not you drink will change nothing!"

I ran from the apartment. I knew Kolia's moods inside out.

When he was drinking, as he was now, he would stay on the same subject until he passed out.

I walked to the river and sat for a while thinking. I couldn't accept the idea that my father was dead, but I knew I would if I had to. I was not the child Kolia said I was, and I wasn't living out a movie fantasy. If Irina Kirk sent us bad news, then I would somehow find the strength to accept it. I hadn't survived this long by turning my life into a series of fantasies that I could dream away.

Whatever I had once felt for Kolia was over. I realized for the first time that I had fallen in love with the screenwriter and confused it with the man. He lived only for drinking and writing, and he destroyed anyone who came near him. Even the heart attack that had put him in the hospital—and I, like the devoted fool I was, cooked his dinner and brought it to him every night out of some feeling of guilt that I was responsible for his illness—couldn't stop his drinking. He began again the day he was discharged.

I could go on admiring his talent, but I had to free myself from the man. To stay with Kolia was to die with him. But how was I to get free? Whenever Mamula and I had thrown him out of the apartment, he always came back as if nothing had happened. His ego was such that it didn't allow for rejection. The idea that someone he wanted did not want him was something he could not understand.

Mamula finally hit on a way to get rid of him. It happened on one of the many evenings when Kolia was drunk and carrying on about something in a long tirade. We weren't even certain of what he was saying. That was how slurred his speech had become. I said to Mamula, "If only they could see him like this for once, then maybe we would be rid of him at last."

She knew what I was talking about. Whenever I had complained about Kolia to any of his Communist friends or members of his writers' society, they had looked at me as if I were telling lies. "He drinks a little," one of them told me, "but he is always a gentleman."

Mamula went to her room. I could hear her speaking to someone on the telephone. Then people started arriving—the chairman of Kolia's writers' society, a member of the police, a doctor, and the head of Kolia's Communist group. Kolia was in the bathroom when they first came in.

"I have called you gentlemen here," Mamula said politely, "so that you will see the face of your respected Kolia as we know it. When he comes out of the bathroom, you will see the man we have lifted from puddles in the street where he could have drowned."

There were murmurs of protest. I said, "Do any of you know how he lost his four front teeth?" I looked at the doctor.

"Well, I am not his dentist," the doctor said, "but I believe he slipped and fell in the snow."

I laughed. "It has never snowed inside this room, doctor. Kolia passed out right here and fell face down against the back of that chair."

At this moment Kolia stepped into the room. He stopped. He glared at me and Mamula, and put his hand to his chest. "What are you two up to? Do you want me to have another heart attack?"

"Go ahead," Mamula said. "Your doctor is here."

Kolia turned away. "I am going to bed." He started for Mamula's room.

The police officer stepped forward. "You cannot sleep here. You are not registered to live in this apartment."

Kolia turned back and, losing his balance, clutched the wall to keep from falling. The Communist said, "You are a disgrace, Kolia. You have received the highest award that can be given to a party member in this country, and you are disgracing it."

"It is true," Mamula said. "So long as this man insists on staying here where it is not even legal for him to be, he will go on being a disgrace to the Communist Party. We are two women alone, without power to control him."

Kolia looked wildly around the room but he knew he was trapped, and he left meekly with the men.

He telephoned me the next day to say he was coming back. Luckily, I was leaving to make a picture in Moldavia. Kolia said, "I do not believe you."

"I do not care what you believe. If you want, come around. You will meet only Mamula and her rolling pin."

"I will be here when you come back."

"Kolia, listen to me. I never want to see you again as long as I live. I mean it."

His voice softened. "Vikka, my darling, you don't mean that. You know how it is with us."

"Yes, I do. And that is why if you come anywhere near me or Mamula again, I swear I will call the police!"

"Vikka!"

I hung up.

IRINA KIRK

Irina Kirk returned to her Connecticut home determined to find Jackson Tate again. She had not been able to shake Victoria's tear-stained face from her mind. Yet she did nothing immediately. Something held her back, something she could only describe as a strong instinct not to look for the admiral for a week.

A week later, at 11 P.M., she went to her bedroom. It was an odd time to begin a search, but the instinct she trusted told her the time was right. She went through her address book, not knowing for whom she was looking. Suddenly, she came upon the telephone number of a naval lieutenant who had invited her, the year before, to lecture on Russian literature at Annapolis. She telephoned him and asked if he could locate Admiral Jackson Tate's grave. She gave him the last address—Virginia Beach—that she had.

The lieutenant called back the next evening. "Guess what? Your admiral is alive." He gave her Jackson Tate's address and telephone number in Orange Park, Florida. The lieutenant said, "It's a good thing you didn't call me any sooner. They just received the admiral's new address yesterday."

Irina thanked him and silently blessed her instincts. She dialed Jack's number. She heard the telephone receiver—and an extension receiver—being picked up. She was offended by his lack of response. First, he couldn't place her name and he seemed a bit put out at anyone's calling so late in the evening. Irina didn't take into account that Jackson Tate was one month shy of being 75 years old. She only saw Victoria's face in front of her. She told him to tell whoever else was on the phone to hang up. That was when she learned that he had married. It increased her impatience with this man, who didn't seem to understand the urgency she felt in the situation. She told him that she thought the KGB was after Victoria and Zoya.

He said, "KGB?" and sounded as if he hadn't even heard of them.

"The Secret Police!"

"Oh, you mean the NKVD."

"That was your day, Admiral. It is now the KGB."

Remembering that telephone call, Irina has stated: "I thought, how can I get a response out of this man who doesn't respond well, at least in the way I felt he could have? Then I remembered that he was military, and I thought the only thing to do was to give him a command."

She said to him, "Admiral, I want you to do the following: I want you to send me your picture. I want you to write on the picture 'To my beloved daughter, Victoria,' and I want you to write a letter to the mother and to the daughter."

Jack interrupted her to say; "They'll never get them through the mail."

Irina said, "That is none of your affair. I will see that they get there."

Surprisingly enough, Jackson Tate, who was used to giving orders, not taking them, took it all from Irina Kirk. He asked what type of pictures she wanted, and she told him, "I want a picture of you the way Zoya remembers you in 1946, and one the way you look today."

Although Jack agreed, the conversation deepened his distrust of Irina Kirk, a woman he didn't know who suddenly seemed to be stepping into his life and taking charge of it.

Using the same brusque tone as in her telephone conversation, Irina Kirk wrote to Jackson Tate on September 8, 1973, beginning:

Dear Admiral Tate,

It was rather a shock to find you. I had just told Victoria that most probably you were not alive.

She then proceeded to recap everything that had happened during her stay in Moscow, including the discovery of Victoria's screenwriter and her drinking problem. Irina wrote:

As for drinking I didn't know, but it was explained to me later by some of my dissident friends. They said that beautiful girls like that were certainly rare in Russia. Victoria is spectacular but she is also proud, fierce, independent. The KGB would like nothing better than to be able to use her to sleep with foreign diplomats for obvious reasons.

So long as she is the way she is they can't force her to do any such thing. So they begin to look for sources of personal dignity in order to destroy that first. They found that having an American father gave her some kind of a source of a different identity, so they destroyed that with that tale of lies. Now they are trying to make her an alcoholic in order to be able to use her when she reaches the state of being willing to do anything for a drink.

On the last page of her letter, Irina wrote:

I don't know you and, frankly, can't care about you, but I've seen Victoria, her grief and what is coming, and my only thought is to help her. The news that it was a lie, that you hadn't thrown her picture away, did help. But how long will it last? We must maintain that small fire that was lit in her soul and not let the others extinguish it.

Irina Kirk had taken charge, and Jackson Tate floundered along in her wake. He sent the pictures and the letters she had asked for rather quickly because she wrote to him on September 20, 1973, thanking him for them. One can only guess at what he said in his cover letter to her. Obviously, she had made him feel guilty for his lack of action, because she wrote back:

Why did you decide that I thought you were a heel and a heartless person? Did I say that? No, I didn't and I don't think that you are any of these things. I just think that you must be a very weak man, that's all.

Irina then told Jack what he should do, or might do. She offered him the name of a lawyer who handled the rights of Soviet writers, saying that Jack could consult him if he was really interested in doing something for his daughter. She wrote:

> I would also write a postcard just to see if it goes through the official mail. We can estimate their attitude. Just say the following, 'Dear Zoya and Victoria, I hope you received my letter and photos which I just sent you. I know the mail is slow, but on the whole the post service is good and eventually letters get there. Please write me when you get my letter. Love.' Nothing more, let's see if it gets there. I'll write you the address, but please write Zoya's name in Russian.

There can be no question that Irina Kirk's intentions were of the best and most honorable. She knew how to deal with the Russian mentality and how to put pressure on the Soviet government. While neither Zoya nor Victoria was a dissident, such as those Irina had worked with, the procedure was the same. She knew it and Jackson Tate did not, so she had to take charge. Irina might wish she could work without him, but he was necessary to the project. That she must, secretly, have regarded him as a reluctant child seems to come through from her many letters to him. She would have to lead him every step of the way, and with everything spelled out for him down to the smallest detail.

One can only guess what Jackson Tate felt and thought. He acknowledged his daughter as his own, and he obviously cared about her fate as well as Zoya's. But still he was 75 and had married for companionship in the last years of his life. "I'm at the end of the road" was a statement he made often to family and friends. And he never said it to evoke sympathy or protests. He meant it. It was part of Jackson Rogers Tate's clear-eyed realism about himself.

But suddenly the peace and quiet he had sought in Orange Park, Florida—a place that offered only a dog track and one each of every major fast-food chain to halt the tourists passing through on their way deeper into Florida—had been shattered by a memory from the past.

Jack Tate didn't want to escape his responsibility to this daughter he had never seen, but he wasn't certain what to do. He knew he wasn't in good health—his body told him so every day—and he was too old to travel to Russia even if he could get in. And he was certain that they would never let him into the country again.

This Irene Kirk seemed to be the only solution, but he neither liked her nor trusted her. She seemed to be a woman who was always giving orders, and there was too much talk of dissidents in her letters. How did he know that if he did cooperate with her, she might not get Zoya arrested again—and Victoria, too? But if he did not cooperate, what would happen to Victoria? According to the Kirk woman, his daughter's entire emotional state—not to mention her drinking problem—hung by a thread attached to Jack.

If only there were time to think it all through, perhaps he could take the whole thing out of Kirk's hands. After all, Victoria was his child, his family, not hers. But he knew that a man at the end of the road doesn't have time. His body might give it to him, but his mind, which swam with memories that wouldn't stay in place, would never be what it once was. The man who had worked his way up through the ranks to rear admiral just wasn't there anymore. He could still make the noises of command, but he knew he was no longer in charge. Like it or not, this Kirk woman was, and he would have to tag along.

He bought a postcard with a tourist view of Orange Park on it and copied Zoya's name in Russian on the address side. Then word for word, he wrote the message Irina Kirk had told him to send.

Shortly after her letter of September 20, 1973, to Jackson Tate, Irina Kirk got a telephone call from a man who said his name was Hugh Tate.

"I'm Jack's adopted son. My mother was his second wife. I'm a retired navy captain. When you talk to Victoria, say hello to her from her brother."

Irina said she would, and waited. Surely, he hadn't called just for that.

Hugh said, "I have to tell you that my father has gone into the hospital for open-heart surgery, and his chances aren't good."

Irina gasped, and Victoria's face looking up at her from the bed in the dacha flashed across her mind. If her father died now, it would kill Victoria, too.

Hugh continued, "Just before he was wheeled into surgery, the skipper—that's what I call him—told me to look in a little box he keeps in his bedroom, and I would find your letters, which would fill me in on everything. That's why I'm calling. I guess you'll want to tell Victoria."

"Hugh," Irina said, "you must keep in touch with me. I must know what happens with the admiral."

Irina placed a call to Zoya and waited for the operator to call her back. Finally, the telephone rang. The operator said there was no one home at the number Irina had called. Irina hung up, wondering if indeed there was no one home, or if her call had been blocked. "No one home" was the excuse given when the Soviet government did not want an outsider to reach a citizen.

Perhaps it was for the best. Let Victoria enjoy her father's pictures and letters for a little while longer. If he died, there would be time enough to tell her.

VICTORIA

I was in Moldavia making the film *Cruelty* when Mamula telephoned me at my hotel. "What is it, Mamula?" I said, suddenly tense. It was not like her to telephone me, and especially not at a hotel where we knew people listened in on our conversations.

She laughed. "No, no, do not worry, Vikka. It is good news. I have a *letter* for you."

"Oh?" I could tell by the way she had said "letter" that it was important. I could only think of my papa. Was it possible? "Can you say who it is from?"

Mamula laughed again. "Let it be a surprise. I will fly to you tomorrow morning with the letter."

"All right," I said as casually as I could, but inside I felt as if there were rockets going off.

When I returned from the studio the next day, Mamula was waiting for me. I threw my arms around her and kissed her. Then I leaned close to her ear and whispered, "Tell me! The letter? Is it from Papatchka?"

"Yes," Mamula said. "Let us take a walk to the park."

It was the only safe place. I knew that my room at the hotel had been searched twice during my stay, though I had no idea by whom or what they were looking for.

We found a bench near a lamp and sat down. After looking around to see that there was no one watching us, Mamula reached into her coat pocket. "There is a letter. And two pictures. Irina has translated the letter into Russian." Mamula handed me a picture of a man in a navy uniform sitting at a table, putting a cigarette into his mouth. "This is how your papa looked when I knew him. It says on the back that it was 1947, but he looked the same."

Tears ran down my cheeks as I looked at the face Mamula had loved. My papa, I had him at last. "See," Mamula said, "the dark hair, even the eyebrows, just like yours. And look there"—she pointed to a shadow in the center of the chin— "you even have the cleft as he does."

Then she handed me the other photograph. It was Papatchka again, but now much older and heavier, standing in front of a desk and wearing a very colorful shirt over his trousers. "And this is how he looks today. I think he is still a handsome man."

I just nodded. I couldn't speak, and I couldn't take my eyes away from that face. Papa. Papatchka! If only I could touch that face just once. "I love you," I whispered to the man in the picture.

Mamula handed me her handkerchief. "And now the letter. It is addressed to me, but you will see that it is for you, too."

September 12, 1973

My dear Zoya,

It is inconceivable to me to believe that a great nation could feel any danger from us after so long a time or cause sorrow to a child who was only the result of a great love between us. I am now 75 years old and my life is far behind me. The road is very short.

I will never forget the wonderful night of V-E Day when you lay in my arms and Victoria was conceived and we decided if it was a boy, it would be Victor and if a girl, Victoria, for the great victory the world had achieved.

We have done no harm to anyone, only loved each other. Why should we be the subject of malice from a powerful political organization or government, and certainly there can be no onus to Victoria, the innocent child of our union.

And to you Victoria, my darling daughter, I can only say I am sorry that my love for Zoya has caused you so much trouble and unhappiness.

I loved you then, Zoya, and I still love you and cherish the memories of the short year we had together.

Jackson

I collapsed against Mamula, sobbing out of control. He had called me his darling daughter.

Mamula pushed me up. "Vikka, you must sit up and pull yourself together. Someone could be watching."

I sat up, but I couldn't control my tears. "My darling daughter." I was truly a daughter at last, and with a papatchka I no longer had to imagine. I felt wonderful, glorious. Twenty-seven years of shame had washed out of me in three words—my darling daughter.

That evening, my mind still spinning, I wrote my first letter to my father so that Mamula could take it with her when she returned to Moscow the next day.

Hello my dear man,

I really don't know what to call you, but I assume that because you called me your daughter in your letter, so I can call you my father. Now, one of the most beautiful and unexpected things has happened in my life. Finally, people have helped us to find each other.

I really have dreamed about this my whole life, and I always subconsciously believed and trusted that we would meet each other some day.

I was about 15 or 16 years old when Mama told me everything about you, and I asked a lot of questions. Is he handsome? Is he tall? Is he kind, and so on and so on. For me, as for every girl in the world, I had a wish that my Mama and Papa would be the most beautiful and kind people in the world. I think Irina told you under what tragic circumstances I lost my mother for several years. I lived in Kazakhstan with my mother's sister, and I was sure that she was my mother because nobody told me about my real mother. That was because she received a 25-year sentence in prison, and nobody had the hope that she would ever come back. But she stood everything and endured everything. And she came back, and she got me back. She has given everything to me and to her work, but I suppose she will write you herself about herself.

My dear Papa, I am right now far from Moscow in a little town in Moldavia where I am making a new movie in which I play the leading female role, but I think Irina has told you many of the details of my life.

I want to write to you about so many things, to tell you every-thing about my life, but because of what happened—I found you, and it is so unexpected—I cannot gather my thoughts together right now. I have been waiting all these years for some sign from you. Just a few words, and finally I have them. Of course the true happiness for me would be if I really could see you. I can just imagine that we would sit down—just the three of us, no one else—and we would talk, talk, and talk. I think we have so many things to talk about.

I don't know how such a meeting can take place, but when my mother is back in Moscow she will think about that.

I have been working for around ten years in films. The picture of me that Irina Kirk sent to you is from a movie. But back then I wasn't too interested in being an actress. I thought I wanted to be a psychiatrist. My mother was horrified at the idea. With her sense of humor, she said, "All right, you can be a Doctor of Psy-chiatry, but your patient will be your mother."

So I am an actress now. I had a nice role in a movie called *Dvoe,* or *Ballad of Love.* This movie was bought by a lot of coun-tries in the world, and one premiere was in San Francisco. I kept a wish hidden in my heart that you would see that movie and recognize me as your daughter.

Now, there has been a boyfriend in my life who is a script writer. As Irina Kirk has probably told you, he drinks a great deal. He is 53 years old. For the sake of my mother and for you, I have stopped the relationship and my drinking.

Soon my mother will be flying back to Moscow, so I am writ-ing this letter in the last minutes. I know this letter is a little somber, but I think you can understand my condition at this moment.

I thank you very much for the pictures you sent to me, and of course I recognized you immediately. I am very sorry that I can-not send you any pictures of myself from here, because I don't have any, but my mother will include a picture with this letter when she gets to Moscow.

I wish you a lot of happiness, health, and a long, long life, and of course, the most beautiful things in the world. I kiss you very tenderly.

Your daughter,
Victoria

I gave the letter to Mamula. The next morning, before she left, I read my father's letter again and looked at his pictures. It hurt me terribly to give the pictures and the letter to Mamula, but I knew that I couldn't keep them with me at the hotel where someone could find them.

When I returned from Moldavia, I was certain that there would be another letter from my father waiting for me. But there was nothing. At first, I was terribly disappointed, but then I told myself I was behaving like a child. I had had a letter from my father, and he had called me his daughter. My world had changed with that letter, but that didn't mean that the world I lived in had changed. Letters from outside the Soviet Union were still very hard to get. Perhaps he had written me several letters since that first one, but it would take time for them to reach me. Irina had to make elaborate arrangements and find people coming to Moscow whom she could trust.

But as the weeks went by and no letters came, I began to feel that one letter was all I would ever have. My father had done his duty, and that was all. Mamula tried to console me with the thought that he might have died since that letter. I refused to accept that. I preferred to believe that he no longer wanted to write me.

Kolia came back as I knew he would, and because I was frightened and upset I turned to him again for comfort, the last thing one should ever turn to Kolia for. Of course, he turned on me. "Why do you always talk about your father? It's Papatchka this, and Papatchka that, and it is very boring. You would do much better to pay attention to me. At least I am here. The man obviously doesn't care about you at all. He wrote a letter! One letter!"

I lunged toward Kolia, ready to claw his face with my fingernails and he backed away from me. For once I saw fear in his eyes. I chased him out of the apartment and refused to see him ever again. I think he knew that this time I would not allow him to come back, because he stopped telephoning me.

I faced New Year's Day 1974 free of Kolia and alcohol and certain that any day there would be another letter from my father.

But winter gave way to spring, and then it was summer. And there was nothing. Not one letter, and not one telephone call from Irina Kirk. Had she lost interest in me? Didn't my father care? Was he even alive?

The questions spun around in my brain day after day. At one moment, I would tell myself that he was writing to me, but the letters didn't get through. The next minute, I was convinced that one letter was the extent of his caring for me. I would never see my father.

I walked through my days, not really interested in anything. I tried to lose myself in the film I was making, but the work became secondary. There was only my father. His photographs dominated my life.

I would go home each evening and Mamula and I would eat dinner together in silence. I would look up and catch her watching me. I would see her worried expression, and I would force a smile. "Don't worry, Mamula, I will live."

IRINA KIRK

She had to give the admiral credit. He was a tough old bird to have survived open-heart surgery at the age of 75. When he had finally gotten back in touch with her, close to two months after Hugh's telephone call, he had told her with some pride that he had been on the operating table for five hours and twenty minutes.

Jack started writing to Victoria again, and Irina forwarded the letters to a man in France whom she believed could get them into Russia and to Victoria. But any hope Irina had of convincing Jackson Tate of trying to go into the Soviet Union to see his daughter was now out of the question. The surgery, plus his "old-age diabetes," made the idea impossible.

Victoria had asked Irina to get an invitation from her father to visit him. Irina knew how desperately Victoria wanted to see him, and she assumed that Victoria might even risk whatever came as the result of her applying for a visa. It worried Irina that she had not been able to reach Victoria in months. Whenever she placed a call to Zoya's apartment, she got the inevitable "no one home."

Victoria still didn't know how close she had come to losing her father for all time. Well, she would tell her in person when she went to Europe in the summer for her sabbatical year. That is, if she got into Russia at all. Irina had no doubts that the Russians knew about the book she was working on, and of her involvement with the dissident movement. The question was, how much did they know?

As spring turned to summer 1974, Irina learned that the man in France was not getting the letters through to Victoria. She had to find a new way, a new person who could get through.

She decided on Michael Agursky. He had been a professor of cybernetics and philosophy. A Jew, Agursky had shown great courage in challenging the Soviet system. Only a man with "great guts"—her description of him—would have met in a forest with CBS newsmen and spoken of conditions within Russia.*

Irina made arrangements for Jack Tate's letters as well as her own to get into the hands of Agursky.

* Michael Agursky lives in Israel today.

VICTORIA

It seemed like an ordinary summer day. I was standing in a long line waiting to arrange for my car's annual tune-up. I had been on line for at least two hours, and it looked like I would be there for another two hours before my turn came. I asked the man behind me if he would hold my place while I used the telephone.

When I called Mamula to tell her not to wait with dinner, she interrupted me. "Come home! Quickly! I have great news for you!"

"I can't. I will lose my place. Can you tell me on the phone what it is?"

"No!" Mamula shouted. "Absolutely not. Forget your automobile, and come home!"

I ran for my car and drove home. There were several letters from Irina Kirk and four letters from my father. It was like the greatest holiday in the world. He was alive! He cared! I devoured his letters, brushing away tears each time the pages blurred in front of my eyes.

Later Mamula told me how she had gotten them. A man had telephoned and without introducing himself said, "Are you expecting any letters from the West?"

Mamula hemmed and hawed, not committing herself. The man said, "Well, I have something for you that I think you want. Can I see you?"

Mamula arranged to meet him. It was Michael Agursky, who was to take tremendous risks for me.

IRINA KIRK

She arrived in Moscow in August 1974, but she didn't see Victoria right away. First, she met with Michael Agursky to talk over the problem of Victoria and her father. "Is there a chance that he will come to see her?" Michael asked.

Irina shook her head. "No. He is old and very ill. It is out of the question."

"Then she will have to go to him. Do you think he would initiate her visit?"

"The trouble with him," Irina said, thinking of her past dealings with Jack Tate, "is that he doesn't know how to deal with the situation, how to work around the Russians."

Michael thought about it. "Since her father is an important man, an admiral, I think an invitation from him to his daughter to visit him is the way it should happen."

Irina and Michael decided that the best way to move Jack Tate to action was to have the American consulate in Moscow write him and suggest that he invite his daughter to the United States. Irina liked the idea. "I am certain Admiral Tate will respond much better to an official letter than to one from me. If I write, he will just think it is that woman again pushing him into an impossible situation. Jackson Tate remembers his last time in Russia, when they threw him out. He doesn't think he could get in, or that Victoria can get out."

Michael smiled. "He may be right, but let's find out."

"First I'd better see Victoria," Irina said.

When she went to Zoya's apartment and told the two women that Jack was seriously ill, Zoya shook her head and said, "Terrible. Jackson is old. I cannot picture that."

Victoria said flatly, "He cannot die. I must see him once."

Irina said, "I assure you he cannot come to you. Would you go to him if you could?"

Victoria didn't hesitate. "Of course."

Irina said, "It could destroy everything you have here forever. And you still might not be allowed to go."

Zoya nodded. "Listen to her, Vikka. What she says is true."

"I don't care. I have dreamed of my father my whole life. I want to go to him."

"All right," Irina said. "Then we begin."

The meeting with James G. Huff of the American Consulate took place in Red Square. Michael Agursky was there with Victoria and Irina. Huff agreed to write to Admiral Tate to inform him that he could invite his daughter to visit him.

VICTORIA

September 7, 1974
Dear Mr. Tate,

Your daughter Vicki asked me to translate her letter to you. I've fulfilled it with pleasure but not with the appropriate skill. Excuse me for mistakes.

Michael Agursky

My dear, my nice Daddy,

How do you do? We were extremely glad to have got your letter. I was very excited but at the same time distressed after finishing it. How many disasters can befall a single man? Your health is the main thing! You ought to gather all your strength to defeat the illness. If I've understood your letter in the right way, the worst is already behind you.

Mother always talked about you as about a very courageous man, a very strong one who was able to defeat everything. You need only to have the tremendous wish to recover, and everything will be okay, don't you think? You are likely not to imagine how dear is each line from you to me.

Each moment I pray for you in my mind for your illness to go away. There was more bad than good in our life. I hope for the brightest future.

Sometimes when I sign an autograph for fans, I wish them happiness as big as an elephant. I wish you health and happiness as big as all the elephants in the world.

Daddy, my dear, I don't know exactly how to draw the day of our meeting near. It is very sorrowful that Irene was away from us for so long and any channel which gave us information about you was disrupted.

We have no possibility to apply to the appropriate office for the permission to travel to you. But as I was able to find out, everything rests on some formalities. I am not sure if you will have strength to occupy yourself with these problems.

It would be very good if you could do the following:

1) adopt me

2) inform the American Embassy in Moscow (and personally, the head of the Consulate—James Huff) about your wish to see me in the U.S.A. Don't do this if you think there will be political problems.

If this is done as soon as possible, I hope we'll be able to see each other. Daddy, my best, my dearest, I don't need anything besides our meeting. I am longing for it as for the best minute in my life. Since the first account about you from my mother, about your existence, I was sure that I would find you and that some day we should see each other.

I am very, very sorry that you are ill and not able to travel. Gather your strength and patience, and everything will be okay. By the way, I think that the political situation now is most favorable for our meeting. In any case, I am not afraid of anything. I have no other reason to go to the U.S.A. besides this simple one—to see you. If it is difficult for you to occupy yourself with this problem, you don't have to do it. I won't be distressed because I will be able to understand it. I kiss you tenderly in all the places which cause you pain so that they will never hurt.

> With enormous love,
> Always your Victoria

P.S. Daddy, I have written this letter yesterday but today I've decided to write some more lines. Please try to send me an official invitation by mail, in the usual way, to my address. It will be very interesting to see if I get such a letter. For our meeting you have to go through all these formalities which I've written you about. I kiss you once more.

> Your daughter,
> Vicki

My address: Soviet Union, Moscow 121248 Kutuzovsky Prospekt. 4/2 apt. 243

IRINA KIRK

In October of 1974 Irina Kirk was in Rome staying with friends, but her mind was still in Moscow. Looking at the forms from the American Embassy, she realized that Victoria would soon be running risks if the Soviet government did not look kindly on her request to visit her father. She would need all the protection she could get. It was the citizen who was unknown outside the Soviet borders who was treated most severely, but if Victoria was known in the West they would move more cautiously against her. She thought of Hollywood. Why not? Victoria was an actress and a beautiful woman. But Irina knew no one out there.

Then she thought of her friend Leonard Bernstein, who was conducting in Vienna right at that moment. Surely he must know someone. Irina placed a call to him and stressed the urgency of speaking with him. He told her to meet him in London, where he would be going next. In London she told him the entire story and said that she wanted to interest someone in Hollywood in Victoria and her story. The more famous she could make Victoria, the safer she would be. Bernstein told her to contact Mike Mindlin, a producer at Paramount Pictures, and to use Bernstein's name.

On her return to Rome, she wrote to Jackson Tate and prodded him to complete the necessary forms and write the letter of invitation. She also stated that she would be going back to Moscow in case he wanted to send his daughter a Christmas present. And she argued for Jack's adopting Victoria as a way of protecting her.

Jack was well enough to respond within two weeks to Irina's request for a *vyzov*, an invitation, for Victoria, and to send a $200 check to buy her Christmas presents. With the money Irina bought Victoria a suede jacket with a lambskin lining, skirts, sweaters, and blouses.

She took the forms and invitation that Jack had sent and had copies made. To test the political climate, she had copies sent to Victoria from Switzerland, England, and Italy. None of them got through. But the copy she gave to a diplomat to carry in personally in his pouch and deliver to James Huff reached him. Irina also carried in a copy, which she gave to Victoria.

Irina arrived in Moscow in November 1974 for a ten-day stay. Before going to see Victoria and Zoya, she met with Michael Agursky and learned that Victoria was going to take the first step toward her hoped-for visit to her father. She was going to the head of her film studio for a character reference. That worried Irina.

Victoria would be declaring herself officially the child of an American citizen and stating her desire to leave the country to see her father. Irina knew that Victoria was no dissident, but would the Soviet government believe it? And what if Jackson Tate died before Victoria got permission to go to him? Where would that leave her? For that matter, what if she got a bad character reference? Victoria would have risked everything, and she might accomplish nothing—and be punished for the attempt.

VICTORIA

When I looked at the beautiful presents Irina brought me from my father, I wanted to cry. I would have sent him the world for Christmas, but there was so little I could get for him in Moscow. Just a little set of wooden cups and bowls decorated in red, black, and gold paint. "They are tourist souvenirs, Irina, but what can I do?"

"It doesn't matter, Vikka. He will love them because they are from you."

I got my father's telephone number from Irina, and one evening when Michael was with us, I decided to call him. I placed the call and was told that all lines to the United States were busy with official calls and they were not accepting call requests from civilians.

"I am going to try to call from the main telegraph office," I said to Michael. "Will you come with me? I need someone to speak with him."

Michael warned me that he was a known dissident and that it would be a risk for me to be seen with him. I said I didn't care.

I cursed myself for not paying attention during my school years when Mamula told me to study English. If I had, I would not have had to ask Michael to come with me. But I had no choice.

We went to the main telegraph office on Gorki Street, and I asked to place a call to Orange Park, Florida, in the United States. They didn't say that the lines were busy, just that there would be a wait. I began trembling. Soon I would hear his voice. "Oh my God, Michael, what can I say?"

Michael printed the words "I am your daughter" on a piece of paper, told me what they meant and how to pronounce them.

"But what should I call him?"

Michael said, "Daddy."

"What is daddy?"

"It is papa, like children say in English."

I rejected that. I was not a child anymore.

We waited 45 minutes. Then a woman in the telegraph office signaled to me that America was on the line. I went into the booth with Michael. "Hal-lo?"

I heard a rough masculine voice. "Who is this?"

I burst into tears. "Victoria," I said between sobs.

"Who?"

"Victoria!" I found the piece of paper. "I am your daughter, Papatchka," I managed to get out, and then I dropped the receiver and ran from the booth and buried my face in my hands.

It was Michael who told him that I had received his invitation. "But the connection wasn't very good, and probably my language wasn't good either or he couldn't hear me well. But I did hear him say one thing. He will telephone you on your birthday."

I fell against Michael in a new flood of tears. I felt like such a fool. To have risked so much to place the call and then not to be able to speak. But I had heard my father's voice. It was worth it all.

The next day, I went to see the head of my department at Mosfilm to request a character reference. He read the invitation from my father, then said, "What is this nonsense?"

"It is not nonsense. I am going to see my father, and I need a character reference." I felt myself growing tense and I tried to force myself to stay calm and pleasant.

"All right," he said. "Our department will have a meeting to discuss your request. Then we will tell you yes or no." He sounded completely uninterested.

I flared up. "I don't need a yes or a no. I am not asking permission to travel. I am not going there to work. I am going to see my father, and he doesn't care what you write on that paper."

He smiled, and it was not a pleasant smile. "Maybe your father doesn't care, but if your reputation is not good enough you will not go."

"How long will I have to wait?" I asked, knowing that by law he could keep me waiting for only one month. But I had heard of other cases where people had waited much longer because they didn't dare to complain. I was fully prepared— though I didn't say so—to scream the place down if necessary to get my character reference. My father was not going to die without my seeing him just because some people wanted to show me how important they were.

The man shrugged. "There are many people to speak with about you, and then there must be a meeting among the heads of each department. When the material is all gathered and a decision is reached, then it must go to the head of the studio."

I left the studio, hopeful but nervous. There was nothing I could do for the next month except wait and pray that they would not drag it out for the full month.

IRINA KIRK

Before she left Moscow on December 4, 1974, Irina Kirk saw Christopher Wren of *The New York Times*, while Michael Agursky spoke with Robert Toth of *The Los Angeles Times*. The two journalists were given a brief outline of Victoria's story. Both men agreed to sit on the story until they received word to release it. It was the only way she could think of to protect Victoria should action be taken against her for trying to get a visa.

She next saw Victoria and told her what she had done. She advised her to contact the journalists the minute she thought the tide might be turning against her. "If the world learns of your story, the publicity can protect you within Russia."

Irina also left a postcard with Zoya, addressed to herself in Connecticut. It was a standard tourist view of Red Square, and on the back Irina had written: "I am in Moscow having a wonderful time. Wish you were here. Mary." She explained it to Zoya. "I do not know what will happen with Victoria and you, but if things start to go bad, put this postcard in the mail. It is an ordinary tourist message and it will get through. When I receive it, I will do everything I can to make your story known and to arouse the world.

Zoya put her arms around Irina. She kissed her. "Iritchka, you have been very, very good to my Vikka and me."

When Irina left Moscow, she flew to Los Angeles to tackle the film colony. She was hoping to sell Victoria's story to the movies and to interest Hollywood in Victoria herself. She telephoned Jack and told him what she planned to do, asking him for the names of any big shots he still knew in Hollywood. Jack could only give her one name, the widow of a Hollywood producer, and neither that lead nor the one Bernstein had given her was fruitful. The general attitude was that there was no interest in cold-war stories. Discouraged and angry, Irina began having chest pains and was taken to the hospital. She wrote to Jack, filling him in on her lack of success and reminding him to call Victoria on her birthday, January 18. "Give me an idea what time you'll be calling, so one of my English-speaking friends will be there."

Her letter included an address in Hawaii where she was going for a brief rest.

When she returned to Connecticut, she found a postcard waiting for her from Moscow. It said: "I am in Moscow having a wonderful time. Wish you were here. Mary."

VICTORIA

I waited all month for my character reference. While I waited,
I gathered the mass of statements and facts that had to be presented to Ovir, the office that would issue the visa: How much
I earned, where I lived and with whom I lived, and on and on
and on. But still no character reference. I called the head of my
department. "Are you trying to break me? By law I am entitled
to have my character reference within a month. Yet I've heard
nothing from you."

He sounded indifferent over the telephone, as if I had asked
him about the weather. "One of the men who should be at the
meeting has been ill, so it has been postponed until the end of
the week. We meant to call you. Come in on Friday."

Once again Michael agreed to go with me, though he again
reminded me about the risk I was taking being seen with him.
I told him I was proud to have him as a friend. While he
waited outside, I went into the meeting room. Chairs were
drawn into a semicircle facing one chair that I knew was for
me. I looked at the men waiting for me. Though I knew few of
them personally, their faces were all familiar. I had seen them
in the studio corridors.

There was one face I did know, in the center of the semicircle. It belonged to a man named Smirnoff, who was the secretary of the Communist Party in the section of the studio where I worked. But I knew him before he had started to climb the Communist ladder. He had been an actor assigned to a film in which I was to appear. Only Smirnoff never even got to the first scene, because he had no talent, and because he was an alcoholic. He fell down dead drunk during his first rehearsal. As far as I knew, that was the end of his acting career.

Now, this alcoholic was a man with power in the Communist Party. He looked first at me and then at the men seated on either side of him. "We are here to discuss whether or not Comrade Fyodorova is to be allowed to go to the United States of America."

I smiled and tried to look pleasant. I knew that Smirnoff still drank, and I thought there was a slight slur to his speech, but I couldn't be certain. His next words were: "After serious consideration and much examination of the facts, we don't think she should be allowed to go."

I felt myself growing tense. "Oh, and why is that?"

"Because we believe you are an immoral person!"

"Immoral? Immoral?" I didn't believe what I was hearing.

"Yes, immoral. First, you have been married and divorced twice."

"Does *that* make me immoral?"

"Furthermore, you have shown no interest in Communist life or society. You have never come to any of the lectures on Communism or Marxism that are given twice weekly at the studio."

I could still see him passing out during the film rehearsal, and now he dared to sit in judgment of me. "Listen, I am an actress, and I studied at the Institute for four years where there were more lectures on Marxism than on acting, and that was enough for me without attending *your* lectures!"

He smiled. "Very brave, Comrade Fyodorova, and very foolish. You were warned way back, when you did not appear at our lectures, that you could have cause to regret it, and now you have. Do you think we want an ignorant woman running around in other countries? How would that look? Do you even know what is happening now in our country?"

"Yes, it is a big mess!" I knew I shouldn't be saying these things, but as I was already set to receive a bad character reference, what did it matter?

Smirnoff smiled. "That is very funny, but not exactly the right answer. Do you know that right at this minute there is a large and important Communist convention going on?"

I leaned forward, looking straight at Smirnoff. "Do you think that when I get to this small town where my father lives, he is going to say, 'Tell me what is going on in Russia, my darling. Is there a Communist convention?' "

Smirnoff raised his eyebrows. "You have a delightful sense of humor, though a little sarcastic, but we will see who ends up laughing and who crying." He looked down at the paper in front of him. "I see also that you have a serious drinking problem."

I exploded. "*You* dare to talk to me of a drinking problem? I had the strength to stop drinking. And when I *was* drinking, I never drank while I was making a film. I never was in trouble, I never was late, and I never held up a picture by even one minute because of it! I am a disciplined actress, and everybody knows it . . ."

He interrupted to say, "Unfortunately, it does say that you are a good actress."

I held up my hand. "I haven't finished yet. Do your great comrades here know about your drinking problem? Do they know that when you tried to be an actor at this studio you fell down drunk in front of 50 people? How dare you speak about my drinking problem?"

He didn't even blush. "We are not here to discuss me. It is you who came to us for a reference, and that is what we are discussing."

"That is right," I said. "I came to you for a character reference, and that is all I want, good or bad. There is no need for everyone to talk about what I eat, how much I sleep, when I go to the bathroom, and what I do or do not know about your Communist conventions. It is all games that you are playing with me. Games!" I got up and ran from the room.

ZOYA

December 14, 1974

Dear Jackson,

It was such a big surprise for Victoria and myself to receive your letter and your photographs. My heart was full of emotions, and it was very hard for me to concentrate my thoughts so that I could write you a letter. Yes, a lot of time has gone by since that time, and a lot of things have happened since then, but I am very happy that it is already behind me. Vikka and I are very happy about that little note* that you sent us, and it would be so beautiful if you as a father could hug your daughter.

My whole life is Vikka. She definitely looks like you, and it seems to me that she also has your character and temperament. I still cannot believe that we have found each other. I keep hoping that you and Victoria will meet someday, somehow.

I wish you, my dear Jackson, good health, and it is my main wish because if you have your health the rest will come. I remember you as a very strong and a very energetic man. I kiss you.

Yours,
Zoya

P.S. I really had a wish to write you in English, but I am afraid of my terrible mistakes.

* A reference to Jack's invitation to Victoria.

VICTORIA

When I told Mamula about my meeting at the studio, she became terribly upset. "How could you, Vikka? How could you! You are not an ignorant child. You know what happened to me because I defied them."

"Did you expect me to sit there and let that drunkard Smirnoff call me immoral?" I knew Mamula was right, but I didn't want to admit it.

"No one said he was right, Vikka, but what would it have cost you to let him think it?" Mamula took my hand. "I am an old woman, Vikka. I don't want to go back to prison again. This time I would not come out."

She mailed the postcard to Irina Kirk that night.

It was New Year's Day 1975 and I still had heard nothing about the second and, I hoped, final meeting on my character reference. On January 18 I gave myself a twenty-ninth birthday party and invited all my friends to our apartment. I think it was a happy party for them, but it was not for me. I kept waiting for the telephone to ring with the call my father promised to make on the birthday card he had sent me. As it grew late, all the old fears started. He was dead. He no longer cared. He had forgotten about me.

At two in the morning I couldn't wait any longer. I took a friend aside who spoke English and asked if he would translate for me. Then I placed the call. It would be only six in the evening where Papatchka was. The call went through in a very short time.

I heard the voice. "Who is this?"

"Papatchka. It is Victoria."

I gave the telephone to my friend and told him to ask why he hadn't called me. My friend said something I couldn't understand, and then listened. He told me that my father had tried to telephone and had been told that all circuits were busy.

I grabbed the phone back. I had prepared the words all day. "I love you, daddy," I said.

And he said, "*Yah lyooblyoo tebya ochen.*" I started to cry. He had said, "I love you very much."

But then he said something else in English, and I had to give the telephone to my friend again. My friend smiled. "He said, 'And I remember when I said the same words to your mother.'"

I took the phone back to say, "I love you very much," again, and then, "Good-bye, Papatchka."

And it was suddenly the happiest birthday of my life.

The second meeting on my character reference was scheduled for the morning of January 26, at the main studio of Mosfilm.

About 25 men were seated at a long table, and in the center was a dry stick of a man with gray hair, wearing a black suit so old I could see the shine at the elbows from the doorway. This was the head of the KGB at the studio, a man who never smiled, a man who worked among creative people but understood nothing about them. I couldn't help contrasting him with James Huff of the American Consulate staff who had greeted me with smiles and warmth.

I knew there were other KGB people present, but I could only recognize some department heads. There was no one anywhere along the table who really knew me—just faces one nodded to in the corridors—and yet these people were going to judge my character. Or at least they would pretend to. They knew and I knew that only one person in the room counted, and that was the man from the KGB.

It was the same thing all over again except that no one discussed my being an alcoholic. It began with "Why do you wish to go to America?"

"To see my father. He is an old man, and he is very ill."

Papers were examined and passed along the table. The KGB man said, "We have nothing about your father being ill. If that is so, you must provide us with a medical statement as to his health."

I said I would try to get some proof of Papatchka's illness. Then we went again into why I never appeared at the lectures on Marxism and Leninism, and from there to the fact that I was divorced. "Yes, I am. What is wrong with that?"

Black Suit shook his head. "We do not consider it a good idea for a person who is divorced to leave the country."

"Why? It is not shameful."

"It is not shameful, but it is much better if a person going out of the country has family within the country."

I smiled. "Do you think I won't come back? Well, I have a mother here, and you know it very well. I am going to see my father, not to escape." My anger was starting up again. I silently asked Mamula to forgive me if I couldn't control myself.

"You have a lover," Black Suit said. It was not a question, but a statement.

"I *had* a lover," I corrected him, "but it is over. And when I had this lover, we lived together openly without shame."

I said the words looking directly at the man sitting next to Black Suit. He was high up in the studio, and everyone knew that although he was married, an actress had been his mistress for many years. The man lowered his eyes. "Do you regard that as more shameful than sneaking back and forth between a wife and a mistress?"

Black Suit said, "We are here only to discuss you and your character."

"Why don't you discuss me as an actress? At least there you might know something! As a woman, you know nothing about me, and yet you decide that I am good or bad."

Black Suit nodded. "Very well, as an actress you are quite

good, and as a woman you are much less. Do you think with such an opinion we could permit you to represent the Soviet Union abroad?"

I stood up, shaking. "Do you think I care about anything but seeing my father? Do you think he is going to ask me what kind of Russian I am? He is an old man, and I am twenty-nine years old and we have never seen each other. *That* and what we feel for each other are all we are going to talk about."

Black Suit gave a dry smile. "How simple you try to make life. There are rules for Soviet citizens, and those who obey them are rewarded and those who don't obey them . . ."

"You dare to tell me about your rules!" I raged. "Do you think I don't know them, and how they change? Why do you think I have never seen my father? Your rules are why! And my mother suffered from your rules, until a new regime made new rules! Every day of my life I have lived with the brand of illegitimate, and whose fault is it? Yours, each one of you!"

All of the men at the table seemed uncomfortable by my outburst. Only Black Suit seemed as calm as ever. One medal hung from the pocket of his suit, a cheap medal that was given to every citizen who stayed in Moscow when the Nazis were approaching. It was so common that most citizens never wore it. But this little man flaunted his openly as if it were some high award that had been presented only to him. This was the man who was trying to prevent me from seeing a true hero, my father, an American admiral.

Black Suit stood up. "I know I speak for everyone here when I say that we find you completely ill-informed and unsympathetic to the Communist cause, and secondly, a woman who has led an immoral life. This is the character reference we will send to Ovir. With it, you will never see your father or America. You will not even see Kiev."

"Just send the paper," I said through clenched teeth.

"You will see your father the day you see your two ears!" He turned and left the room, and the other men hurried after him.

We will see about that, I said to myself, and then burst into tears.

From the meeting room I went directly to the picture studio and told the man I needed a picture for my passport. He told me to come back when my face looked better. "I don't care what my face looks like. Just take the picture. I need it!"

By the time I left his studio, I knew that word had gotten around about my scene at the meeting. Gossip always traveled with lightning speed at the studio. People who usually spoke to me, or at least smiled, turned away when I passed.

Mamula was waiting for me at the apartment. The minute she saw my face she knew the meeting had gone badly. I told her what had happened. She put her hand to her breast. "We will go to prison for sure," she said.

"Mamula, we are in prison already."

She turned away. "I am going to make some tea."

I went to her and told her what I planned to do. She nodded, but didn't turn around. I put my hands on her shoulders. "Mamula, do you remember how you fought for yourself when you were arrested? How they made a hell of your life to get you to tell them your secret name? And one day, you told them it was Chiang Kaishek."

She turned around, and there was a little smile on her face. "Of course I remember."

I put my arms around her and pressed my cheek to hers. "Well, now it is time for me to fight for my life and my pride and dignity. You must understand."

I felt a strength come into her body. She kissed me and said, "Then let's do it."

I got the slip of paper with the name and telephone number on it that Irina Kirk had left with us, and made the call. A man answered in fluent Russian.

"Is this Chris Wren of *The New York Times?*"

"Speaking."

"Did Irina Kirk ever mention the name Victoria Fyodorova to you?"

"Are you willing to talk to me?"

"Yes," I said, looking at the paper again. "You and Robert Toth of *The Los Angeles Times.* Can you come to our apartment now?"

IRINA KIRK

When she read the "Mary" postcard on her return from Hawaii, Irina Kirk called Jack Tate and told him that she had received the signal to start telling the story to the world.

It was a story she had wanted to write for years, but had held off out of her concern for Zoya's and Victoria's safety. Her writer's instincts told her that the story, with its emotional impact, was highly salable.

But it was only a few days after her return that she saw *The New York Times* of January 27, 1975. Her eye stopped on an article four columns wide and five and one-quarter inches deep. It was headlined: SOVIET CHILD OF WAR WANTS TO VISIT U.S. FATHER.

Irina felt as if her heart were going to stop as she read the story of Victoria's news conference. The story was old news to Irina—she had lived with it for 16 years—but it contained information she wanted to know. "In an interview with two American correspondents. . . ." Good, that meant that Los Angeles had the story, too. It would be picked up by the wire services, and the whole country would know in a matter of hours. That would help to protect Victoria and Zoya.

In another paragraph she found what she most wanted to

know: why Zoya had sent her the "Mary" postcard, and why Victoria had held the news conference.

> The daughter, who is 29 years old and divorced, said there was nothing political in her decision to apply for an exit visa, and that she intended to return to her mother in Moscow. She has received no reply from the authorities, but she feels that since she applied, her film colleagues have grown cool toward her.
>
> Her portrait, she said, was immediately removed from the public office of Sovfilm-Export in downtown Moscow, and the security agent at her studio told her that he disapproved of her wish to go to America.

There were two paragraphs telling of Irina's part in the affair. Irina wasn't certain how she felt about them. She knew that she couldn't be left out, but her inclusion had probably finished off any further trips into the Soviet Union, and that hurt. Victoria and Zoya weren't the only Russians who had sought Irina's help. What would become of the others now? She took it philosophically. In a few months her book of interviews with Russian dissidents, *Profiles in Russian Resistance*, would be published, and that would probably close off the Soviet Union to her anyway.

Irina left the University of Connecticut campus and got into her car to drive home. There was going to be so much to do now that Victoria had thrown the fat into the fire. Irina only wished that she felt stronger. The stay in Hawaii hadn't been long enough for her to recover completely from her experience in Los Angeles. She simply would have to do what she could and be careful.

It was obvious that the Russians weren't going to make it easy for Victoria to get to her father. The question was, how tough were they going to make it? Irina smiled to herself. Well, Victoria wasn't going to be another Zoya and just quietly disappear. Irina knew how to fight the Russians with worldwide publicity. She'd keep Victoria in the headlines until they had to let her come. And Jack Tate was going to help do it. Irina Kirk would show him how.

As she pulled into her driveway, she could hear the telephone ringing. Fine, Irina thought, everybody call. I'll talk to the whole world.

Later on, when she was able to get a copy of the story in *The Los Angeles Times,* she had to laugh at the secondary feature on Jack Tate. The story by Robert Kistler, headlined " 'IT'S ALL TRUE,' ADMIRAL SAYS OF 30-YEAR-OLD STORY," began with a statement that seemed so typical of the man she knew only by letter and long-distance telephone: " 'I don't know why the world is interested in something that is 30 years old,' Jackson Rogers Tate said of his 1944 [sic] Moscow love affair with Zoya Fyodorova." Only Jack, who tried to keep his emotions so hidden, wouldn't know.

Irina had to take the receiver off her telephone to get any rest. But the minute she replaced it, the calls started coming in again. All but the one call she was waiting for—from Jack Tate. She had so much to say to him, things he had to do. Knowing him, he probably thought everyone could just sit back and wait for Victoria's visa to come through. He wouldn't even realize the seriousness of Victoria's picture being removed from the film company office.

She telephoned Victoria in Moscow. Victoria and Zoya didn't know what an impact their story had created in the world outside of the Soviet Union. And Victoria told Irina that she needed some sort of medical statement about Jack's heart condition. Irina said she would try to reach Jack.

Finally, he telephoned, and his first words to Irina infuriated her. She had expected some statement of his gratitude. Instead she got, "Well, we did it!"

He cut her even deeper with what he told her next. "You don't have to worry about the movie rights anymore. I've given them to my old buddy, Jack Cummings."

Irina could feel the tension that had so recently hospitalized her starting up again. "Who is Jack Cummings? When I asked you if you knew anyone in Hollywood, you gave me only the name of that woman who brushed me aside."

"Oh well," Jack said, "he was retired, but I've asked him to come out of retirement just to make this picture."

On January 30, 1975, Irina read a UPI story headlined, "U.S. MOVIE BIZ PLOTTING TO MELT SOVIET RESISTANCE." It told her that "Producer Jack Cummings said yesterday he is contacting several studios about filming the story of retired Admiral Jackson Tate and the bittersweet affair with Zoya Fyodorova, who went to prison for eight years for her political indiscretion."

Only three days after the world learned of the incredible story that Irina had kept to herself for 16 years, she was losing it to people who knew nothing about Victoria and Zoya, and had never even gone inside Russia. Now, when she should have been her busiest working for Victoria's safe coming out of Russia, she was reduced to standing on the sidelines of her story and writing letters to Jack Tate telling him what he must do to help Victoria ("I suggest that you buy a dozen different postcards, write a couple of sentences on each, like 'thinking of you,' or 'this is how Florida looks, hope to be able to show it to you soon myself,' and leave it with Mrs. Tate or Hugh, so if you are ill again, they could send them once a week"). She continued to telephone Victoria to keep her spirits up and even chatted with her by telephone while the television cameras of Channel 3 in Hartford, Connecticut, recorded the event.

Meanwhile, in Moscow, a new character was entering Victoria Fyodorova's life, a man who was to push Irina Kirk, the woman who had begun it all, into the background completely.

HENRY GRIS

In January 1975 Henry Gris and William Dick were in Moscow on a story concerning Russian work in parapsychology. Their paper was the *National Enquirer*.* Gris was its roving editor, and Dick the articles editor. Of the two men, only Gris, who had been born in Latvia, spoke Russian, and he spoke it fluently.

Six feet tall, slim, and gray-haired, Henry Gris was the right man in the right place when the Fyodorova story broke in the world press. Not that he knew about it. There had been nothing about Victoria's news conference printed in Moscow. And when he did learn about it from a call from his editorial offices in Lantana, Florida, he wasn't much interested. He and Bill Dick were much more excited about the important Russian parapsychologist who had consented to see them. But the edi-

---

*The *National Enquirer* is a weekly tabloid owned by Generoso Pope, Jr., and published in Lantana, Florida, a small town outside of Palm Beach. Founded in 1926, the paper became an instant success when Pope took it over in 1952 and souped it up with scandalous stories of celebrity behavior and shocking headlines (MOM BOILED HER BABY AND ATE HER). In 1966, under Pope's editorial leadership, the *Enquirer* started cleaning up its image and became respectable enough to be sold in supermarkets across the country. A recent figure reports its circulation to be 4,000,000 copies a week.

tor in Florida brushed that aside. The Fyodorova story was big news. "We would like to get an exclusive angle on the story of her reunion with the admiral."

He briefly filled Henry in on the story.

Henry asked for an address on the Fyodorova women and was told, "We don't know. Look them up in the phone book."

Henry explained that there were no telephone books in Moscow. The editor said, "Look, they're both actresses, and the mother is very well known. You shouldn't have any trouble."

Henry hung up. In a city of nine million people, he was supposed to locate two of them without any trouble. He turned and told William Dick the good news. "The idea is that we are supposed to help the girl get over to the United States in any way we can, and get an exclusive on it."

The two men were staying at the old National Hotel on Gorki Street. They decided to go into the bar for a drink and dinner. The maitre d', who knew them both, smiled and led them to a table shared by two men. One was a stocky, elderly Russian; the other, a gaunt man, was obviously a foreigner.

Henry and Bill began to discuss the problem of locating Victoria and Zoya. The former, with 30 years of experience behind him with the United Press, is a man who is at ease with anyone and not at all shy about going after what he wants on a story. He turned to the two strangers at the table and struck up a conversation. Once he determined that the gaunt man was from East Berlin, Henry zeroed in on the stocky Russian and hit it lucky. The man was a concertmaster for the Bolshoi and knew people throughout the arts in Moscow. Henry listened politely while the man reminisced about the way it was with the Bolshoi in the past and how shoddy so many of the artistes were today. Finally, Henry asked if the man happened to know an actress by the name of Zoya Fyodorova. The man's eyes lit up. "Of course. A charming woman and a dear friend."

"And her daughter Victoria?"

"Vikka, certainly. The longest legs in Moscow. But why do you ask?"

"My friend and I are trying to locate them for our newspaper."

The man reached into his breast pocket and pulled out a

leather address book. "But how fortunate that we happened to meet. Would you like their telephone number?"

Henry and Bill went to Henry's room right after dinner, and Henry called the telephone number he had been given. Zoya answered the phone. When Henry explained why he was calling, Zoya asked, "What paper is it?"

"It is the *National Enquirer*, but I don't think you would know it," he said. "It is published in Florida."

He heard a pleased gasp from the other end. "Florida? Then you must know the admiral."

Henry explained that Florida was a large place, but still the idea of their working on a newspaper from the same place as Jackson Tate created an opening wedge. Zoya invited the two men to come to see her and her daughter the next afternoon.

It was a brief visit. The men were two hours late for the appointment because the parapsychologist turned out to be a fascinating interview. There was barely time to establish contact with the two women before Gris and Dick had to leave to catch a plane for Riga in connection with their parapsychology article.

But by the time they left, Henry felt that a rapport had been established. He told them they would call when they got to Leningrad, the stop after Riga on their story, and perhaps another meeting could be set up on their return to Moscow. And he assured Victoria that he and his newspaper were prepared to do everything in their power to help her in any way with her visit to her father.

On February 10 Henry called from Leningrad to say that he and Bill Dick would be back in Moscow the next day. Zoya invited them both to dinner at the apartment.

Victoria served her specialty, *pelmeni*, Siberian boiled meat dumplings. The wine that Henry brought was served, but Victoria didn't touch it.

Again the topic of the *National Enquirer* helping Victoria was brought up. "And naturally," Henry said, "we would be willing to pay you for an exclusive story."

"What is exclusive?" Zoya asked.

Henry explained, but the women were uncertain what to say. Finally, Victoria said, "I think you should talk to my father. Whatever he decides we will do."

Henry got out his tape recorder, and the women taped messages to the admiral. Henry said it would help to prove to Victoria's father that he did indeed know them. He even took pictures of the mother and daughter in their apartment.

When they returned to Florida, Henry called Jack Tate. "My co-worker William Dick and I are just back from Moscow and we would like to come and pay our respects to you, Admiral."

Henry couldn't understand the growl that came over the telephone, but it didn't sound friendly. He acted as if it were, however, and sailed right on. "And we have brought photographs and taped messages for you from your daughter and her mother. May we bring them to you?"

Jack told them to come over.

When they arrived at the Club Continental, a 52-unit apartment sprawl—"an inspiration from the fabled Côte d'Azur," according to its membership offering—on the banks of the St. Johns River in Orange Park, they found Jackson Tate waiting for them among the cacti and other plants that cluttered the small patio of his ground-floor apartment. He led the two men into his office and seated himself behind his desk. Henry could tell immediately that Jack Tate was not going to respond to the European charm and manners—tinted with an accent reminiscent of Bela Lugosi's—that had, he thought, appealed to Zoya and Victoria.

He played the tape for Jack and translated. Victoria said, "I love you very much, Papa, and I am looking forward to seeing you," and Zoya said, "I love you very much, Jackson, and I hope that you are in good spirits and in good health."

Jack listened to the tapes and looked at the pictures without saying anything. Henry felt the admiral was not untouched, but that he was playing a waiting game with them. "Well, what do you fellows want? If it's an interview, I've given every last one I plan to give. There isn't a thing I've got to say that isn't already a matter of public record."

His attitude seemed to be more one of irritation than hostility. He was an old man and his nerves were frazzled. "We thought we might be able to help you in some way, Admiral," Henry said.

"Help?" Jack said. "I don't know your newspaper, and I don't need any help. Vicky hasn't even got her visa yet, and if you know the Russians the way I do, she might never get one."

Henry nodded in agreement. "That is true, sir, but if she does get her visa to come over here, how are you going to handle the crush of newspaper reporters that descend on you?"

Jack smiled for the first time. "You know, gentlemen, you don't get the title of admiral by sitting quietly in a corner. I plan to take full charge. I will establish worldwide coverage of the event. I'll tell the press, the radio, and the television, and whatever the hell else there is when they can show up here to see Vicky, talk with her, and take their damn pictures. Then I'm going to send the whole goddamn pack of them away, and Vicky and I will get to know each other in peace and quiet."

As Henry listened, he realized the old man really thought he was going to handle it all as if it were World War II and he was in charge on the bridge of an aircraft carrier. He had no understanding of what the story of himself, Zoya, and Victoria had meant to the whole world. Jack and Zoya had been elevated to the romantic status of Romeo and Juliet. One paper had even compared them to Pinkerton and Butterfly, and Victoria was some long-suffering virginal waif, an Evangeline. If Jack actually handled the press as he said he planned, Victoria would be torn limb from limb and probably have a breakdown before it was over. And Jack would be turned into a cheap clown answering stupid questions with stupid answers.

But this wasn't the time to say any of this. "I understand," Henry said. "We would have liked to have an exclusive arrangement with you and your daughter, for which we would pay, of course, and we would guarantee you both peace and privacy for your first meeting. . . ."

Jack interrupted. "Guarantee peace and privacy, bull! It can't be done."

Henry smiled. "You have your plans, and we will abide with them."

Jack stood up. "Then I guess that finishes this meeting."

Henry had been looking around the walls of Jack's den-office, and he spotted a picture of a younger Jack Tate sitting across from a man he recognized as Jack Cummings. Henry pointed to the picture. "How odd, Admiral, that I should come to Orange Park and see a picture of a friend of mine on your wall. How do you know Jack Cummings?"

"You know him?" Jack said suspiciously. "He's an old buddy of mine from way back when I did some stunt work at M-G-M."

"Certainly, I know him. I would even like to call him."

Jack shrugged, still suspicious. "Okay by me, if you pay for the call."

Henry got out his address book and his telephone credit card and placed the call. "Jack? Henry Gris, and you will never guess where I'm calling from."

As he spoke with Cummings, Henry watched Jack Tate out of the corner of his eye. The face softened, and the suspicion melted away.

Henry finished the conversation with, "Well, I've met Victoria, and I even have some photographs of her. Why don't I call you when I get back to Los Angeles, and we can get together and talk?"

Henry Gris and William Dick said good-bye to Jack Tate and thanked him for his time. No deal had been set.

Henry went to the paper's offices in Lantana and reported that Tate's plans were suicidal. The admiral had no idea what would happen to him and to Victoria but he wasn't going to listen to anyone anyway. "I've done my duty," Henry said. "Now could I please go back to the parapsychology story?"

That was vetoed in favor of Henry meeting with Jack Cummings to see if something couldn't be worked out.

Henry Gris flew to California, and when he met Jack Cummings for lunch in the Polo Lounge of the Beverly Hills Hotel, he realized he had the right man to get Tate to change his mind. Jack Cummings and Jack Tate were old friends and he was advising Tate on getting Victoria out of Russia.

Henry explained the situation, and his personal concern for Jack Tate, to Cummings. "You must talk some sense into him. He looks bad, and Victoria says he is dying, and having seen him, I believe it. Why must he kill himself for this grand press conference? It makes no sense, and it wouldn't work anyway. I think you are the only person who can get through to him."

Jack Cummings said he would call the admiral, but only if the *National Enquirer* would agree to pay Victoria's expenses. Henry said, "I really think it would be better if you went to see him. If you will agree to put in a good word for the *National Enquirer*, I know I can get the paper to pay all the expenses."

JACKSON TATE

Jack had to admit he liked the way Henry Gris operated. Flying Jack Cummings down to see him showed style.

Jack listened to his friend and what he said started to make sense. Henry Gris would personally go into Russia and bring Victoria out and stay with her all the way to Florida. Since the girl had never been outside of the Soviet Union, what did she know about handling herself in the West, especially with all the press of the world after her?

Furthermore, the *National Enquirer* would guarantee Jack and Victoria a chance to spend time together in complete seclusion with luxurious accommodations.

When the deal was finally set, it was agreed that the *National Enquirer* would put in trust for Victoria Fyodorova—this was Jack Tate's stipulation; he didn't want to touch the money—the sum of $10,000 for her use when she arrived in the United States. Furthermore, they agreed to pay all the expenses—housing, flights, food, clothing, etc.—for the three weeks of worldwide exclusivity on the story of the father-daughter reunion that the *Enquirer* wanted. (It can only be guessed at, but $100,000 is a likely figure that the *National Enquirer* ended up spending on its three-week exclusive.)

After the details were worked out between Jack Tate and the legal staff of the *Enquirer*, Henry Gris placed a call to Moscow and put Jack on the telephone with Zoya. Henry remembers the call as a fiasco. Jack tried to use what Russian he could remember, and Zoya tried to speak to him in English. Finally, Henry took over the telephone and explained the *Enquirer*'s deal to Zoya and Victoria. They understood that no interviews were to be given by either of them from the day Henry arrived to bring Victoria out, through the three weeks she would be with her father in a hideaway to be selected by the *Enquirer*.

When Jack finally signed the contract, he grinned at Henry. "This is going to cost you people a lot of money if she ever can come out."

Henry knew the whole deal was academic and would cost nothing unless Victoria got her visa. "What do you mean, *if?* I will get her out."*

Jack shook his head. "No one can *get* her out."

"I'll bet you I can."

Jack said, "How much?"

"Ten bucks."

Jack stuck out his hand. "You got yourself a bet."

The two men shook hands.

"And furthermore," Jack said, "if your paper thinks it can keep a story like this one away from every other newspaper in the world for three weeks, they're crazy."

"We will see," Henry said.

---

* At the moment that Henry Gris told Jack Tate flatly that he would get Victoria out of the Soviet Union, the idea came to Jack Tate that Henry Gris was a member of the KGB. After all, who else could make such a statement with such certainty? It was an idea that was to grow into a fact in Jack's mind.

Henry Gris, recalling the statement, said it was based not on his own ability, but on Jack Tate's denial of the reality of the situation. With the world press continually writing about the wartime lovers and the beautiful daughter who wanted to see her dying father, the pressure of world opinion was on the Soviet government to let Victoria out. They'd have to capitulate sooner or later.

Jack Tate, somewhere along the way in his relationship with Henry Gris, told him that he believed him to be a member of the KGB and that he had "blown his cover"—a favorite expression of Jack's—on the Victoria story. At one of their last meetings, Henry Gris presented Jack Tate with a desk set—a letter opener and scissors—slipcased in black leather. Down the length of the leather sleeve, there were silver letters that read, "With love from the KGB."

IRINA KIRK

These are excerpts from two letters to Jack Tate:

Jan. 31, Saturday
  I thought over your kind invitation to come to Orange Park with Victoria. I think it would be a good idea for the first week or two to be with her. She would want to say things to you that would be too intimate; she would not say it through an interpreter whom she doesn't know. She is rather reticent anyway. And also, since all this will be so exciting, tiring, and emotional she will need someone to talk to at night. Being alone in the Country Club* is new to her, she is very close to her mother and always has had her mother to talk to when she comes home at night, to share things. So I guess it would be better to have me there at first. Please tell me what the Club charges. I was on my sabbatical all of 1974 (this means on half pay) and have to plan to borrow money for this.
  If the reporters ask you about where Zoya spent the eight years, it was in Vladimir Prison. This is probably the most horrendous place there is. Tell them to look up a book, *My Testimony*, by Marchenko.

* A reference to the Club Continental and villas where Jack Tate lived.

Feb. 10, 1975

Of course no one wants to commercialize on this story, but at the same time why should other people make money on Victoria? The *National Enquirer* people who came to see you sent correspondents to Moscow to try to make a deal with Vikka. They offered her plane fare, accommodations, tours of Florida, etc., in exchange for an exclusive interview. She replied that she had to ask me first. She did when I spoke to her over the phone and I said not to make any deals with anyone until she gets here. It can hurt her chances for a visa and she doesn't know whom she is dealing with. So they came here yesterday* (without calling first) because Victoria told them that I will make the decision about that. She has known me for 15 years and trusts me, since she knows very well I could have sold that story long ago and didn't, as I promised her mother I wouldn't. I talked to the man and said that she is buying her own ticket; she doesn't need theirs. Her father is paying her accommodations, so she doesn't need theirs, and she will have enough tour offers as it is, so what is so great about the offer? He asked me what I would suggest. I said that *if* she decided to give an interview to them when she gets here, and only after she gets here, then they will decide how to reimburse her.

---

* A reference to the *National Enquirer*, as represented by Alastair Gregor, a reporter.

VICTORIA

In the days after the press conference with the two American journalists, the telephone rang continually. It was always newsmen from foreign papers wanting to know what was happening. I could only tell them that I was waiting for permission to visit my father. I knew that my character reference was not a good one, but still I was hopeful.

Mamula would put on a brave face whenever she looked at me, but I knew she was very worried. I told her that she had nothing to worry about, and she said, "You have never seen Vladimir."

In February I received the medical report on my father's health through Irina, and I was happy that I couldn't read English. I took it to the Ovir office, and they told me they didn't need it. "Then why was it asked for?" I said.

The man shrugged. "I don't know. If you want we can put it in your file, but it is not necessary."

"Put it in my file," I said and left.

The days all seemed the same, and they moved at a terribly slow pace. I saw few of my friends because I stayed home by the telephone, waiting. Maybe it was just as well, because I didn't want to know how many of my friends felt it was no longer safe to know me.

Of course Kolia called to torture me. "I am really just checking to see if you are still there. Who knows, with the stupid thing you have done, how long you will be at home to answer the telephone?"

"I am hanging up," I said.

"Wait!" he shouted, and then his voice softened. "Please, my Vikka, I need you. And you need me, too. Remember the good times together."

"And I remember the bad times, too, and there were more of those," I said and slammed down the telephone.

Aside from Mamula, the only person I saw with great frequency was Boris—or Borya as I called him—a dancer with the Bolshoi who was sweet and affectionate to me, but who came into my life at the wrong time. He told me he loved me, and he was a kind man, but I couldn't focus my feelings on him. My father was always in my mind, and getting to him while he was still alive was all I could really think about.

The only good sign I had as the month of February slowly dragged by was the telephone calls from Irina Kirk. It had to mean something in my favor that they let her calls get through to me.

It was Irina who told me that the whole world was reading about my desire to go to my father. Within Moscow there was only silence. Irina advised me to stay away from the newspaper that wanted an exclusive deal, but I told her that this man, Henry Gris, had telephoned several times to tell Mamula and me that my father had signed an agreement with the paper. Much as I loved and trusted Iritchka, I felt I had to go along with my father's wishes.

During her telephone calls to me, Irina was always mentioning names like Kennedy and Ford and Senator this and Congressman that, names I didn't even know. I would just say "Oh" and "Really?" as if I thought it was all wonderful and I knew about these people. But I knew what she was doing. She was throwing big names at the KGB, who she was certain monitored her calls to me.

From her I learned about things that were appearing in the

press outside of my country. One newspaper story said that I was going to Siberia to play in a new film. I told her that was a lie. I had spoken with my director, who had promised to try to keep me from being assigned to a new film so I could wait for my permission to go to my father.

Irina asked about John Lind, whom the newspapers said I had had a relationship with similar to that of my parents' until he was thrown out of Russia. I told Irina that John Lind, who was British, was a friend of mine when we were both students at the Institute. If John Lind had been in love with me, I wasn't aware of it.

I hadn't seen John Lind or thought of him in years, but I had received a very nice letter from him when the newspapers started writing about me. He offered to come to Moscow and let the authorities hold him as a hostage for the entire time I was in the United States. I wrote him thanking him for his kindness.

February became March, and I thought I would lose my mind waiting each day for the call telling me to come and get my visa, expecting each day to receive a call that my father had died.

Finally, on March 18 the telephone rang and a dry, crisp, masculine voice said, "Fyodorova, V.?"

"Yes."

"Bring your money—rubles—and your passport. You have been granted a three-month visa." The telephone clicked off.

I screamed and Mamula came running from her room. She had a hand clutched to her breast. I grabbed her and swung her around. "My visa, I've got it!"

IRINA KIRK

Irina was on her way to a temple in Bridgeport, Connecticut, where she was to speak.

She didn't feel well, hadn't felt really well since Los Angeles, so her son Mark was driving. She had stretched out on the back seat and had asked Mark to leave the radio off.

He woke her as he pulled up near the temple. "Mom, we're here, and something seems to be going on."

Irina sat up, still in a daze, and saw a crowd of people. As she opened the door of the car, a man with a tape recorder and microphone rushed up to her and said, "Dr. Kirk, may we have your reaction?"

"Reaction to what?"

The man moved the microphone to his lips. "You mean you don't know?"

"No."

"Victoria got her visa."

Irina burst into tears.

When she got home, Irina placed a call to Moscow. Zoya answered and said Victoria was out, running all over with her visa. The two women chatted about the joyous occasion, and Zoya said that she would have Victoria call back.

Irina tried to reach Jack Tate, but his line was busy. She understood that. Her telephone rang almost continuously with friends calling to congratulate her and with reporters wanting statements.

Victoria called her the next day. "My father is so wonderful," she said. "He is sending Henry Gris, but you mustn't tell anyone this. My father is paying for Henry Gris' ticket, just so Henry can pick me up. My father doesn't want me to travel alone."

Obviously, Victoria didn't fully understand the deal that had been made with the *Enquirer*. "Vikka, this means that I will not see you," Irina said.

"What do you mean?" Victoria's voice sounded hurt and angry. "You promised me you would be at the airport."

"I know I promised, Vikka, but Gris and his people are not going to let me near you."

"What do you mean? Do they think I am some rag doll to be carried around? I have something to say, too. I told Henry Gris how important you were to me, that if it weren't for you nothing would have ever happened. And I know he understood."

Irina said something soothing. Obviously, Henry Gris was in charge, so why upset Victoria? It was all over.

After she hung up, she called Jack again. A male voice she had never heard before said, "I'm sorry, but you can't speak to him."

Irina said, "I am not a journalist. My name is Irina Kirk."

"You can't speak to him."

"What do you mean?"

"Listen, lady, I have my orders." There was a click, and the line went dead.

Irina sat with the telephone receiver in her hand, hearing the buzz of the open line. She was stunned. Sixteen years of work on her part, and at the moment of triumph she was being completely pushed away.

She never spoke with Jackson Rogers Tate again, though on April 1, 1975, she received a letter from him:

Dear Irene:

Man proposes & God disposes. To achieve accomplishment things had to be done my way. For reasons best known to myself* I felt that Vicky's exit visa would not have been approved without Henry Gris' efforts. Certainly her entrance into the U.S. without fanfare, publicity and a news Roman holiday could not have been accomplished. Also it would not have accomplished the dignity to the occasion I desired.

There are also other reasons personal unto myself. Originally I was not in favor of the plans, but my friend Jack Cummings convinced me it was the best idea and now I realize it was best. I am sorry it interfered with your plans but Victoria's welfare and happiness are paramount with me. None of these plans were done for the financial betterment of myself. I do not and Victoria will not commercialize on this visit. She has not & will not sign any contracts for anything. She will visit Hollywood as a social guest of Jack Cummings and Glenn Ford—old friends of mine. This trip has no significance except to meet socially various people connected with American motion pictures.

Both Zoya and Victoria are in accord with my plans.

There will be a reception on April 19th at Orange Park for my friends to meet Victoria and as soon as printed I shall mail you an invitation.

Also as soon as we return home I shall have Vicky call you.

Sincerely,
Jack Tate

P.S. Please—this is not for publication.

The reception was held, but Irina Kirk never received an invitation.

Jackson Tate's letter with its direct, gruff style was his way of explaining things to Irina Kirk. There is no doubt that in some strange way he hoped it would soothe her. For Irina it was the final touch to the whole story, the sour icing on the cake.

* A reference to Jack's belief that Henry Gris was a KGB member and held Victoria's future in his hands.

HENRY GRIS

Henry had kept his visa to enter Russia operative since he had
signed the papers with Jackson Tate. And he had his plan
ready.

The hideaway had already been selected. It was John's Island, a strip of land on the Atlantic Ocean off Vero Beach,
Florida, where 24-hour security was offered to the owners of
the 350 condominiums. The hardbound portfolio for prospec-
tive owners states frankly that John's Island does not want just
anybody. "Our decision was to build a community compatible
with the taste and standards nice people have always lived by.
Our goal was simply to create a place where these people can
live extremely well." The *National Enquirer* was able to rent
three condominiums on Silver Moss Drive, which faced the Atlantic Ocean across State Road A-1-A. They had hoped to get
three units in a row but one owner refused to rent, so they
took two together—one for Jack and Hazy Tate, the other for
Victoria—and the third, one house away, was for security and
National Enquirer staff.

When Henry learned that Victoria had received her exit
visa, he immediately called Jack Tate to tell him the good
news, and to tell him that an *Enquirer* reporter would be com-

ing to take over the telephones. A beige phone with a direct line to the *Enquirer* editorial offices had already been installed in Jack's den next to his white telephone. Jack, as prearranged, was not to answer either one.

A few hours later, Rod Gibson, a reporter for the *Enquirer* who was to be the admiral's official spokesman, arrived. He drew the blinds on all the windows in Tate's four-room apartment. Whenever Jack's phone rang, he would answer and tell people that the admiral was asleep, away, anything that would misdirect them. It was he who refused to let Irina Kirk speak with Jack.

Gibson slept on the couch in Jack Tate's office and never left the apartment while final plans were being drawn for the reunion on John's Island.

On the SAS flight from Los Angeles to Copenhagen where he would transfer, the following morning, to the Russian Aeroflot plane, Henry Gris went over his plans to bring Victoria from Moscow to John's Island in complete secrecy. He knew that Zoya and Victoria were not expecting him this early, but that was part of his plan. The quicker he brought Victoria out, the less likelihood there would be of any slips or leaks. He especially worried about Zoya's talking. Despite everything she had been through, there was still a trusting quality about her that might cause her inadvertently to sink the whole scheme.

He arrived in Copenhagen in the evening and went directly to a hotel to sleep. The next morning he returned to the airport at 10:30 A.M. with plenty of time to spare before the Aeroflot flight was due to arrive. When Henry checked at what gate it would be, there was no Aeroflot listing. He was nervous, but he wasn't worried. He knew how the Russians worked. Aeroflot would leave Moscow, arrive in Copenhagen, be there only long enough to disembark passengers and take on passengers for the return flight. The plane would be in and out of Copenhagen within the hour.

But as the time neared when the Aeroflot listing should have gone up on the arrivals board and nothing appeared, Henry decided to act. He asked at the information desk if there was any other flight out of Copenhagen to Moscow that day, and was told that there was a JAL flight to Tokyo at 3 P.M. that stopped briefly in Moscow. At Japan Air Lines, he asked if they had a seat on that flight. The clerk looked and shook his head. "I am sorry, sir, but there is an excursion group to Tokyo filling the plane."

"It is imperative that I get to Moscow today."

The clerk made a call, and then said, "If it is only to Moscow, we can give you the stewardess's seat. She does not have to sit between Copenhagen and Moscow."

Just as Henry got his JAL ticket, the announcement came over the loudspeaker that the Aeroflot flight to Moscow was canceled, but all tickets would be valid for the next flight, 24 hours later. Henry breathed a sigh of relief. Had he not acted, his entire plan would have been wrecked by the delay.

And JAL was better for his purposes anyway. Anyone watching for his arrival—and he had no idea if anyone was—would be expecting him on Aeroflot 24 hours later. He telephoned Victoria to say he would be in Moscow that evening and wanted to see her. He would telephone again from Sheremetyevo Airport as soon as he arrived.

The JAL flight was uneventful, and no one seemed to notice his arrival at Sheremetyevo. He telephoned Victoria. He was going directly to the Hotel Berlin, he said, to freshen up and get a bite to eat, and then he wanted to see her and her mother. He set a time, and Victoria said she would pick him up in her car.

It was after ten in the evening, a Thursday night, when he arrived at the Hotel Berlin, in the heart of Moscow. Victoria picked him up at 10:45 P.M. in her baby-blue car. There was a man seated beside her who had a pleasant Russian face and hair that came down over his ears. She introduced Henry to her special friend Boris Groshikov, Borya. Henry was annoyed. Now there was another person in on his plans.

When they arrived at Zoya's apartment she was delighted to see him, but when he told her that Victoria was leaving on Saturday, she became agitated and tears came into her eyes. "So soon?"

Victoria said, "I am ready, but I have a ticket for next week."

Henry shook his head. "No, it must be Saturday, and I have tickets for both of us, first class."

Henry had ordered two tickets for the Pan Am Sunday morning flight from Moscow to New York under the names Victoria Fyodorova and Henry Gris. He had no intention of using them, but he wanted the people in the Moscow office of Pan Am to have that information, knowing that someone would be sure to leak it to the foreign press corps (the Russian press had no interest in Victoria).

He could picture the crush of reporters and photographers at the Pan Am gate on Sunday morning looking for Victoria, who would already have been out of the country for 24 hours.

"But I have told so many people that my Vikka will not go to her father until next week," Zoya complained.

"Fine," Henry said. "Leave it that way. Now where will you be during the three weeks we have Victoria and her father in seclusion?"

Zoya said, "Four days from Saturday I leave on a theatrical tour."

"Good. That means only four days in which you must not speak with anyone about where Victoria is. It would even be better if you didn't answer your telephone."

"I will not tell," Zoya said.

Henry opened his attaché case and brought out a curly wig with grayish-blond streaks in it. "Here, try this on," he said to Victoria.

Then he handed her a pair of dark sunglasses with huge round lenses. "Do you have a coat that will conceal your figure? You know, not every girl in Moscow looks like you."

Victoria got her long gray overcoat and put it on. It came down almost to her ankles. Henry nodded approval. With the wig, the glasses, and the coat, she didn't look like the Victoria Fyodorova whose picture had appeared in the free press all over the world.

Victoria studied herself in the mirror. "I look crazy."

It was now almost one, Friday morning, and Henry went back to the Hotel Berlin. Before leaving he again reminded Victoria, Zoya, and Borya that nothing must be said to anyone about Victoria's leaving on Saturday morning, or her whereabouts for the next three weeks.

VICTORIA

Friday. The streets of Moscow suddenly looked different and new to me. This was the last day I would see them for three months. I still could not believe my dream was coming true. In only hours—I had no idea of how many—I would see my papa for the first time. I could not stop thinking about it, and yet it was beyond imagining.

Henry Gris had called us the first thing in the morning while Mamula and I were still having our first coffees of the day. He wanted to know what I was doing, who had called, and a million more questions. I wondered if he was taping our conversation. In all the time I had known Henry Gris, his tape recorder was always with him. It was like another ear attached to him.

I told him that Borya and I were going to exchange my rubles for dollars. Henry told me I shouldn't, that he would give me money. "I am going," I said stubbornly. I was beginning to become annoyed with the man. He didn't seem to trust any of us for a minute out of his sight.

"Very well," he said, "but remember . . ."

"I know," I said. "If anyone asks me, I will say that I do not know when I am going to America."

We arranged to meet in front of the Hotel Berlin at four in the afternoon.

When I met Henry, he rushed me into a car after looking every which way, like in a spy movie. We were driven to the airport, where Henry told me to go to the girl at the Aeroflot desk and get us two seats on the Saturday morning flight from Moscow to Brussels. I looked at him. Was he going crazy? "Why Brussels?"

"Exactly," Henry said and smiled. "And when you give our names for the tickets ask the woman as a favor not to tell anyone that you are going on this flight."

I could see he was not going to explain, at least not here, so I did as he told me.

When I was back in the car, he said, "All right, we are going to Brussels for many reasons. One, because no one would expect you to fly to Brussels of all places, and because we already have reservations on Sabena from Brussels to New York City. Secondly, Brussels is one of the few airports that has a hotel that is available to in-transit passengers, which means you can rest between flights without having to show your visa, so no one will even have to know you are there at all."

I had to admit that Henry, though annoying at times, was a brilliant thinker—maybe a schemer was a better word.

"The reason I had you buy the tickets is because you are a Russian and the woman behind the desk is a Russian. If you ask her not to tell anyone, she won't. If I asked, she might think, 'What do I care about the capitalist press?' and tell someone, and then that whole mob that will be at Pan Am on Sunday morning would be over here tomorrow morning. You understand now?"

I nodded. I thought Henry Gris was acting like a spy in a comedy. "Did you get your money changed?" he asked.

"Yes," I said, "and no one asked any questions. I just showed them my visa, and there was no trouble. And what did you do?"

Henry smiled. "There were many, many calls to make concerning your meeting with your father. Then I went to see your mother to interview her for the story I will write about all of you."

"Did Mamula tell you about tonight?"

Henry nodded. He did not seem pleased. "Yes, and I wish she had not done it. It means more people will know about your going."

"It is not a party," I said. "Just a few very close friends. And Mamula did not say when I would go, so it is all right. There will be just Borya and Yosh and her daughter—Yosh was with Mamula in Vladimir—and Mama who is my Aunt Alexandra. That is all."

Mamula seemed upset when I came home. She already had the table set, and things were cooking on the stove. A bottle of cognac and a bottle of vodka were on the table, and there was also a carafe of wine. "What is wrong?" I asked.

"It is that Henry Gris with that machine of his," she said. "He was here with questions, questions, terrible questions about your father and me."

"Well, he is a journalist," I said.

Mamula shook her head angrily. "The questions he was asking. I have never seen such things in a newspaper."

"You should have told him to shut up and leave you alone."

"He is not such an easy man to control."

It was a happy evening at the beginning. Mamula wore her curly blond wig, and she made me put on the one Henry had brought. I could see an angry look cross Henry's face, as if the wig gave his secrets away.

I didn't drink, of course, but Mamula had at least three glasses of wine, which is more than I had ever seen her drink before.

Yosh suddenly stood up and raised her glass. She looked slyly at Mamula and then said, "Do not worry, ladies. The Americans will save us all!"

She and Mamula laughed hysterically as they remembered the time in Vladimir when Yosh had said that.

It was a warm and lovely evening until Henry took out his tape recorder and leaned close to Mamula to say something. I saw her stiffen and her face grew red with anger. "No!"

I knew he was at her again for the intimate facts of her time with my father. "Stop it, Henry," I said, "don't you see that you are hurting her?"

He apologized and sat back, but the tape recorder stayed in his lap.

Yosh started on some incredible story about Vladimir that she swore was true, which made us all laugh, but then Henry said something to Mamula again. She burst into tears. "Help me, Vikka, he keeps pestering me."

I stood up. "Go home, Henry. I am very angry with you."

He said, "Neither of you understands that I have to have all the details if I am to write this story."

"Well, all the details are not available to you. I want you to leave!"

Henry shrugged and put away his tape recorder. "Very well, but I will see you early tomorrow morning. You know what time."

HENRY GRIS

It was after midnight when Henry Gris left the party. He would pick Victoria up at five in the morning to go to the airport. He decided to walk to the Hotel Berlin. There were still telephone calls to make to the United States and he needed the cold night air to clear the wine and cigarette smoke from his brain.

He hoped he was right in not having tried to stop the party from taking place. It was a risk, since none of them really seemed to understand how important secrecy was to Victoria's departure. Well, he couldn't play the Gestapo with them too much. He had already offended Zoya and Victoria. But what had he asked? In the United States he doubted it would even be regarded as an intimate question. Why did Zoya want to have Jack's baby? If Jack didn't realize that their chances of being together after the war were slight, surely Zoya must have. But Zoya took offense, as if he were asking her to describe their sexual positions. Russians, a strange breed!

At the hotel he placed a call to the newspaper in Florida. Yes, Jack and his wife had been moved out in the middle of the night to the hideaway retreat. No one had seen the fleet of cars departing. Okay, so one half of the cast of characters had gotten away safely. Now, the rest was up to him and all the other *Enquirer* people who would be joining them as Victoria and he made their way more than halfway around the world.

Moscow was still asleep at 5 A.M. on Saturday, March 22, 1975. Henry sat in the back of the rented car and looked out at the streets. There was no one. He was pleased at the light dusting of snow. Anyone hiding in a building entrance would leave footprints.

Henry leaned forward and spoke to the driver in Russian. He made his voice crisp and official-sounding, and he could see the driver's back stiffen to attention. "I want you to know that I am taking the actress Victoria Fyodorova to America. This is an official mission, and I want you to protect us from any foreign correspondents who might try to come close to her. This car must not be interfered with, do you understand?"

The Russian driver touched his fingertips to his cap. "Certainly, comrade. I will make sure."

The car turned onto Kutuzovsky Prospekt. They came alongside the gates to the apartment building, and Henry scanned the first entranceway. The snow was unbroken. The car went across the park and through the low entranceway to the section in which Zoya lived. He told the driver to park immediately inside the courtyard and to keep watch.

Henry entered the building and went up the stairs, wondering what mood he would find the two women in. He had to admit that he felt a faint twinge of guilt at how the evening before had ended. He did not think of himself as a hard, indifferent reporter, though he suspected that was how Victoria and her mother saw him.

The women were at the dining table opposite each other, doing their faces in mirrors propped up in front of them. Borya hovered in the background. Happily, both Zoya and Victoria were pleasant. The incident that had ended the previous evening seemed forgotten. Zoya offered Henry a coffee, and Victoria said she had barely slept because of the excitement of the coming trip. She already had the wig on. She slipped on the sunglasses and stood up. She was wearing dark slacks and a jacket. She got her overcoat and put it on. Henry smiled in approval. "I am ready," she said and pointed to the small suit-case and the bag that contained the presents she had bought for her father and his wife.

Henry told Borya to go down and look around to make certain there was no one lurking about. Zoya got up and went for her coat. "What are you doing?" Henry said.

"I am going to the airport."

"You can't," Henry said. "You are too well known. You will attract attention."

Zoya burst into tears. Victoria put her arms around her mother. She turned on Henry. "Of course she is coming. And Borya, too. There is no one there. The whole world thinks I am going tomorrow. You said it yourself."

Henry said, "All right, but they must both say good-bye in the car. They cannot come with us into the airport."

Zoya accepted that.

Borya came back to say there was no one but the car and driver. Henry insisted that they go down by the stairs, not the elevator.

Outside he took a quick look around to see that there was no one hidden anywhere. Then he signaled for Victoria, Zoya, and Borya to come out. To his annoyance, Zoya insisted on sitting up front with the driver, because "that is where I always sit." Henry put Victoria in the middle of the back seat.

They started out for the half-hour drive to Sheremetyevo. It was growing light, but the sun had not become visible yet. There were only a few people on the streets.

Henry had the driver stop several yards from the Aeroflot building. Borya kissed Victoria and whispered something to her. She nodded. Then Henry signaled to him and they both got out of the car so that Victoria and her mother could say their good-byes in private.

VICTORIA

Mamula began to cry as we kissed good-bye. "Why, Mamula, why? It is only for three months, and then I will be back."

"I know," she said, "but it is so far away."

I kissed her again. "You know that you are being silly. Is it so different than if I were in Moldavia or any of the other places where I have gone to make films? Think of it that way."

She nodded and dabbed her eyes. "I know, but for me there are always those years when we were not together. It is always hard for me to give you up for even a minute."

Henry was signaling. Mamula and I kissed again. "I love you the best in the whole world," I whispered against her cheek. And then I left the car.

Henry took a camera case on a strap from his shoulder and put it on mine. I guess I was supposed to look like an American tourist. I felt foolish in the wig and big sunglasses, but Henry seemed satisfied.

Of course we were much too early for the 9 A.M. flight to Brussels, but I had given up asking Henry questions. He got us onto the check-in line, which was short at this early hour, and then he took me straight to the departure gate. The whole time we stood there, Henry kept looking around to see if anyone was watching. I was certain he would sprain his neck.

Finally, the gate opened. Henry grabbed my arm and rushed me onto the plane. We were the first on board and I was embarrassed when he made a scene with the stewardess, insisting that we had first-class accommodations. So this was the man who knew everything? He didn't even know that all Aeroflot flights were one class.

But he got what he seemed to want. We were given the two very front seats. Henry told me to get inside against the window, then with one more look around, he seated himself beside me.

"What was that foolishness about?" I whispered to him. "In the Soviet Union there is no such thing as first class. You should know that."

Henry smiled. "Of course I do. I just wanted to make certain I got these two seats with no one in front of us. Now all anyone can see is the back of your head."

We took off, and I looked down on Moscow disappearing as the clouds moved in. I couldn't believe it. I was actually going outside of the Soviet Union, and with each minute that passed I was a minute nearer to my father. I took out my handkerchief and wiped at my eyes under the sunglasses.

"Are you all right?" Henry asked.

I nodded.

"In about three hours we will arrive in Brussels, where we will be met by John Checkley, a reporter from our London office. He will act as another bodyguard for you. We will take you to a hotel within the airport, where you can have a rest, because it is several hours until the Sabena flight to New York."

I turned back to the window, but there was nothing visible outside except for the clouds.

Henry turned around to the man and woman seated directly behind us. "Pardon me, do you have the time?" He asked the question in Russian.

The man said in German that they did not understand.

Henry nodded. That was what he wanted to know.

Henry got out his tape recorder. "I want you to tell me everything you can remember about your entire life."

I told him that I didn't feel like talking just yet. My emotions were still churning around inside of me. "Please, let it wait until after Brussels," I said. "There will be time then, and I will feel better."

He put his tape recorder away. The stewardess brought us a lunch of cold chicken, a thick piece of black bread with butter, a glass of red wine, and a glass of soda water. I thought it was very good, but Henry barely touched his food. "Don't your countrymen ever feed their chickens? This one is old and skinny and tough."

"I like it."

"Wait," he said. "When we are on Sabena, you will see what first-class service is."

"Okay," I said, and continued eating. The chicken *was* tough, but I wouldn't admit it to Henry. Somehow, because I was leaving my country, I felt very defensive about it, even as I was excited about seeing what the capitalist countries looked like.

For the hundredth time, I checked the flight bag under my seat to make certain it was still there. It contained a little metal jewel box and a nest of painted wooden dolls that sat one inside the other for my father's wife, and there was an amber medallion for my father.

When we landed at Brussels, Henry waited until half the passengers on the plane disembarked before we stepped into the aisle. "Stay in the middle of the crowd when we leave," he said.

He had a tight grip on my arm. "Do not speak in Russian." I started to tell him he was hurting my arm, but he said, "Better not speak at all."

I really thought he was crazy. Who was looking for me in Brussels? And I almost burst out laughing when we came off the plane and there was no one waiting there for us. "We'll go into the airport," Henry said.

We started up the long corridor. Two men wearing Sabena caps were walking toward us. As they passed, one of the men took a disinterested glance at us, but continued walking. Henry turned around. "John?"

The other man stopped and looked from Henry to me. I realized that each of these two super international agents didn't even know what the other looked like. John Checkley came over. "Henry Gris?"

Checkley was a tall man wearing glasses and not the bodyguard type. The two men shook hands, and then Checkley introduced the Sabena official. John Checkley said, looking at me, "Is that Victoria Fyod—"

Henry cut him off. "Shhh. Yes."

The official led us to the hotel and up to a bedroom.

"You can sleep here if you wish," Henry told me. "Bathe, do whatever you want. It is five hours until the New York flight. I have things to do. You are not to use the telephone."

I laughed. "I do not know anyone in Brussels."

"Nevertheless," he said, "do not answer the telephone if it should ring. Do not open the door for anyone other than myself. I will send you up something to eat later on."

"I need some cigarettes. Can't I go out and see the airport?"

"I am sorry, no. It is too risky. I will get you cigarettes." He started for the door. "Fix your watch. Brussels is not on the same time as Moscow." He gave me the correct Brussels time.

"Can I take off the wig and the glasses?"

"Of course," he said, as if I had asked a stupid question. But he came back into the room and drew the drapes over the window. "Leave them closed."

After examining everything in the room and in the bathroom—I was impressed with it all, such luxury—I finally lay down. It was so good to take off the wig, which made my head itch, and the sunglasses, which I found annoying. I closed my eyes, not expecting to sleep. But the next thing I knew there was a knocking on the door. It was Henry with cigarettes, a lemonade, and a sandwich with something in it I didn't recognize. He told me it was tuna fish salad. I liked it.

Then he said if I was going to shower before the flight I should do so now.

"I cannot meet my father this way. See what that wig does to my hair. There must be a hairdresser when we get to New York."

"Yes, yes, everything is arranged," Henry said, but I didn't think he was paying attention to me. "I will be back for you in two hours. I have some more calls to make."

And he was gone again.

I didn't put on the wig until Henry came back. John Checkley and the man from Sabena were with him, as were two other Sabena men.

"We are going directly to the plane now," Henry said. "We will be on every side of you. If someone should come toward you, you are to look straight ahead and keep walking. And speak to no one, no matter what."

I nodded. Henry and John fell in on either side of me. I insisted on holding the flight bag myself, but John took my suitcase. The three Sabena men walked with us, one in front and two behind. I was amazed that no one turned to stare. I thought we looked like a small army. And I wanted to laugh at Henry and John, looking every which way as we walked. Two middle-aged men acting like little boys playing spies, and nobody in the airport cared.

The Sabena men took us directly onto the 747 jet. A stewardess led us to first class and we had the front two seats again. John sat back on the aisle at the head of tourist class so that he could stop anybody suspicious who might try to get through to where we were.

Henry made me take the window seat again. "Can I speak?" I asked.

"Not in Russian."

"That is all I know. That and a few words of English."

"Then don't speak."

"But there is no one on the plane."

"They are coming," Henry said.

"At least let me talk until the other passengers come. I want to know what happens next. How many hours until we get to New York?"

"We will be in New York this evening. There will be a short delay between flights and then we will fly to Miami."

"Will I see my father then?"

"No. We will drive to where he is."

"How many hours?"

"Just a few more."

The first passengers started to board, and Henry put his finger to his lips.

I sat back.

Of course, there was no one on the flight the least bit interested in me. In time, even Henry believed it and allowed me to go to the bathroom. The first thing I did was take off the wig, which was giving me a headache. I could have stayed in that bathroom for an hour just for the pleasure of not having that elastic around my head, but I knew that any minute Henry would come and probably break the door down.

When I returned to my seat, Henry had the tape recorder out again. He wanted to know every fact I could remember about my life. It helped to pass the time.

There was only one bad moment, and that was when the stewardess came around to take our food orders.

I didn't understand her. I said only one word in Russian, the one for "what," and I got a kick in the ankle from Henry.

He ordered something for me and told the stewardess, who was looking curiously at me, that I was from East Berlin and couldn't understand her.

My dinner turned out to be shish kebab, which was delicious. I had never tasted meat so good, and I couldn't believe that in the West they just gave it away free on the airplanes. Of course I said nothing when Henry leaned toward me and said, "Do you still prefer the Aeroflot chicken?"

"That was very good, too." I cannot explain my sudden need to defend everything Russian, but I think it had something to do with the fear that was starting to build in me the nearer we got to my father. I had looked forward to the moment of our meeting for so long, and now when it was no longer a dream I was beginning to be afraid. What if he didn't like me?

And so I was hanging onto the only thing I had, my Russianness.

HENRY GRIS

Henry looked over at Victoria. She had finally fallen asleep. He glanced at his wristwatch. They would be in New York within the hour.

He smiled at her. She was a tough cookie, all right. It was funny the way she defended everything Russian all of a sudden. He had never had any impression before that she was chauvinistic. He suspected that inside she was scared stiff, but she would never admit that. Well, that was her problem.

He envied her being able to sleep. Even if he could, he didn't dare. He had to stay alert. Who could say what would happen? Of course, Victoria thought he was a fool. She didn't understand half of what was going on around her, or what a miracle of journalism was being pulled off right in front of her. He smiled at the thought of the crush at Sheremetyevo on Sunday morning.

He got out his notebook to check details of the next step of their trip. The New York airport would be a problem because Victoria would have to show her papers there. But the admiral had called the immigration authorities in Washington and explained the need for his daughter to go through as quickly as possible, and with little fuss. The man at the other end of the phone had told him that he would personally alert the men on duty at Kennedy.

Tate and his wife were already at John's Island, and so were Rod Gibson, and Diane—Dee Dee—Albright, an editorial assistant who would be Victoria's companion on the island.

A call to the editorial offices had assured Henry that four *Enquirer* reporters would be waiting by the customs area to surround Victoria when she came through. The cars would be just outside the building at the nearest parking space.

While in Brussels Henry had also placed a call to Zoya's apartment and was pleased when he was told that there was no answer.

"Remember, no talking from now on. Only to the man who will ask for your papers, and nothing more with him than you have to."

Victoria nodded wearily.

They stayed in the middle of the passengers disembarking in New York. John Checkley stepped to Victoria's side as soon as she and Henry cleared the first-class exit. The three of them walked swiftly. They walked her directly to the gate for foreign visitors. John, a British citizen, stayed right behind her while Henry, an American citizen, went to his line.

While he was waiting, Henry scanned the entire area beyond the gates. There was one man standing beside the exit door to the waiting rooms who looked like a newspaperman. There was something about his extremely casual air. Henry signaled to John, then nodded his head toward the man. John saw him and nodded back.

Henry had only his attaché case. He cleared customs just as Victoria came abreast of the inspector, who looked from her photograph to the woman standing before him. "Fyodorova? We are expecting an admiral's daughter named . . ."

"Yes, yes," John said before the man could say the name aloud again. "This is she. And please, as you have been told, speed is essential in clearing her."

"Of course," the inspector said and stamped her visa. "Good luck, Miss Fyodorova, and a happy reunion."

Henry grabbed her as she stepped free. "Turn your back to the door."

They waited for John to come through. "You see him?" Henry said.

John nodded. "I'll bump into him, and while I'm apologizing, you and the girl slip by."

But when they came to the door, there was no one there. The man, whoever he was, had gone. As they came through, four men quietly stepped forward and casually surrounded them. Nothing was said.

Outside there was a limousine, and Henry helped Victoria into the center of the back seat. Two men sat on the jump seats facing her.

They went straight to the International Inn only minutes away. As they got out of the car, Henry said to Victoria, "Don't look around. Just walk straight into the lobby and stay close to me."

VICTORIA

I didn't even look up. All I saw was the carpeting as I walked beside Henry. Then we were at a table and someone had pulled out a chair for me. I heard piano music and a woman's voice singing. I thought it was a record, and then I looked up. There was a woman in an evening gown sitting at a piano, accompanying herself as she sang. I looked around. From films I had seen, I knew this was a cocktail lounge, something we did not have in Moscow.

"Would you like something to drink?" Henry asked.

"Something," I said, "but not alcohol."

I think it was a lemonade, only sort of bitter. It didn't matter. I was trembling. We would sit in this place for an hour or so, and then there was only one more plane ride between me and my father. Suddenly I wanted more time. I wasn't ready.

Henry was speaking to the other men at the table. I understood very little of what they were saying. And the woman kept singing. I was in the middle of a crowd and I felt terribly alone, and frightened. What was I doing here at night somewhere in New York City? There was no one at any of the tables that I could see in the dimly lit room who was dressed anything like me. I felt like a fool, certain that I stood out as a freak. I heard a man and a woman laughing and I didn't dare look at their table. I knew they were laughing at that crazy woman in the long overcoat with the insane wig and glasses. Dear God, why had I agreed to all of this just to go to someplace called Florida to meet a man I had never seen before? He was my father only because of a physical act with my mother. There were no emotional bonds between us. We had never shared one second of our lives. Maybe Kolia was right. I should have just settled for a photograph.

I felt tears coming to my eyes. Thank God for the glasses. Then there was a sob, and I saw Henry look at me. "Are you all right?"

I nodded. That brought me out of myself. What was I doing? Torturing myself, that was all. Hadn't my father bought Henry Gris's ticket so he could come for me? My father did feel for me; he did want me.

I felt better. It was exhaustion, and that damn wig pressing against my head.

Finally, Henry touched my arm. He put some money on the table and stood up. We all got up, and again the men surrounded me, and we went back to the limousine. The night felt cool, but not as cold as Moscow. Then I was inside the limousine again and we were heading for LaGuardia Airport. "I want to say something, Henry."

He looked at me. "Yes?"

"I asked for someone to do something with my hair, and you said yes. But now we are going to the airport again. I mean what I say, Henry, I will not have my father see me for the first time looking terrible. I must bathe and do something with my hair."

I could tell the way he looked at me that he knew I meant it. I did not take my eyes from his. Finally, he nodded. "I will call Miami from the airport and arrange for someone."

"Don't forget."

HENRY GRIS

It was the first time he had heard that tone in her voice, and Henry Gris didn't doubt for a minute that Victoria would refuse to see her father unless her hair was properly done. She was the admiral's daughter all right.

He called the newspaper in Florida from the airport lounge. The editor at the other end sounded exasperated. "Are you going soft in the head, Henry? Where the hell are we supposed to get a hairdresser at this hour? Forget it."

"I tell you she wants one, and she is a most stubborn young woman. We've got to do something."

"Well, we're sure as hell not going to rouse a hairdresser in the middle of the night. You think he or she wouldn't be suspicious, and all we need is for someone to recognize her and blow this whole story wide open."

"True," Henry said, "so find someone on the staff to help her."

"I'll think about it and get word to you at Miami."

Henry told Victoria it had been arranged for her hair to be done in Florida. They got on the plane. It was well after 10 P.M. Saturday night. John Checkley stayed in New York to fly back to London the next day. Just Henry, Victoria, and two of the four reporters who had met them went. There were only a handful of passengers, so it was easy to seat Victoria next to a window, with Henry beside her and one reporter in front of her, the other behind.

As soon as they were in the air, Victoria said, "You are sure about the hairdresser, Henry?"

"I called about it. The editor I spoke with said he would do something. I don't know what you think goes on in this country, but beauty parlors do not stay open all night here."

"And I have not waited 29 years for this moment to look like something my father will be ashamed of."

There was that tone again. Henry could hear her father speaking the same way when they first met and Jack told him he was going to run the press conference.

Henry leaned back in his seat and closed his eyes. He doubted that he would sleep but he wanted to try. His eyes burned and his jaw ached from the tension that had been building up since they had left Moscow. That had to be over 24 hours ago, but he was too tired to work out all the time zones they had passed through.

He opened his eyes and glanced over at Victoria. She was staring out the window at the dark night.

VICTORIA

It was too dark to see anything out of the window. I only knew that somehow I was flying over the United States, maybe even Florida, and soon I would be standing looking at Papatchka.

The fear I had felt before didn't come. I was too tired. My whole body ached and my head burned with the heat of the wig. When I could finally take it off, I would tear it to shreds and burn it. The glasses, too.

I thought about Mamula and wondered what she was doing at this minute. I didn't even know if it was night or day, or what day it was in Moscow. How I wished she could be here with me right now. This moment was hers, too, maybe even more than it was mine. She should have the pride of showing Jackson the child they had made with their love. She could even talk to him with her few words of English.

I felt a tear slide down my cheek. I didn't bother to wipe it away. Henry was asleep. Who could see? Poor Mamula. She had had so much of her life destroyed because she had loved a man she was not supposed to. And now, at the moment when her story became complete, she would not even be there. Life was unfair.

A little bell sounded and some words that I could not read lit up. I knew it was the signal that we were going to land. Henry opened his eyes and looked at his wristwatch. "Miami," he said.

Again, another army of men surrounded us, and this time there were three cars. Henry and I got into the middle one. I was outside for only a minute, but I was amazed by the warmth of the air. In Moscow it was still winter. Even in New York it was cold.

The first car pulled away from the curb, and ours followed. Henry and I were in the back seat. There were two *National Enquirer* men in front. "Well, it looks like we are going to pull this off, Henry," one of them said.

Henry laughed. "We? Where were you in Moscow when all this started?"

I tugged at his sleeve. "The hairdresser, Henry." I saw an annoyed look cross his face as he leaned forward to talk to one of the men. I knew he thought I was a silly female, but I didn't care. It was important that my father see me for the first time with pride in his eyes.

Henry sat back. "We are stopping along the way. There is a woman waiting who will help you."

I turned back to the window trying to see Florida, but all I saw was an occasional palm tree and the jackrabbits that ran across the road in front of the car lights.

The car in front of us began to slow, and our driver slowed down, too. There was a car up ahead on the side of the road that flashed its lights and pulled out in front of our lead car. "What is the matter, Henry?"

Henry said, "That is Iain Calder, our editorial director. He is leading us to his house in Boynton Beach where you can shower and have your hair done."

"Can I take off this wig now?"

"When we get to his house."

HENRY GRIS

Jane Calder was standing out on their front lawn as the cars pulled up. When Victoria stepped out, Jane went to her as if they were old friends, put an arm around her shoulder, and led her into the house.

Iain led the men into the huge living room of the two-story house. A table with coffee and sandwiches on it stood in front of the stone fireplace. Henry was too tired to eat. He just wanted coffee. A council of war was held while Victoria was upstairs. A photographer told them they must not arrive until approximately 6:40 A.M. "We'll want the sun coming up behind her as she comes into the house, and it would be best if there were light coming through the windows. Sunrise is 6:27 A.M., so you ought to give it at least 10 minutes before you start up to the house."

Henry looked at his watch. It was only 2:46. "What are we supposed to do for four hours? It's not that far to Vero Beach and John's Island."

Someone said, "Well, we ought to be able to keep her here until after three at least. Surely she doesn't expect her father to be up in the middle of the night waiting for her."

"I don't know what she expects," Henry said, "but I know

she has waited her entire life for this meeting. I don't see how we can hold her back."

"Oh, come on, Henry. This isn't the first story you've ever handled. You'll think of some way to stall."

Henry nodded. "I suppose so."

Victoria came down at five minutes after three. She had showered and applied fresh makeup. Her hair had been washed, and then dried and arranged by Jane Calder. It hung simply on either side of her face, with a slight wave to it. She looked at Henry questioningly.

He went to her. "You look lovely. Your father will be very proud."

"I hope so. I won't wear the wig anymore, Henry."

Henry smiled. "No, of course not."

Iain Calder fixed her a cup of coffee and a plate of sandwiches. Victoria tried to refuse. "No, we should go," she said in Russian.

Henry told her there was time and she should eat. "We still have a few hours' drive."

It was 3:30 when they left the Calder house. The night air was chilly and Victoria pulled her coat around her as she stepped back into the white Lincoln. Henry slipped in beside her.

The lead car swung out from the curb. It was a short drive back to the highway. The road was dark and deserted. "Aren't we going slower?" Victoria asked.

"I don't think so," Henry said. "I think it is because you are excited that it seems that way."

VICTORIA

I don't know why I kept staring out the window. There was nothing out there to see except the night and an occasional palm frond caught in the headlights. But I kept looking as if I suddenly expected a sign that would say THIS IS WHERE YOUR FATHER LIVES.

I wished I had changed into a dress. At least my hair looked nice again, that was something.

Suddenly there were lights up ahead and the car in front pulled in beside a building.

"What is this place?" I asked Henry.

"It is an all-night restaurant."

I didn't understand. "But we have just eaten."

I saw Henry glance at his wristwatch as he opened the car door. "I'll find out."

He went up to the head car. Then he came back. "It is one of the men. He wants bacon and eggs."

"Now?" I felt my nerves snapping. I couldn't believe it. I had traveled who knows how many hours, had come within a few miles of my father, and now they expected me to sit still while some man ate bacon and eggs.

Henry put his lips close to my ear. "I believe the man has a certain illness like diabetes. He has to eat certain things at certain times or it could be very bad for him. You must understand."

So we all went into this restaurant. We were the only people there. Henry sat me with my back to the front door, and this photographer ordered bacon and eggs and coffee. Henry ordered coffee for me.

It seemed to take forever for the man's food to come, and then I swear I have never seen a human being eat so slowly, one little bite of food at a time. I kept looking up at the clock on the wall, watching the hands move toward five o'clock, and still the man ate.

We didn't leave the restaurant until twenty minutes after five. I wanted to go and hit that man. I had had two cups of coffee that I didn't want, and I do not know how many cigarettes, waiting for him to finish.

At last, we were moving again, three cars in the night on an empty highway, and then the coffee started catching up with me. I had to go to the bathroom. I tried to think of something else. I didn't want us to stop again. Someone else might want bacon and eggs, and I would never see my father.

Finally, I had to tell Henry. He leaned over to the driver. "There is a rest area just a little way ahead."

The driver of our car tapped his horn to signal the car up ahead. When we came to the rest area he hit his horn again and put on his turn signal and we swung in. Everyone got out. I went inside the ladies room and into a booth and fixed the lock behind me.

When I was ready to leave, I couldn't unlock the door. I twisted at the lock, but it wouldn't give and the door came down almost to the floor so that I couldn't crawl under.

I was nearly hysterical. I didn't know whether to laugh or to cry. Twenty-nine years of waiting and here I was locked in a toilet. I started pounding on the door, but no one heard me.

Suddenly I saw that the lock didn't twist but slid up and down into a groove. I raised the lock and the door opened easily. I came out laughing.

Our caravan started up again. Several miles farther on, Henry pointed as a sign came into view. "That's Vero Beach. The island where your father is waiting is near there."

Suddenly I felt my insides churn and I began to tremble. Then I was sobbing, deep aching sobs from way inside me. I couldn't control them.

Henry put his arm around me. "What is it? Tell me."

"I am afraid. I am afraid."

Henry patted my back. "Come now, this is the happiest moment of your life. There is nothing to be afraid of."

"I know," I said, but I continued sobbing. Henry gave me his handkerchief. "If he sees you with red eyes, your father will think his daughter is a rabbit."

I took a deep breath and clenched my teeth to stop my tears. "There, that is better. It is over."

I wiped my eyes.

I could see the ocean and long, tall palm trees leaning against the wind. There was the faintest touch of light on the horizon like a silver-pink streak along the top of the ocean. "Dawn is coming," Henry said, and I felt the car slowing down.

"Are we there?" I asked.

"Almost," Henry said.

"Then why are we slowing down?"

Henry had glanced at his watch again. "The driver of the car ahead got a ticket for speeding in Vero Beach. They are very strict here, so he has to be very careful or he will lose his license."

The streak of light far out where the water met the sky had widened, and there was an orange-pink glow to the sky. I could hear birds waking up.

We pulled up to a little white stone house, and a man in a white cap stepped out. "What is it?" I asked Henry.

"The security guard for John's Island."

He spoke with the driver of the lead car, then pointed down the road. We started off again.

HENRY GRIS

It was only a short drive to the condominium in which Jackson Tate, his wife, and at least one *Enquirer* photographer were waiting, and there were ten minutes to kill until the sun would be fully up.

Henry checked the numbers of the condominiums. Jackson Tate was in the first one. Victoria's was right after his. Henry told the driver to head for the second one. He turned to Victoria. "We will go first to the house you will stay in. It is right next door to where your father is. You can fix your face so that he won't see that you have been crying, and then we will go in to him."

Victoria nodded. She seemed numb.

The car rolled to a stop in front of 39 Silver Moss Drive. A slender young woman with dark hair came running down to the car. Henry helped Victoria out. "This is Diane Albright—Dee Dee—who will be your secretary-companion. Dee Dee, why don't you take Victoria inside and help her with her face while I go see if her father is ready?"

Henry tapped his wristwatch for Dee Dee to see. "I'll come back for Victoria in exactly ten minutes, you understand?"

Henry cut across the lawn to number 40. There was a reporter just inside the doorway, and another one in an alcove with an open phone line to the *Enquirer*. Hazel Tate sat on a sofa at the far end of the room, twisting a handkerchief. Jackson Tate stood in the center of the living room, his feet braced as if he were on a rolling ship's deck. He was wearing one of those garishly colored sport shirts that he seemed to favor. "Well, Henry?" he boomed out, but his voice sounded tight. "Where is she?"

Henry went to the admiral and shook his hand. "Having a last minute touch-up to look her best for you."

Jack shook his head. "It's a hell of a day, Henry, a hell of a day."

"Are you nervous, Admiral?"

Jack snorted. "What do you think?" He slapped at his belly. "You know I'm no longer the man her mother told her about. I only hope she's not expecting too much."

Henry slapped him on the back. "She's expecting to meet the father she already loves, that's all."

"I hope so," Jack said.

The windows were brightening with the rising sun. "I'll go and get her," Henry said.

VICTORIA

Henry asked me if I were ready. "He's waiting for you."

I nodded, but I couldn't speak. My throat felt closed.

"Don't you want to take off that overcoat?"

I shook my head. For some strange reason, I needed that coat from Moscow at that moment. It was my security blanket, as if Mamula was with me protecting me.

Henry took my arm and we started along the path to the place next door. I looked toward the ocean, which had turned to gold in the rising sun. The color blurred as my eyes filled. I fought back the tears. I didn't want my father to see me crying.

The path curved out and up to the door, which stood open. There were photographers walking behind us, I think, and I saw someone with a camera run ahead into the house, but I was paying no attention to anything but that door ahead of me coming closer and closer. Behind it was my father, my Papatchka for whom I had waited my whole life. We were almost at the front stoop when I felt my feet giving out from under me, and I started sinking to the ground.

Henry's hand tightened on me, pulling me up. "I can't make it," I said. "Please, I can't."

"You must," Henry said. "You have traveled across two continents for 33 hours for this one moment. There are only a few more steps."

I dug my feet against the grass and pushed myself up with Henry holding onto me. "That's it," he said. "Keep going, keep going."

Each time he said it, I took another step. And then we were in the doorway, and I looked into the room and there was a man in a funny shirt holding out his arms to me. I saw that he was crying.

I opened my arms and stepped into his and felt them close around me. I was crying, too. We just stood there, holding each other, saying nothing, crying in each other's arms. I think the moment was too big for us.

It was Henry who broke it. "Hey, Admiral, you owe me ten bucks."

"You're damn right I do," I heard my father sob. And then he kissed me, and I couldn't stop my tears. "Papa, Papa, Papa . . ." I couldn't stop saying the word.

"Shhh, shhh, baby, it's all right now. I'm here." He patted my back as if I were an infant. Then he put his lips close to my ear so that no one else could hear, and began to sing the waltz from *The Gypsy Baron*, the love song he had shared with Mamula so many years ago.

EPILOGUE

Henry Gris and the *National Enquirer* did indeed pull off their exclusive coverage of the meeting between Victoria and her father. They kept the two of them in seclusion at John's Island for three weeks while three stories, with photographs, of their meeting appeared in the *Enquirer*. Then they arranged for a press conference to allow the rest of the world press access to the story the *Enquirer* had already given its readers. Today Henry Gris is senior roving editor with the *National Enquirer*. He resides in California.

On June 7, 1975, Victoria Fyodorova became the wife of Frederick Richard Pouy, a first officer with Pan American World Airways. They met at a cocktail reception given for Victoria in New York City. Pouy had read about Victoria's desire to meet her American father in *People* magazine. He wrote to Jackson Tate stating that he often flew to Russia, and should there be anything he could take into Moscow from the admiral to his daughter he would be more than happy to oblige. When Victoria came to the United States and was presented with a poodle, Sailor, which she wanted to take back with her, the admiral remembered the note from the Pan Am copilot and had an invitation to the cocktail reception sent to Pouy.

The Pouys live in southern Connecticut with their son, Christopher Alexander (named in part for Fred Pouy's father and for Victoria's aunt), born on May 3, 1976. Sailor also lives with them.

Zoya Fyodorova resides in Moscow, where she is still a popular actress in Russian films. She has been granted a three-month visa each year to visit with her daughter, son-in-law, and grandchild.

On April 27, 1976, Zoya met her Jackson again for a very brief visit at his home in Orange Park. They talked mostly about Victoria and the grandchild that was due momentarily. They never saw each other again.

Dr. Irina Kirk is still on the faculty of the University of Connecticut. She speaks to Victoria on the telephone with some frequency, and they meet occasionally.

Jackson Rogers Tate died of cancer on July 19, 1978, at the age of 79. He cooperated fully in the researching of his part of this story. He was able to read the first half of the manuscript, but did not live to see its completion.

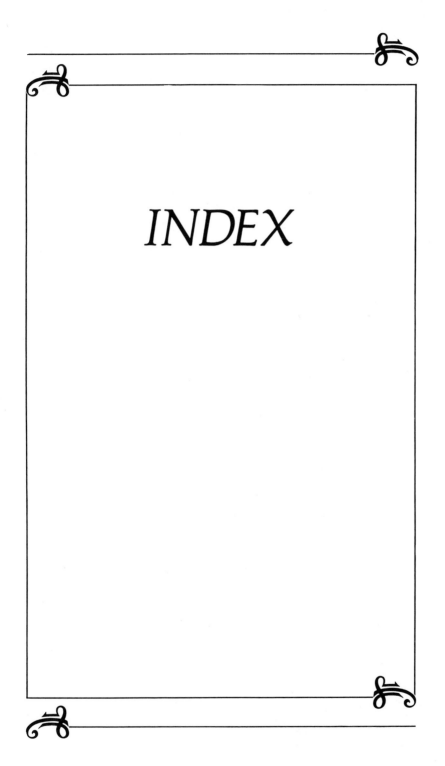

INDEX